FATAL ATTACHMENTS

The Instigation to Suicide

Viola Mecke

PRAEGER

Westport, Connecticut
London

Library of Congress Cataloging-in-Publication Data

Mecke, Viola, 1928–
  Fatal attachments : the instigation to suicide / Viola Mecke.
    p. cm.
  Includes bibliographical references and index.
  ISBN 0–275–98253–X (alk. paper)
  1. Suicide victims—Psychology. 2. Suicide victims—Family relationships. 3. Suicide—Psychological aspects. I. Title.
  HV6545.M37   2004
  362.28'1—dc22   2004044385

British Library Cataloguing in Publication Data is available.

Library of Congress Catalog Card Number: 2004044385
ISBN: 0–275–98253–X

First published in 2004

Praeger Publishers, 88 Post Road West, Westport, CT 06881
An imprint of Greenwood Publishing Group, Inc.
www.praeger.com

Printed in the United States of America

The paper used in this book complies with the Permanent Paper Standard issued by the National Information Standards Organization (Z39.48–1984).

10 9 8 7 6 5 4 3 2 1

This book is dedicated to
the memory of my beloved husband
Günter Mecke

Contents

Preface   *ix*

CHAPTER 1   Fatal Attachments
Love Betrayed   *1*

CHAPTER 2   Instigators
From the Hellespont to Seattle   *13*

CHAPTER 3   Terrorized Children
From Innocence to Instigator   *25*

CHAPTER 4   Passive Instigators
Walking By on the Other Side   *36*

CHAPTER 5   Passive Instigators II
But I Was Doing the Best I Could   *52*

CHAPTER 6   Ambivalence and Instigators
He Loves Me; She Loves Me Not   *69*

CHAPTER 7   Self-Attached Instigators
The Jilted Lover   *85*

CHAPTER 8   Passive Instigators III
On Looking a Gift Horse in the Mouth   *96*

CHAPTER 9   Provocateur Instigators
From the Outer to the Inner Force   *108*

Contents

CHAPTER 10   Heroic Provocateurs
Riddles and Rhymes, Music and Massacre   119

CHAPTER 11   The Internal Instigator
Death in the Soul   124

CHAPTER 12   The Internal Instigator II
Double and Triple Tragedies   140

CHAPTER 13   Cult Instigators
The False Path   154

CHAPTER 14   Instigation Foiled
Getting Out Alive   168

CHAPTER 15   Loving Attachment to Life   181

Notes   187

Selected Bibliography   197

Index   203

Preface

Two events in life led me to study suicide. One was the shock I suffered when Tommy, a five-year-old boy whom I had seen for a psychological evaluation, deliberately killed himself. The other was the experience of seeing my own husband's turmoil as he occasionally struggled against suicidal impulses. Through these events I was drawn to the idea that at times someone so deeply wishes the death of another person that that other person would kill himself or herself. Tommy's father had declared that he wished Tommy were dead; my husband's father punished him as a toddler by holding him outside a second-story window, threatening to drop him to his death. Although my husband's childhood story is much like Tommy's, fortunately he overcame his demons and survived.

These two experiences, among others, alerted me to search for the forces that push one to suicide. Although the terrorist attacks of September 11 did not precipitate my writing of this book, the suicide-terrorists are prime examples of the theme I explore—that often enough another person plays an instigating role in a suicidal act.

The facts are incontrovertible. We will never know the reasons for many suicides, but it is undeniable that some persons kill themselves because they become trapped in ill-fated attachments. The role of a leader who urges and even compels the suicidal actions is easily recognized, as in suicides of cult members. Sometimes the person who induces the suicidal action is not as easily identified. Several psychotherapists have influenced me, for they call suicide a murder. For instance, Otto Wills suggested, in cases of suicide, ask who wanted the patient dead. However, it was my husband who developed the concept of the instigator from his knowledge of the ancient method of punishing crime by defenestration. This book arose from the conversations we shared before his death.

There are more suicides than homicides in the United States, over 30,000 each year. Suicide has been a topic of significance throughout history, but in the last thirty-five years hundreds of books and an overwhelming number of articles on suicide have appeared. Edwin Shneidman was a pioneer in the field, and, in 1958 with others, he founded the Los Angeles Suicide Prevention Center. Then, in 1968 Shneidman took a lead in founding the American Association of Suicidology. In 1987, under the leadership of Dr. Herbert Hendin, the American Suicide Foundation was incorporated in order to fund research in the United States.

Most research deals primarily with the phenomena of the behavior of groups of people. I wanted more in-depth information about the individuals whose lives are destroyed by suicide. My search took me to the rich history of myths, legends and modern literature that present suicide as a theme. In these stories I found my passageway to a further understanding of the suicidal actions of individuals. As I read them, I saw that there is often a destructive relationship between the suicide victims and a key person in their lives.

I have written this book to help stem the riotous tide of suicide and to provide a background to help understand the forces that extinguish a person's will to live. The violence of mankind against each other has always wounded and astounded me. Rape, neglect, deprivation, physical attacks, emotional abuse, murder, war and suicide are all failures of individuals, of families and of society.

The stories that I tell in this book will leave the reader with little doubt that, at times, the suicide victims have acted on the wishes of other persons who should have been nurturing and sustaining influences.

Suicide occurs under many conditions and with many stresses that act upon individuals. My aim is to illuminate one of the forces that may lead to suicide in the hope that many individuals will learn to defend themselves more successfully against those malignant forces that engender the idea of self-murder. And, of course, I hope to stimulate more research so that psychotherapists will more readily use these concepts in working with those agonized and despairing persons fighting their impulses to kill themselves.

I have never had a patient kill himself or herself while I was working with them in psychotherapy, although the despair of some of my patients has been profound, and they needed extra care and attention during those crisis times. In this book I have taken every precaution to protect the identity of those patients whose stories I tell. One note: For ease in writing, I occasionally use the pronoun *he* to refer to both genders.

I bear responsibility for the concepts presented in this book. Some are elaborations of previous relevant theories, others emerge from research findings that are more adequately described by other writers. Most of what you read here is my own reflections about the role of suicide in human relationships.

To identify all the contributions that others have brought to my thinking would be a Herculean research task. As for me, I have studied, taught and practiced clinical psychology for more than 40 years. My theoretical bent has been toward psychoanalytic theory, which itself has been enriched by notable thinkers over the past 100 years. Contributions to the theories of human behavior continue to extend our understanding of the human psyche, to enhance our ability to help patients, and to provide insight into societal problems. To all those incredibly intuitive thinkers and meticulous researchers, I say, "Thank you for enriching my life and my work."

Because this book has been in the making for several arduous years, it seems impossible to thank all those who have encouraged and helped me. Bill Fontana and Margrith Raspotnik provided help during the early stages of this undertaking by translating from German some of my husband's writings. My friends, amazed that I would spend my time in retirement writing a book, have understood my need to share what I have learned and have encouraged me every step of the way. My brother and his wife, Bill and Barbara Bloom, have provided constant support, both emotionally and physically, even though listening and talking about suicide has not always provided the most pleasant dinner conversation. I would like to thank Dr. Jerry Clark of Montecito and Dr. Jo Linder-Crowe of the Glendon Association in Santa Barbara, who read parts of the manuscript and provided suggestions. My dear friends, Beth and Derek Westen, have been a major cheering section for me, with their in-depth understanding of psychological concepts and their unfailing interest in reading and making insightful suggestions. Mostly, I would like to thank Lowell Dabbs, for without him the book probably would never have been written. He has read and edited every chapter, often rewriting sentences or clarifying ideas that at times must have seemed muddled. I thank him warmly for all his care and his work.

CHAPTER 1

Fatal Attachments

Love Betrayed

Tommy was dead. A beautiful child, only five years old, he had killed himself with his own small hands. How do I know this? I first saw Tommy when he was only nine months old. His parents had brought him to the clinic for an evaluation because they thought he was retarded. His father, Dr. Jerome, vehemently claimed that he did not want him—that Tommy was a deficient child. "Place him in an institution," he said. "He should not have been born. I don't want him at home!" I saw him only for an evaluation.

Tommy was an appealing infant with blond, curly hair who crawled timidly toward the stuffed animals that I placed on the floor for him. He was very quiet, even shy. After talking with his parents, I asked to be alone with Tommy for a few minutes. Strangely, he did not fuss when his parents left the room as would be expected of an infant. Tommy sat placidly on the floor, head down, and gave no notice of their leaving him. When they returned he did not look at them or cry to be held, although he did glance surreptitiously at his mother. During this and the following sessions with Tommy and his parents, neither parent cuddled him, and Tommy never approached his parents for comfort, assurance or guidance.[1] Lack of attachment to his parents seemed problematic and suggested nurturing negligence or deprivation at home. Nevertheless, his behavior was typical of most infants. He crawled about on the floor. He grasped toys, holding them firmly, shaking them for a sound and tasting them. He uttered delightful babbling sounds. He had good motor coordination, with age-appropriate learning and memory skills.

1

Pleased, I told the parents that according to all measures of physical and cognitive abilities, Tommy fell well within normal bounds of development. I discussed important areas of nurturing to further his healthy development—holding him, talking to him and playing with him. Tommy's mother smiled guardedly at the information but could not express her relief. Tommy's father, however, was incensed. "I never wanted that child. . . . My older son is perfect. . . . I do not want Tommy! He belongs in an institution!"

When Tommy was nineteen months old, the parents returned with him to the clinic. Again, the father insisted—*in Tommy's presence*—that he was retarded, that Tommy should not have been born and that he, the father, did not want him. I reevaluated Tommy's physical and intellectual growth, and again, he scored within the normal range of the developmental milestones, including verbal and social skills. For instance, he could say baby, mama, cookie, bye-bye and similar words that many children that age can say. At first he seemed afraid to play with the toys—blocks, little wooden cars, stuffed animals and others—but when I gave him permission, he played, but cautiously, always checking the face of his father. One aspect was striking: Tommy's face, like that of his mother's, showed no emotion.

When Tommy was three years of age, the parents arrived again at the clinic. This time the evaluation team suggested that the parents enroll Tommy in the nursery school at our clinic so that we could evaluate his development more carefully and his social adjustment more thoroughly. For three months Tommy came to the nursery. At first he seemed a bit frightened and avoided playing with the other children, but day by day he ventured into activities with them more eagerly, learning it was possible to enjoy himself and to play with other children. After three months, however, Dr. Jerome complained that he could no longer afford to have Tommy in the nursery. Although we offered a scholarship, his father refused to bring him anymore.

Dr. Jerome, the father, was a highly educated professional who had made significant contributions to his field of nuclear physics. He was a brusque, pompous, portly and balding man of medium height. He seemed an angry man with an air of self-importance that was demeaning of other persons. He could easily have afforded nursery school for Tommy. Tommy's mother, Anna, was a quiet, timid woman of thirty-six with mousy blond hair pulled straight back. She wore dark print dresses that hung down limply from her shoulders, making her look quite old-fashioned. She seemed very frightened of her husband and mutely agreed with his every word. She never uttered a contrary word when Dr. Jerome insisted he wanted to be rid of Tommy. When pushed for her response, she would reply meekly that she agreed with her husband. She never said, "No, he is my son, our son; I will take care of him, I want him."

At four, Tommy found the psychotropic pills that his mother kept at her bedside and ate them. His mother rushed him to the hospital, where he was treated, and he recovered. Both his parents impressed upon him that if he were to do that again, he would die. He listened. A year later, at five, Tommy once more ferreted out his mother's pills, still lying enticingly and in open view by her bedside. He swallowed them all and died.

Too often, as you will see in the pages that follow, a person commits suicide because the essential human attachment—crucial to normal growth and survival—is openly denied and cruelly withheld, even from a child. With older persons the attachment failure may be less obvious, but it is just as damaging to them. Tommy's father carried that curse deep inside him.

I struggled with the word *instigation* because it sounds harsh to my ears. Yet no other word seemed as appropriate. *Incitement* has an active connotation that, to me, does not provide room for important unconscious factors. I considered *facilitation*, but to facilitate sounds more like the act of handing someone the pills or the gun. *Instigation*, however, can denote both the conscious and unconscious dynamics that are at work within this phenomenon. The very idea that one person may have some responsibility for the suicide of another is troublesome, and many people will shy away from it. No one, including myself, really likes to believe there is someone who can be that instrumental in inducing a suicidal action. *Instigation* seemed the best-fitting term.

Therefore, I call individuals like Tommy's father the *instigators*. In reality, all Tommy yearned for so desperately was to rest in his father's loving arms. Instead, he heard repeatedly that his father wanted him dead. So Tommy did as his father wished. He took his medicine. The attachment to his father, so necessary for growth, became a fatal attachment.

I realized that suicide might spring from hopes of satisfying the wishes of a rejecting person, the victim's instigator, during discussions with my husband. Seated in the library, reading, as was our custom after a late dinner, my husband said in a somber voice, "I would like to talk." Books laid aside, I waited for him to begin. His voice quivering, he told me how he had somehow known, since he was a lad of three or four, that his father wanted him dead. He described the rage of his parents toward him that resulted in beatings, in threats, in enemas.

I listened in horror as he described how his father would attack him. In Günter's own words, from his journal,

> Again and again, my father [is] coming for me. The nearer he comes, the blinder is his fury. So when he now is all over me and attacks me and is pummeling me and knocking me about he himself is so blinded by fury that he doesn't know where he is turning to hit me—at my head or body. He becomes quite unpredictable to me, I can't see, can't predict where to turn to escape his fists and blows. I don't really have reliable cues as to how to dodge him and in which direction to run to escape. He finally catches me and hangs me out of the second story window by the back of my pants, and now there is no escape. I am too terrified to cry.

His father would be yelling that he should just drop this brat and see the end of all their troubles. At that moment, and only then, would Günter's mother intervene, for she, too, thought that this little boy had destroyed her life, especially her sexual life. She told him so when he was a child and again when he was an adult.

Although he had to battle the specter of this abuse most of his adult life, Günter did not commit suicide. He often claimed that he was rescued only because his parents sent him away to school during his adolescence. And while his parents remained basically rejecting of him, at times they also indulged him with praise and toys. Günter's constant battle between life and death was rooted in trying to ward off his father's wishes that he should not have been born and that he should die and, to a lesser extent, his mother's cruelty in blaming him for impairing her sexual life.

By contrast, Tommy's father was a consistent instigator. So Tommy acted out his father's spoken wishes, perhaps feeling with a five-year-old's logic that his death would bring his father's love. Günter knew and absorbed his father's wishes for him to be dead; but because his father's rejection was not as consistent, he did not act on them. Yet Günter's life was torn with inner turmoil. Only in therapy, as an adult, could he acknowledge that deep inside him he had been haunted his entire life by the knowledge that his father wanted him dead. Günter never had the essential attachment with his father, and the inner conviction that his father never wanted him and wished him dead paralyzed much of his life. To the end of his father's life, his father never softened. Lying on his death bed, his father said, "I do not want to see him."

In Tommy's case, his father poisoned the relationship to Tommy with open hostility. It was not only a negative attachment, with any bond between them denied and impugned, but a malevolent one. The father consciously and actively wished Tommy evil. The unconscious, internal dynamic that his father projected onto Tommy was a hatred of himself, deeply rooted in the sense that he, the father, should not be alive. Therefore, Tommy should not be alive.

The origins of self-hatred resided deeply within Tommy's father, Jerome. He was the second son of his parents, born in Austria during the days when Hitler took over the country. As Jews, the parents decided it was wise to escape the Nazis. Packing what they could carry, the parents took their two boys, Jerome, then twelve months old, and his brother, four years old, and began their walk toward Switzerland. Little Jerome became very ill on the journey and the parents believed he was dying. Rather than carry this sick, crying baby with them and risk being discovered, his parents abandoned Jerome on the doorstep of a church and plodded on their way. But Jerome survived and was reared by the Catholic priests—never again to see his parents. The little boy grew up feeling unloved, abandoned, despised by his parents and self-hating. He described himself as a fearful and shy youngster. Perhaps because Tommy was his second son, as he had been, Dr. Jerome unconsciously selected him and denied him affection, love or protective feelings. The victim of his own infancy, he was unconsciously compelled to reenact his life history with Tommy.

Spurred on by these two real-life dramas, I began searching for the extent and meaning of suicides and their instigators, starting with suicide stories in myths and legends. Then I matched these ancient legends with modern stories and with actual case histories, hoping for a better understanding of some suicides. Surprisingly, the basic phenomenon that emerges from fiction is that many a seemingly lonely suicide has in reality a partner, an instigator—silent or not so silent. These instigators carry their own wounds or stigmas that in turn trigger the death wish of the suicide victim. My aim has been to understand how the instigator and the suicide victim interact, and thus to clarify the death-wishing forces between them that ultimately result in tragedy.

It is significant that in English, we refer to a suicide as a "suicide victim." Victims are usually taken to be passive recipients of some kind of abuse. According to *Merriam-Webster's Collegiate Dictionary*, a victim is someone "who has been destroyed, ruined, seriously injured by some ruthless person before whom he has been helpless." Thus our victim terminology seems to acknowledge that profound forces outside the victims of suicide are central. My thesis is that an instigator is often a crucial force in suicides. That is, sometimes external instigators' wishes, either conscious or unconscious, become demands that their dependent victims destroy their own lives.

The origin of the word *suicide* in the dictionary provides an additional insight. The word *suicide* grew from the ancient Latin word components *sui* (self) and *cide* (cut), that is, to cut oneself. These roots lie behind the modern interpretations of suicide in terms of self-judgment, self-condemnation and self-execution. Thus a person may feel morally repugnant and create an inner voice like a harsh judge who hands down a secret death sentence. The condemned one may go on living—but only until the instigator, as a sly prosecutor, leads the person to the conscious acknowledgment of his wish to "sui-cide." The root words aptly indicate another important aspect of suicide—the aggression and anger toward one's self and toward others that cry for expiation in acts of suicide.

Suicide has stolen the lives of individuals around the world and throughout the centuries. It exacts a relentless toll from the individual who commits suicide and from those who survive the victim. On May 2, 2001, the surgeon general reported that every year more than 650,000 Americans attempt suicide and more than 30,000 succeed.[2] It is estimated that over 5 million Americans have attempted to kill themselves. Every seventeen minutes an American takes his or her own life. It is startling that, for every two victims of homicide, three persons take their own lives. And with every suicide, the lives of at least six other people are deeply affected.

Statistics show the astonishingly huge problem of suicide. Numbers are powerless, however, to take us very far along our journey to understand the conditions of an individual who succumbs to suicide. Statistics conceal and dehumanize, making mere objects of the real people that you and I may know, dismissing the narrative of their lives, their relationships with others, their feelings about life and their crying need for intervention.

Many stories of suicides have been reported over the ages, and many notable persons have committed suicide: Empedocles, Crasus,

Gracchus, Cato, Lucretia, Antony, Cleopatra, Brutus Coccius, Nerva, Seneca, Calpurnius, Hero and Saul come to mind. Circa 1610, John Donne, a poet and an Anglican clergyman, wrote a treatise entitled *Biathanatos*, which included a three-page list of suicides in the classical world.[3] Even this list was not exhaustive. Further, the number of famous—and infamous—persons who have committed suicide in modern times is just as shocking: Virginia Woolf; Marilyn Monroe; Ernest Hemingway, his father and one of his daughters; Sylvia Plath; Vincent Foster; Admiral Boorda and others too many to enumerate.

The option to choose to live or die has always been a question of morality and cultural attitudes. The ethical and legal issues are as strongly debated today as they were in earlier times. In many cultures, suicide is a crime, or a sin, and the surviving relatives are steeped in shame. Suicide victims were often mutilated after death and refused a proper burial. The next of kin could not claim inheritance rights. Such has been the reaction to suicide when viewed as a shameful and terrifying mystery.[4] And the shame and terror still haunt many of us in the course of our present lives.

Philosophers have argued for and against the morality of suicide since the earliest of times. Plato and Aristotle took slightly different positions in discussing the morality of suicide. Plato saw man as the property of the gods, so that suicide could not be tolerated insofar as it seemed disrespectful to the gods. A public burial should be refused to "someone who slays himself, violently robbing himself of his fate-given share of life." Yet Plato was more tolerant when the suicide's life had become unbearable through painful and incurable illness, abject poverty or shame.

Aristotle was rigid. He condemned suicide "as an offense against the state" because it damaged the welfare of the city through the loss of a contributing citizen and was also a crime against one's own person, an act of cowardice in the face of responsibilities.

But then, as today, there were philosophers who, operating under different premises, espoused suicide as a moral right. For instance, the Cyrenaic philosophy (a minor Socratic school in North Africa) and later the Epicurean philosophy both embraced hedonism, which was based on the pleasures of the senses as the goal of life.[5] According to Cyrenaic and Epicurean philosophy, when after mature reflection one concludes that life becomes intolerable, one should be allowed to commit suicide without fear. In fact, one of the leaders of the Cyrenaics, Hegasus, was expelled from Egypt for persuading too many young people to commit suicide.

To summarize briefly, on the one hand there are arguments that support the right of the individual to make a free choice to live or die. On the other hand is the opposing view, that suicide is a form of murder and threatens the whole of society. Perhaps in this view suicide is shameful because it implies—often correctly—that someone has failed in the care of another.[6]

Suicide victims use diverse methods. In ancient tradition and frequently today, many jump from a height that ensures death. In ancient Grecian culture, the Leucadian Cliff, which rises over 2,000 feet above the Ionean Sea on the island of Leucas, was an ideal spot for suicides. According to myth, this cliff was an arena for testing the innocence of a criminal or proving the love of a rejected lover. If a person suspected of a crime was thrown off the cliff and lived or was rescued by some other means, the suspect's innocence was proven. If a rejected lover jumped and lived or was saved miraculously, the lover's devotion was abundantly demonstrated for all to see.

A notable suicide platform in the United States is the Golden Gate Bridge in San Francisco, from which over a thousand persons have leaped to their death. Other cliffs known for suicides include the Maiden Rock of the Sioux people, the craters of certain Japanese volcanoes, some waterfalls on the Island of Bali and Beachy Head in England. Beachy Head apparently has more suicides per year than the Golden Gate Bridge.[7] It has a sheer drop of 550 feet straight down to the rocks by the sea. Ordinarily it is a place to picnic and to play, to experience blissful repose in the loveliness of nature, but never far from consciousness lurks the possible encounter with death. Its very beauty may call one to death.

Hanging or jumping from a height remains a frequently reported method of suicide in many countries. For instance, Pierre Boelle reports that hanging was the main method of suicide among young men in France and the United Kingdom during the years 1993–1995;[8] P. S. Yip and R. C. Tan report that jumping from a height is the most frequent method of suicide in Hong Kong and Singapore.[9] Jumping or hanging was the method most often used for suicide in Ethiopia.[10] Plato reports that hanging exerted a particularly malignant impact upon the Greeks, being the most shameful of deaths. Today with the availability of firearms in many countries, guns have become the most frequent method for suicide among males; poison or drugs are the most common means among females, especially in the United States.

These methods tell us how it is done. They do not describe why it is done, or why suicides are so rampant. We hear about a mangled body, an unbearable disappointment in love, the loss of a fortune or honor, advancing old age, illness, madness or idiocy. These seemingly self-evident reasons sound hollow, like superficial rationalizations. They spring from our anxiety, inviting us to grasp at any straw of external plausibility rather than face the discomfort of looking closer and deeper into the problems of life and the mysteries of death.

Clinicians have not been any more successful than anyone else in understanding the forces that lead to suicide. In the study of the frequency of suicides, Alec Roy claims that a tendency to suicide may be hereditary.[11] Likewise, the search for a metabolic explanation for suicide in terms of a low level of serotonin (5HT) has received extensive attention.[12] These may be too facile attempts to explain why some individuals self-destruct, however. Others with similar genetics or biology do not kill themselves.

A few clinicians have indeed wondered about the role of other people in suicidal actions. Sigmund Freud himself pondered the impetus behind suicide and concluded, "It is true we have long known that no neurotic harbours thoughts of suicide which are not murderous impulses against others re-directed upon himself."[13]

Karl Menninger agreed and wrote, "First of all, suicide is obviously a murder," a murder of the self-incorporated love-hate figure, that is, a person from whom the suicide victim wants love. He stated:

> Suicide must thus be regarded as a peculiar kind of death which entails three basic internal elements and modifying ones. There is the element of dying, the element of killing and the element of being killed. Each is a condensation for which there exist complexes of motive, conscious and unconscious. What we call a suicide is for the individual himself an attempt to burst into life or to save his life. It may be to avoid something far more dreadful, to avoid committing murder or going mad.[14]

These concepts border on the role of an instigator, but they do little to explicate the instigator-victim relationship. Other psychiatrists have recognized the partnership in many suicides and the complex dynamics that are involved. One psychoanalyst, M. Straker, also had an understanding of the peculiar relationship between the instigator and the suicide victim. He wrote, "A decisive factor in the successful suicide attempt appears to be an implied consent or unconscious collusion between the patient and the person most involved in the psychic struggle."[15] It is this collusion that I will explore, that is, the relationship between two persons that results ultimately in the suicidal death of one.

Clinicians presently seem to share a conviction that suicide is an act of an abnormal individual suffering a mental illness, probably depression or schizophrenia. Keep in mind, however, that there are many more depressed and schizophrenic people who do not self-destruct. Words such as *depression* and *schizophrenia* are often merely convenient labels given after the fact. Neither word adequately addresses the inner state or external circumstances of the individuals who chose to kill themselves.

Most of today's psychological thinking about suicide avoids investigating the fatal attachments that may occur between people, that is, between an instigator and a suicidal victim. My contention is that in many cases a deeper examination reveals that instigators are haunted from early life by damaging, death-frightening experiences. The terror is repressed, only to reverberate as hostility or withdrawal throughout their lives, especially in critical relationships of closeness or intimacy. The hostility is projected onto the other, energizes that person's fears of loss and abandonment and ultimately results in the suicidal action. The instigators, trying to protect themselves from reliving their terrorizing experiences, instead restage the trauma, casting their selected partner as the victim, and that person, instead of the suffering instigator, commits self-murder. These principles will also show how the death wishes of the leaders of cults and terrorist leaders such as Osama bin Laden are transplanted to their doomed followers. Although this relationship has been hinted at in the literature, I believe that no one has ever attempted to look at attachments not just from the view of the victim but also from the viewpoint of the instigator. We need to know what happens within the instigator that demands the death of another person. We must also investigate what makes the instigator's personality attractive to the victim.

Focusing on the instigator or the death-wisher, however, entails entering into forbidden territory. There is a lot of resistance, even resentment, from those who want to protect instigators from any awareness of their death-wishing toward the victims. It is easy to tell the survivors, "It is not your fault; they (the suicide victims) made their own decision for themselves!" But this kind of exculpatory rationale could similarly be applied to the present-day suicidal terrorists as well. The

10

present widespread anger against the suicide-terrorists provides the incentive and latitude to look closely at these fatal attachments.

I will try to identify the instigators and clarify their roles in many suicides. We should ask, what made Tommy's father hate his lovable infant son so virulently? Conversely, I will try to determine the forces behind the susceptibility of the potential suicide victims to the instigators. What makes the instigator so central to their lives? How do they become so fatally attached to the instigators? What happens to destroy the victims' pleasures or the meaningfulness of their living?

In the search for as much information and insight as possible about instigators, I became convinced that the terror of the present suicide bombings and the growing ferocity of suicidal attacks in the rest of the world might affect any objectivity. I sought a longer historical perspective. Knowing that since the beginning of creative thought bards, poets and dramatists have provided us the deepest possible insights into human nature, I turned to the myths, legends and stories from ancient and present times. I found that the toxic relationships between instigators and their victims have long been vividly revealed. To further define the character of the instigator I looked at modern stories of suicide victims and then, finally, to case histories of real-life suicides.

In this work, I shall utilize these legends and works of literature for illustrative purposes. Revealingly, in many of these tales, the instigators to suicide have themselves had an encounter with death that left them physically and emotionally traumatized or stigmatized. They were desperately attempting to live and to overcome their own inescapable anxiety about death.

Disturbingly, and yet true to the psychology of many fatal attachments, the instigator in these stories often assumes a charming persona that entices the attachment of the suicidal person. The beguiling instigator engages the self-orientation of the suicidal person that becomes an implacable, narcissistic core that propels them toward death. In the myth of Narcissus, for instance, Narcissus' pathological self-involvement overwhelms his will to live and to respond to love. In the recent story of *Roderick Hudson*, Henry James depicts a troublesome psychologically entwined relationship between Roderick, an unstable young sculptor, and Rowland, his would-be benefactor, that enflames their past griefs and rejections.

Other stories illustrate provocateur instigators. These instigators awaken dormant forces in a self-condemning person much as a cult leader with his group members. Other instigators dominate and condemn the victim, arising from earlier identification with a key person whose death, by illness or suicide, came during their early lives. Case histories and several short tales of instigators will be used to supplement these stories. The stories of the suicide of the poet Sylvia Plath and others provide a dramatic example of the inner instigators.

Finally, I will discuss the suicide-instigators of the cult leaders and the terrorist leaders and their suicide-murders. The Kamikaze pilots of Japan during World War II astounded the world. The present suicide-bombers provide new illustrations of the close association between murder and suicide and also between the instigator and suicide victims. Cult leaders choose to die with their members. The terrorist-instigators command only the suicides of their followers, and they themselves remain behind to launch more human bombs but also to survive. Terrorist-suicides force us to consider an interesting dilemma of instigators who induce the suicide of followers while carrying out homicide. Suicide-leaders have an ultimate power of unremitting aggression as their motivating force in life; history has many such tales.

With this background, in the final chapters, I discuss how an instigator and a potential suicide victim, and their therapists and loved ones, can overcome these fatal attractions.

My goal in writing this work is not to focus on the negative or to cast blame, but rather to shed light on an idea that is almost taboo. The key to change is understanding. My deepest wish is that this work will play a role in reducing the agonizing pain of suicide victims and their survivors.

CHAPTER 2

Instigators

From the Hellespont to Seattle

> Ruthless Eros, great bane, great curse to mankind, from you come deadly strifes and lamentations and groans, and countless pains as well have their stormy birth from you.
>
> Apollonius Rhodius, *Argonautica* 4.445

She stood there on the rail of the bridge. Should she jump? For three long hours she debated. And the cars roared by, the drivers and passengers yelling at her, "Jump!" "Go ahead! Jump!" Finally she jumped.[1]

The foregoing scene, brutal but commonplace, illuminates a disturbing feature of ordinary psychology—our distaste, even impatience, with threats of suicide. Still more disturbing is the situation when the taunt comes from someone close to the potential suicide, when it is a loved one who taunts: "You can't live without me? You'll go off the bridge if I don't love you? O.K., let's see you do it. Jump!" Such common phrases are too often thought or uttered. What do these words mean? We see such scenes in literature, but do such instigators really exist? Can the attachments that lead to suicide be recognized before it is too late?

I approach this topic with much trepidation, because it may seem unbelievable that anyone would knowingly be responsible for another's suicide—or would not be filled with horror to discover they were unwittingly responsible. Yet it is unquestionably the case. And with the recent events of the suicidal murder bombing in New York

City and Washington, D.C., on September 11, 2001, the evidence of a suicide-mastermind behind the death of the suicide-bombers is embodied in the ruins of the Twin Towers. These terrorist-leaders made suicide the supreme goal for their brainwashed followers. Such terrorist-leaders never wrap the bombs around themselves; they dress themselves in their power, power that finds its strength in enslaving the impressionable spirits of young people. The terrorist-leaders are obviously instigators, igniting the spirit of youth to self-murder. The deadly influence of such instigators gives us a mandate to look at the instigators of individual suicides.

Suicide events are reported almost daily in the newspapers. These stories seldom provide sufficient detail to enable us to understand the relationships of the suicide victim. For instance, a report in the *Los Angeles Times* stated: "A man shot and killed his mother and sister after an argument in their upscale Glendale home and then took his own life. . . . Neighbors described the family as friendly, devoutly religious and the last people they would expect to see visited by violence."[2]

The paucity of data in this tragic report made me wonder what the relationships among the family members really were, if they really could have been as happy and supportive as neighbors thought, how the interactions disintegrated into homicide or suicide, and what the inner dynamics and personal histories of each family member were. News reports invariably avoid such investigations. My search for incidences of instigators came first from my clinical experience; then I was led to the abundance of literature that tells of suicide. I hope that the myths and legends that are used in the following chapters will provide more clarity and psychological plausibility that can be gleaned from a review of the multiple suicides that are reported almost daily in our culture. Our first story about an instigator comes from a Greek legend.

TIMAGORAS AND MELES

A young man named Timagoras was an immigrant to Greece, probably from Turkey. He fell in love with a handsome Athenian youth, Meles. Time and again Timagoras sought the love and companionship of Meles. But haughty Meles wanted nothing to do with this foreigner. He persistently refused to return the love or friendship of Timagoras. One day, obviously irritated by Timagoras' presence, Meles challenged Timagoras to prove his love by climbing to the highest point of a cliff and throwing himself from it to the rocks below. "Go jump!" he yelled.

All too eager to gratify any request of his beloved, Timagoras immediately climbed the Acropolis and jumped from the highest point, killing himself instantly. Horrified and guilt ridden by his own cruelty and insensitivity, Meles now had to look within himself, recognize his false pride and feel the shame of his prejudice and anger. Meles found he could no longer face himself or life. Racked by remorse, he rushed to the Acropolis and jumped, in his death finally uniting himself with Timagoras. Meles was, without doubt, an instigator.

Enraged by the cruelty shown Timagoras and the implied discrimination against themselves, the other immigrants in Athens built an altar to Anteros,[3] the "avenger of all rejected love."

Anteros was the brother of Eros. In Greek mythology, Eros, the god of love, was the son of Aphrodite and Ares. He was lonely and languished in his loneliness, making it impossible for him to grow.[4] To help him, Eros' mother, Aphrodite, gave him a brother called Anteros. As long as his love was affirmed by the presence of Anteros, Eros grew physically and prospered spiritually. Anteros became the god who reciprocates love and also the god who punishes those who scorn love or do not return the love of others. The immigrants, feeling scorned by the Greeks, built an altar to Anteros, to express their revenge.[5] The other message in this story is that in all of us love is the prerequisite for growth; without it, we shrink emotionally and spiritually.

One theme that will occur over and over again in this investigation is the effect that the failure of love can have on both the instigator and the suicide victim. A suicide kills two—sometimes directly as with Meles and Timagoras, sometimes more indirectly. But as Shneidman suggests, any suicide leaves an "illegacy" to the survivors, an agonizing, self-doubting, self-questioning guilt.[6] Arthur Miller, in his play *After the Fall*, has the hero say, "A suicide kills two!" Unrequited love seeks its revenge.

KATY AND HER MOTHER

Katy provides an excellent example that a wellspring of instigation may surface in the most unexpected situations. I first met Katy in a children's hospital. She was a beautiful, dynamic teenager with long brown hair and dark brown eyes that sparkled when she smiled. She had one brother, ten years older, who was married and lived in a distant city. Her parents were divorced and she lived with her mother. Katy had been riding in an automobile with her friends when a truck struck their car, killing her three friends. Katy lived but was paralyzed from the waist down, never again to walk.

For about three months, Katy was a patient in the hospital in which I worked. As the time for her release approached, her physician referred Katy and her mother to me for counseling in order to prepare them for the physical care and emotional support that Katy would require once she went home. To enable Katy to have some independence, her mother had already remodeled the home to provide an outside ramp from the house to the sidewalk and an enlarged bathroom space to accommodate Katy's wheelchair.

Katy had been quite depressed over her paralysis, but she showed a good spirit for making it in life, for returning to school, and for seeing her other friends. She had received extensive counseling with another psychologist during her time in the hospital, and was as ready for her change in lifestyle as could be expected. Her mother missed several scheduled counseling sessions with me, but since Katy's medical doctor had ordered them, she eventually came for a session. A tall and imposing woman, she stomped into the office and settled down with a huff. Sitting sideways and not looking at Katy, she demanded, "Now what do I have to do? This is the only time I will be here!" Katy's eyes filled with tears.

Several times during the course of our conversation, the mother complained that Katy had ruined her life. Not only did she have to pay for remodeling her home, but in addition, the mother felt that her personal life had been destroyed. She had been ready to marry her present male companion, but now that would never happen. Her life was ruined! The actual words that she snapped were, "Katy should have died, too! She has always been a problem and now she is spoiling my life again." Later in the session the mother looked at Katy and uttered, "I don't know why you lived and your friends all died!"

This was not the mother I had expected to counsel, not a woman who cared deeply about her daughter. She was not a mother who was grieving about her daughter's accident or who was concerned about her future, and not a mother grateful just to have her daughter alive. She certainly was not a mother ready to help Katy meet the challenge of living.

Katy did indeed go home with her mother. Within a month she returned to the hospital. Feeling too intensely her mother's anger at her very existence, Katy had cut both wrists with a razor blade, severing several nerves. She lived. But she lost the use of one hand. Perhaps the saddest part of this sad story is that Katy's attempt at freeing herself from life ended in a kind of living death. Katy was sent to a rehab center and from there to a foster home for disabled young adults.

The hostile reactions of her mother had been too much for Katy to bear. The mother was too selfish to sacrifice her wishes for her own life in order to provide Katy the love she needed. The path to suicide was opened for Katy. Her mother led Katy to despair and to attempt to kill herself; she was an instigator. The mother's rejection of Katy and her grief over her own losses in life were expressed in anger and hostility. It may well be expected that her anger was an old anger, a hostility that ate at the core of her being and now found expression against Katy during this new trauma.

Tommy's father, Katy's mother and Timagoras' beloved Meles angrily pushed their victims toward suicide. Meles even said the famous words "go jump!" They knew what they had done, because they had consciously expressed their wishes for the suicide, though they might not have consciously expressed their malicious intent.

The puzzle of each suicide will never be solved. Nor must every person in a relationship with a suicide victim question his or her intentions or responsibility. Many suicidal tragedies will remain enigmas. Furthermore, our society seems to be gradually accepting suicide—especially assisted suicide for the aged or pain-ridden person—as an acceptable end to one's life.

Nevertheless, my first observation was that many persons in danger of suicide are irresistibly provoked by an antagonist, an instigator who activates the death sentence lurking in the shadows of the already self-condemned suicide victim. The victims are seeking love from an individual who is unable to provide it. The victims' deeper and older fear, that of being unlovable, now asserts itself in the self-killing actions.

The second realization, which surprised me from these stories of fiction and from clinical experiences, was that the instigators were revealed as a physically stigmatized, damaged and psychologically traumatized player. Having been wounded, the instigators are struggling with life and seem unable to embrace love. In their search for inner peace, or even revenge, the instigators engender conflict in the outside world, as cult leaders do with their followers, or they reinforce and stir up the self-hate within the suicide victims. It is the usually unconscious, primitive struggle with their own stigmas or traumas that causes instigators to goad someone who is weary of life toward the suicidal plunge. We shall see how the instigators' internal struggles are acted out upon others. Most individuals do not fall prey to others in their struggle for life, but some unfortunate persons who already feel a pull toward death may succumb to these fatal attachments.

The third observation was that the instigators and the suicide victims are pulled toward each other in unfounded hopes that the relationship will somehow fulfill their inner strivings and gratify their longings for unconditional acceptance. Both are deeply conflicted souls, however, so that the relationship can only prove disastrous; for no one, other than an infant, can have the unconditional love these victims—the instigator and the suicide—crave.

The following story describes another kind of instigator. Sometimes the instigator seems to have been innocent, but as we shall see, this instigator brought about the suicidal death of the hero. It is a classical myth, often interpreted as a tragic love story.

HERO AND LEANDER

More than one poet has immortalized the romantic tragedy of Leander and the beautiful Hero. However, a closer reading of the story reveals a secret: Hero may have deliberately caused the drowning death of Leander.[7] Hero, a priestess of Aphrodite, lived in a high tower, a chaste, beautiful young girl who attended neither dances nor festive gatherings. The story says that her parents kept her isolated, well away from friends, so she could not even mingle with other girls her age. She was permitted to go the temple of Aphrodite, the goddess of fertility and of Eros, whom she appeased through sacrifices rather than gratifying them by enjoying the delights of the couch.

She was exceedingly beautiful. It is said that she "flashed a lovely radiance from her face, and a meadow of roses appeared in her limbs when she moved. From these limbs flowed not three Graces but one hundred."[8] The three usual Graces were Brightness, Joy and Blood of life.

Christopher Marlowe wrote of her:[9]

> But far above, the loveliest Hero shin'd
> And stole away th' inchanged gazers mind,
> So ran the people forth to gaze upon her,
> And all that viewed her were enamour'd on her.

Her beauty was powerful. She used it as a weapon.

So at her presence all surprised and token
Await the sentence of her scornful eyes,
He whom she favors lives, the other dies.

And

Her kirtle (gown) blue, whereon was many a staine,
Made with blood of wretched lovers slaine.[10]

Thus her beauty was flawed by her pride. She caused the deaths of those young men who sought her. Then Leander came upon the scene. He was a comely youth, beautiful and young. His hair had never been cut and it dangled down to his shoulders. Of him, Marlowe wrote:[11]

Some swore he was a woman in man's attire,
For in his looks were all that men desire,
A pleasant smiling cheek, a speaking eye.
A brow for love to banquet royally,
And such as knew he was man would say,
Leander, thou art made for amorous play.

A yearly international festival was celebrated in the town of Sestus in Thrace, where Hero lived, to honor Adonis and Aphrodite. People came from many cities and even such distant places as Thessaly, Cyprus and Lebanon. The young people especially enjoyed these festivities because they had opportunities to meet wonderful partners with whom to spend a lovely time. Because it was a festival in honor of Aphrodite, Hero was permitted to attend.

The young men were so dazzled by Hero's beauty that it is said they became speechless. Many vowed they would accept instant death if they could first sleep with her. They would even choose to marry her rather than become an immortal god. Leander, too, was speechless, but he was a man of action. His love for her proved greater than his fears, and though awestruck and speechless, he approached her with eloquent gestures. Seeing his longing gaze, Hero returned subtle signals of her own. This is how Cupid often introduces himself, for words are too slow when beauty must find its way to the soul. And so Leander and Hero held hands before they uttered a word to each other.

Leander prayed Hero to take pity on his desires. He knelt at her feet, saying that she was like a goddess to him and that he had been shot down by love. (Remember Cupid and his arrows?) He kissed her throat. With more golden words, Leander convinced her that chastity would offend Aphrodite, the goddess of fertility.[12]

> The richest corn dies, if it not be reapt,
> Beauty alone is lost, too warily kept.

At first Hero protested. Yet, after hearing his pleas, she too became speechless. He was a beauteous young man. With a glow warming her heart, she said, "Stranger, likely your words might rouse even a stone"[13] It is still true today that the silver words of a lover win the heart of the maiden!

Leander lived in another town called Abydus, which was on the other side of the Hellespont. Hero told him that her parents would not permit her to marry an alien, and if he stayed in Sestus as an alien, they would not be able to hide their love. She claimed, "That same deed a man does in silence, he hears of in the crossways."

Note that in order for him to have her love, Hero set conditions for him to meet. These seem to be symbols of many a condition that are present today. He should not move to her town; even if they tried to keep their love a secret, everyone would gossip; her parents would not approve of him, and so on. These conditions indicated the beginning of rejection. The conditions that were set were one sided, all on her terms. Leander, the victim, in trying to meet the demands of the love she proffered was undermining himself.

Overwhelmed by his passion, he replied, "for the sake of your love, I will cross even the wild waves." In effect, he said, "I will do anything if only you love me." Already he had become a victim, willing to place himself in mortal danger. He submitted to her impossible demands, but at too great a cost to himself. When such conditions are made and met to satisfy her passion, the victim has already surrendered his own integrity and even placed himself in grave danger.

Hero herself had but one task. At nightfall she was to light a lamp in the tower where she lived so that he could swim across the Hellespont to her, using the lamp as a guide to her bed. She would guard the lamp and shelter it with her cloak. Leander called her lamp his life and the star by which he could set his course. Though he could have followed a true star for navigation as was the custom, Leander had made her his star. Their tryst was made. His doom was set.

The Hellespont, today called the Dardanelles, is a strait of water across which few ever attempt to swim. Akin to the entrance to the San Francisco Bay waters, the currents are strong and treacherous. No one would attempt such a swim except under dire necessity. Leander's father warned him against attempting such a lover's swim. Nevertheless, each night Leander waited in the dusk for her signal. When he saw the light in the tower, he cast off his clothes and swam the mile across the churning waters of the Hellespont, where Hero greeted him with open arms and took him to her bed. Then before dawn Leander crept from their lovebed and swam the treacherous waters back to his hometown. Her parents were never aware of their trysts.

Then the situation deteriorated. Hero imposed more conditions, and meeting those conditions became more difficult. With colder weather, the storms came. Even so, like a moth to a flame, Leander risked his life to swim to his star. There is no suggestion that Hero acknowledged the danger that Leander faced, perhaps unconsciously pushing him to the precipice. Their relationship was unbalanced. One stormy night, struggling against the sea, Leander lost sight of the lamp. Of course it was a suicidal swim, for the waters were even rougher and the currents stronger during the storm. He could not find the lamp because Hero had let it go out. Without his star, he lost his bearings and perished in the waters. Hero had manipulated his suicide-death, not unwittingly, as idealists might claim, but willfully. She knew that especially on a stormy night with no stars shining in the sky he would need the lamp to guide him.

The day Leander washed ashore at the foot of the tower, Hero saw his dead body, beaten by the rocks and storm. Then, like Meles, she was filled with unbearable remorse, not for the loss of Leander but for her own actions. Tearing off her robe, she threw herself down from the tower to lie beside her lover in death.

Ostensibly this is a tale of love gone awry. In the earlier story, Meles was an aggressive instigator who, from the start, could not tolerate Timagoras' love, and so he commanded him to jump. At first glance, Hero and Leander seemed different. They seemed to have loved and to have returned each other's love. Hero had promised to shelter the lamp with her cloak, but she let it go out. It was a betrayal of love. She knew full well that many other unsuccessful and unrequited lovers had died because of her. She knew that on that dark, starless night Leander could not find his way without her.

In this legend we see one way a fatal attachment can work. One person, who will ultimately be the instigator, is essentially caught up in his own narcissistic solitude. Inwardly he may sense the isolation of his existence and have some intuition that to continue without any attachment might mean a slow trudge toward a lonely death. Though this person is too involved in his own charms to change, he may be touched by the earnestness of another person, who seeks an attachment so desperately that he is oblivious to what is readily apparent to others—that the relationship is a one-sided affair. A fatal bargain is made that the person desperate for love has to endure constant danger and hardship or sacrifice as the given condition for the attachment. Often enough this condition enhances the power over the victim-to-be. Eventually, the one who has accepted the love grows bored, or distracted; the love game becomes less interesting and the light goes out. Then comes the death of the needy, desperate partner. The death is more or less accidental, more or less deliberate. And how very often this failed attachment can be observed today: love affairs whose flame burns out. Being dumped by a lover makes the world look black and thunderous. But being rejected is catastrophic when one person has sacrificed so much of himself, of his own life, just to be with the lover. The longing for love and lust brought Hero and Leander together as it has many a couple. It was too one-sided to be fruitful for either; he making the sacrifices, she seeking to fill her own needs.

In this story we begin to see a psychological pattern easily found in everyday life. First comes the rapture of passion as Leander approaches Hero with words, looks and signs of lust or love. Some restrictions are placed on the pursuer, the one needy or pleading for love. Difficulties begin to grow between the couple, and the pursuer tries all the harder to please the loved one. The harder the pursuer tries to please, the more conditions or restrictions are placed. The loved one becomes less enthralled with the game and less fascinated by the pursuing lover; the rejection that comes is often a casual dismissal of the lover. But the lover, rejected and desperate, finds solace only in death, in suicide.

As I continued my search, I found that instigators are not always individuals who angrily and aggressively push the suicide toward his or her death. There appear to be several different kinds of instigators, some not so openly angry as others.

External instigators. These are actual people in the present who incite suicide in another. They are usually individuals who reject or resist an attachment to the suicidal person, even when love or a bond would be expected, as was the case between Tommy and his father. There are two types of external instigators. The *active instigators* are those who angrily and aggressively reject the person and openly wish for his or her death; it may even include a command to die.

The *passive external instigators* are those who silently, consciously or unconsciously, project the wish for another's death. The mode is rejection; the goal is the end of any attachment. Their withdrawal of love may be less evident and their hostility tends to be camouflaged. The result is the same: death for the victim.

Internal instigators. These instigators, either figures from the victim's past or fantasized enhancements of the victim's inner guilt or self-hatred, arise within a victim. Most often these instigators pertain to the victims' intense identification with death, usually the death of someone who was a significant person like a parent. This significant person committed suicide or died by some other means during the childhood of the victim. The death was traumatic for the child. While the relationship between them may not have been a secure or positive attachment, this relationship becomes idealized in the victims' thoughts and can be realized only through death. This identification with the death then takes command of and directs the thoughts and behavior of the individual. The result is an inner persecution that drives the individual toward death. This result can be seen when an adult who experienced the death of a parent as a child is driven to follow in the parent's fatal footsteps to suicide.

Provocateur instigators. These are also external instigators, persons whose self-righteousness covers their own angry wishes for death. Instead of acknowledging their own usually unconscious feelings of guilt or grief, these instigators actively goad the social conscience of the victims, awakening their feelings of grief and guilt, thereby provoking them to self-killing. In effect, they sabotage the life of the suicide victim.

This category includes cult instigators of suicide who have a strong pull toward death. As cult death-leaders, these persons feel condemned to die and, in revenge against life, to lead others to their death with them. Terrorist-instigators similarly use others as pawns. To maintain their power over life, they brainwash other traumatized individuals into committing suicide and simultaneously killing as many other people as possible—all for their "cause," such as a political or religious conviction.

Tommy's father, Katy's mother and Timagoras' Meles have already illustrated the active external instigators. Tommy's mother and Hero give a picture of the passive instigator. We shall now take a look at the experiences that seem to be found in the childhood of instigators.

CHAPTER 3

Terrorized Children

From Innocence to Instigator

And a little child shall lead them.

Isaiah 11:6

How does one become an instigator? What experiences in life lead a person to live in daily dread of death and to make a desperate attempt to escape such a fate by causing the death of others?

The following stories of Paulette, Mary and Osama bin Laden reveal early shocks that left them terrified of both abandonment and death. The attachment to their parents was negated, destroyed in a brutal fashion. They met their silent, unconscious fear of death with a determination to live. They became instigators compelled to overcome the terror caused by their early traumas, and to do so by reenacting their awful experiences with others. This compulsion to restage their losses becomes the gateway to survival, to life and to gaining some control over death—but by shifting their own death sentence onto others. Controlling life in this fashion deeply gratifies the instigator. It would appear that the person who is so beset by trauma and left without a comfortable sense of self-with-others strives to recapture some vestige of identity. Because the early attachments were tenuous or damaged, the inner life of the person may become a barren landscape, as a tree without leaves. That is, the inner life is emptied except for those confusing traumas which now govern the thoughts and the feelings. The person is often without an awareness of the propelling force that the traumas bring. Earlier healthier experiences of attachment, may be stripped of their meaning because the sense of predictability and continuity of life are disrupted.

Unfortunately, however, sometimes the victim does indeed turn instigator and murderer. The following story from a novel by Francois Boyer captures how an intimate exposure to death might shape and deform the horizons of a child.[1] It is a story of fright, of hurt and of emotional ferocity, a story of two children brought together by fate and joined in a morbid game. The experiences of these two children provide food for thought as we try to understand some of the impact of abandonment and death.

PAULETTE

It is June 1940. Paris is being evacuated. Men, women and children, mostly with bleeding feet, with animals such as dogs, cats, calves and horses, form a long column of refugees straggling along on a country road. They are fleeing from the Nazis, to nowhere.

Among them are Paulette, nine years old, and her parents. Her mother is dead, strafed by a German *Jagdflugzeug* (a hunter plane). Paulette thinks her mother's corpse has very likely been kicked into a roadside ditch. There is no time to bury the dead. Just move on. Now the hunter plane returns, strafing and killing more people and animals. Paulette's father is shot in the chest and forehead. Paulette kneels beside him and cries, calling her dead father, "Stupid!" Stupid to let himself be machine-gunned down, stupid to die and abandon her. Stupid is what her father had called her, "That little stupid . . ." Somehow, for some reason, he had disliked her, so she had often disobeyed him. Now he has left her and she is angry at being left alone. She fears she will die, too. She cries some more. She asks herself why she cries. She does not know. Mute and motionless she stays beside her father in a long, long trance. But then a wounded black-and-white dog with an injured foot appears; the dog sniffs at her daddy's corpse and runs across the field. Paulette gives chase, catches it, and sits down with it by a stream. The dog dies.

Paulette comes near a hamlet, Saint-Faix. There is a crossroad by which stands a chapel with a tall iron cross on its belfry. After a recent bombing had shaken the chapel, the cross had bent over a little farther, almost falling down. Michel Dollé is a ten-year-old boy, the youngest son of a farmer who lives in this town. Michel spies a horse, tall, gaunt, black-and-white with a shorn off tail, still wearing a harness. Michel eagerly calls his family. They all come. Hoping to make use of the horse for the family, Michel's adult brother, Georges, grabs for the horse's mane. The horse shakes him off to the ground and attacks. As Georges tries to roll over and get away, the horse tramples on him, his hooves ripping Georges' belly open. In his pain, grief, frustration and anger, Father Dollé turns on Michel, slapping him and shouting, "That's a fine way to look after your COWS!"

Michel himself had been afraid of this tall stray horse. He feels responsible for the terrible accident and avoids looking at his wounded brother. He had called the family to that murderous horse and he was to blame for it all. Could he ever forgive himself? He is sure Georges will die. Michel is furious with himself and his father. He tries to smother his grief with his fury but his grief is choking him.

In this mood of grieving anger and angry grief, Michel runs to the stream, freely crying. Presently, as he sits there by the stream, he becomes aware of little Paulette. She sits alone among the weeping willows lining the stream. By her side lies a dead black-and-white dog. She, too, is crying. Paulette tells Michel that her father and her mother are dead. Incredibly, he then asks her, "Why are you crying?" Paulette sighs. Nor does Michel know why he is crying. These two children seem not to know about grief. They do not know that crying is an expression of grief.

Just as the children do not know what makes them cry, they also do not know what makes them play out the puzzling animal games they will soon invent. They are moved like puppets, overwhelmed by grief and guilt. Paulette and Michel are victimized twice, first by their traumatic exposures and then by their mute, unspoken grief which finds no expression, not to each other or to their elders.

Michel and Paulette are immediately drawn to each other. The Dollés take this strange little girl, quiet and subdued with unblinking eyes, into their home.

Paulette notices that the Dollé family all use hoes to dig out weeds from the garden. She takes a hoe, too, and goes to the stream where she has left the dead, cold black-and-white dog that she now handles tenderly. She raises one of the dog's eyelids and recoils in fright. Silence. She makes the dead dog jump up and down on its hind legs, perhaps to revive it. It is dead. She makes a wreath that she solemnly places on the dog's head. Then she tries to make the dog dance again. "Do it nicely! Dance!" Useless. Paulette digs a hole with the hoe and buries the dog.

The next day Michel finds Paulette at the stream by the dead dog's grave. Michel's dog appears, a dead mole in his jaw. When the dog drops the mole in Michel's hands, he throws the little corpse into the stream. By now, Paulette is already obsessed with the dead. She throws herself on the ground, screams and sobs convulsively. Her arms and legs thrash about; her body arches, shudders and stiffens, as if an electric charge had been steadily growing within the child and now discharges itself in a turbulent outbreak of grief for her parents. Michel senses the meaning of Paulette's attack because the mole, like her parents, was not buried. Wanting to please her, to give her the dead mole to be buried, he retrieves it for her.[2] As she had done with the dog, Paulette caresses and kisses it. Together, the children bury the mole beside the dog. Michel promises her a cross for it.

Soon Paulette has infected the boy with her obsession for making reparation for the death of her parents. Both feel guilty. Michel is susceptible to guilt because he feels responsible for the stray horse's attack on his brother. Michel says about the buried animals, "What we shall have to do is make them crosses." Although Paulette does not understand why, Michel teaches her about the priest, religion and the father in heaven. He teaches her to say the Ave Maria and "blessed is the fruit of thy womb, Jesus" over the graves of the dead animals. Paulette does not know what a womb is. Michel tells her that's where Georges is hurt, in the tummy. Paulette then responds, "And blessed is the fruit of thy tummy, Jesus."

"Thy womb!" shouts Michel.

"Thy womb," amends Paulette.

Michel makes crosses for the dead animals.

In a day or so, Georges dies, leaving Michel overwhelmed with grief and remorse. In his grief's anger, he kills two chicks and takes them to Paulette, who is delighted. She kisses the dead chicks, dances them. "You killed them for me!" she says to Michel. Both children laugh with glee. Then they bury the chicks in their animal graveyard. Michel makes more crosses. In the following days, their graveyard grows—with moles, ants, flies, birds. All must have crosses, too. No longer absorbed in making amends for her feelings about her parents, Paulette now delights in exercising her newfound power over death, even with making death. Michel is smitten with love of Paulette—and he needs relief from his grief, too.

The children go to the funeral for Georges. There is a cross on the hearse and also the letter "D" for Dollé. Paulette must have them, so

Michel steals them. Later, Paulette and Michel wander through the cemetery where all the graves have crosses. For fun, they match the crosses with animals—a cross for a horse, for a sparrow, a nanny goat, a pigeon, a calf, a flea, a chicken, pig, snake, rat, donkey. They are playing burial. And slaughter. There is a tall stone cross. For which animal? "A giraffe!" exclaims Paulette. They take many of the crosses to the stream for their dead animals.

There is just one more cross that Paulette must have, the cross on the top of the chapel. She wants it, wants it. She wants Michel to get it for her. He resists.

Michel says, "We've only just got to wait for it to fall." She wants it right now.

"Pooh! You are frightened." Paulette taunts him; "He's frightened! He's frightened! He's frightened!" Michel is embarrassed. She becomes seductive. "It's not very high, you know. You can see the ocean from up there!"

And so Michel climbs the chapel wall for the cross. He knows it is not safe, but he wants to please Paulette. He knows he might fall. He knows the cross will not support him. But he climbs. And then, just as he takes hold of the cross, the cross tumbles. Michel tumbles, too, falling to his death and sacrificing his life for her love.

Paulette had felt no compunction about asking Michel to risk his life for her. She buries him, planting the cross from the chapel and the letter "D" on his grave. She walks off into the unknown. The author leaves the story here—Paulette leaving, alone. Obsessed as she is with death, she is condemned to repeat her dangerous and futile game in one form or another. She is now a seductress of death.

The development of an instigator seems engendered by early trauma and grief so violent that any attachment to others and to life has been shattered. Bonding with others has been irreparably impaired. Paulette's fears of her own death and having her parents die leave her with a compulsion to overcome her fears. The success of her control over the death of the animals brings her a sense of relief and delight. As the author states, "the children laugh."

It would be easy, at this point, to claim that Paulette is an exception, that she is simply the product of an author's imagination and that her fascination with death is merely the premise for a work of fiction. But, sad to say, Paulette's story is not at all isolated from reality. Here is the case of Mary, a ten-year-old girl whom I saw for an evaluation in my practice as a clinical psychologist.

MARY

A chunky girl, a little large for her age, Mary was in her fourth foster home in four years because all of the previous foster parents had demanded she be removed from their home. A county social worker brought her to the clinic for an assessment of her social problems and for suggestions of a placement and treatment that would help her.

Mary proved to have above-average intelligence and to be especially quick with arithmetic problems and puzzle solving. A clever child, sometimes very charming, with a winning, innocent smile, she could often manipulate others to get what she wanted. She could also be very helpful and quite acquiescent, so that foster parents and other adults would be drawn to her and would want to take care of her.

In the interviews, Mary seemed an unusually open child, talking easily about all her foster parents. She claimed to love the home where she was currently living, saying that these parents were the best parents she had ever had. Further, she emphasized that she loved her foster brother, age three, and foster sister, age six.

Still, the present foster parents were extremely upset over her behavior, not because she had broken the other children's toys or hidden food in her bedroom, or because she would tease the other children until they hit her so she could then "tattle" on them and claim that she was mistreated, and not because of her occasional temper tantrums, though all of these things figured in her behavior.

The problem? Her foster mother had discovered Mary maneuvering her three-year-old brother to jump into the family pool where he was sure to drown. How did this come about? Mary told me her story, one that resembles Paulette's in many ways.

The foster family had three young puppies, one for each child. By putting food on the top of a three-step ladder that Mary placed by the family swimming pool, she carefully trained each of the puppies to climb the ladder, where they eagerly devoured the food. Then one day when the puppies reached the top rung, Mary tied rocks around their legs and pushed the puppies into the pool to drown. Mary smiled to tell how they struggled and sank. Next, Mary told her three-year-old foster brother to jump into the pool. Since he always followed her around and sought her attention, he did jump. She knew, of course, he could not swim. By sheer luck, the foster mother just then walked out of the house to see how the children were playing and saw her son plunge into the pool, where he surely would have drowned.

Mary's life experiences had made her manipulative and even quietly sadistic. She had become fascinated by death and desperately needed knowledge about dying. By three years of age, her father had disappeared, imprisoned, and she never saw him again. To Mary this was the same as if he had died. The next year, she watched in horror as her mother was brutally raped and killed by a man who broke into their home. Any sense of safety or security had been destroyed. By the age of five she was unremittingly wary of the world. Traumatized by the loss of her parents and frightened for her own safety, she became obsessed with terror, loss and death. As each successive set of foster parents "abandoned" her, she was forced to relive the loss of her parents all over again. She longed to find some control over death—and life. Her behavior became more and more sadistic as she gave expression to the anger that raged within her, anger against her fate and an expression of her grief.

The theme of early trauma, grief and the need for power over death will be followed throughout the stories and the case histories in this book. Instigators are made from the terror of trauma. Traumas stir up the fear of death in all of us. In the instigators, a lifelong compulsion may develop to overcome the fear of death through developing a control over dying—sometimes in a need to reenact the key moments through staging the death of others. This can bring a rush of euphoric relief to the instigator.

OSAMA BIN LADEN

I would like now to take a brief look at the childhood of Osama bin Laden, though in truth there is little that is verifiable about his childhood. The one authoritative source that was available at the time of this writing was the book by Adam Robinson, *Bin Laden: Behind the Mask of the Terrorist*.[3]

Osama bin Laden was born in the summer of 1957. He was the seventeenth of fifty-four children (twenty-three brothers and thirty sisters) born to his father, Mohammed bin Laden. His father was very wealthy and provided well for his family. Though he autocratically ruled the family, including his wives and children, he is described as a kind and generous person who engaged in many philanthropic activities. He valued learning, having been faced in his own adulthood with his illiteracy and the need to acquire a belated education. He organized the educational schedule for the children, providing them both group and individual tutoring sessions. The father was determined that his children should have a solid religious foundation and made certain that they received this instruction as well.

Osama's mother, Hamida, was from Damascus. She was said to be stunningly beautiful, a vivacious young woman with a strong personality. Not a suppliant or an unquestioning person but rather one who had her own thoughts and felt free to speak them, Hamida did not marry until she was twenty-two years of age. Hamida was from Syria, so she was alien to the more strict Moslem culture that severely limited the role of women. She struggled with the cultural necessity of wearing a *burka* to cover her face. Because of her streak of independence, the other wives soon scorned her. She was isolated and ostracized by them and spitefully nicknamed *Al Abeda*, the slave, since slave women did not wear the *burka*.

Mohammed was not accustomed to women who were not submissive to men. Even before Osama's birth, a deep rift opened between Osama's mother and father. Wanting Hamida out of his sight, Mohammed forced her to live at the outer edges of the family compound or in some far-away home like Tabuk, a town in northern Saudi Arabia, while her son, Osama, remained with the family in Jeddah where he was reared mostly by nannies and nurses. Osama grew up motherless, never warmed by the love of a mother. Whatever early attachment he may have had with his mother was irreparably ruptured, negated; and even today he remains aloof from her. One can only wonder if Osama's need to keep women submissive stems in part from his father's disdain toward his mother.

Osama was also ostracized by the other children. His brothers refused to play with him and teased him mercilessly about his mother, calling him "Ibn Al Abed," the son of a slave. He often isolated himself in his room. Like many fearful children, he resorted to silly childish antics and mischief in his attempts to gain the attention of adults and of his siblings. He is described as a tall, lanky, introverted boy who was singularly gracious and polite to adults. Missing the close bonding that would have been natural with his mother, he tended to seek substitute attachments with only one person at a time, trying to find that special love. He was unable to feel comfortable as part of a group and thus did not fit in with the family. Osama was dutiful and well behaved around his father who, incidentally, was often absent, traveling on business trips.

There were two activities in which Osama received positive attention from his father. One was during the compulsory Islamic studies, where he avidly read the Koran, shone with his knowledge and participated eagerly in discussions. The second was during the excursions with his father and brothers to the desert. He loved the freedom of the open spaces and surpassed his city-loving brothers in outdoor activities such as riding the camels, learning to shoot and playing in the sand dunes. At home he remained the same shy and isolated boy.

His father died in 1967 when the helicopter in which he was traveling crashed when Osama was ten years old. Profoundly affected by his father's death, Osama retreated to his room and shut the door. Shortly thereafter he was sent, without warning, back to live with his mother. Although Hamida tried, she could not restore a relationship with him where none had ever existed. He shunned her, becoming almost mute in her presence. Remaining angry, aloof and withdrawn from her, he eventually wrote his uncle, asking to come back to the family residence. Now both motherless and fatherless, he returned to Jeddah, a bitter and disillusioned boy.

In Osama we see the frightened, abandoned infant taken from his mother, his first experience with loss. Then the "slave child" taunting from his siblings and especially the loss of his father through his sudden death all heightened his sense of alienation and brought him inconsolable grief. According to reports, these experiences, especially the death of his father, seriously traumatized young Osama. He withdrew to his room, alone with his grief.

His preoccupation with life and death had its early roots in his childhood, for his earliest loss was that of his mother. Death and loss are terror for any child. They bring on a dread of the unknown. Life is without safety or predictability and without protection. As an adult, Osama's fear of death has led him to take unusual preoccupations for his own security. Likewise, he has now justified the death of suicide-bombers.

Children like Paulette, Mary and probably also Osama bin Laden have been quite literally frightened into death's domain. Expectations of death infect them with a sense of terror for their own lives. They have had no control over life and death. Mother and father are gone; they are alone. When will they die?

The terror of death becomes all-possessing. They live with it; they sleep with it. There is no way for them to understand or accept the parents' disappearance into death. When there is no one to comfort them or to explain the deaths to them, they must develop some sense of control over their own existence. Somehow, they need to be able to control death. They become obsessed with death.

Grief is an emotion that demands relief. Grief demands expression. Children must learn of death, of its finality and of its dreadful ache. Comfort and explanations are necessary, for children have no frame of reference for abandonment or death. New attachments and affections must be found. Unfortunately, the younger the child, the more difficult it is for the child to understand death and loss, and the younger the child, the stronger and more lasting will be the impact on the developing personality.

How to defeat death when one cannot grieve? One common way for a traumatized adult to manage his or her distress is to revisit the experience over and over again, sometimes by retelling the experience compulsively, sometimes by having endless nightmares of it, sometimes by acting it out again and again. For children it is the same, with the higher likelihood that they play it out. The repetition of the living-dying cycle is an attempt to understand what happens in death and to remove the inner sense of terror. But no matter how often one rehearses it, the why and the how remain unanswered questions. Since some small relief may follow the repetition of a life-through-death drama, for a child it may become a ritual. But grief remains unallayed. The attachment to life is ruptured.

So they kill to live, reliving death all over again. Paulette with her little animals, burying them, dead, after she has "danced" with them. Then to kill Michel. Mary killing the puppies after she has trained them and fed them, and trying her best to kill her little brother. These children have once been victims of their experiences, but now they have control. They have the power to induce death. The sense of power relieves their fears and they become addicted to this sense of relief. Osama bin Laden, as an adult, exerts that power by convincing his followers that death is desirable.

This feeling of power in children is ironic because it most often results in more violence toward them. Must an adult not punish a child for killing or hurting others? Any additional violence these children experience—as Paulette did when her friend Michel was beaten by his father—stirs up both the fears of death and the fantasies of killing. In her fantasies, Paulette punished Father Dollé by twisting his feet, digging out his eyes with a hoe, cutting off his feet and finally sticking a cross into his head, to carry him up to the clouds and then have him fall into a black well full of fire and boiling water. In her thoughts she had killed her parents, and in her fantasies she killed Father Dollé. Whether or not these children become aggressive or violent depends much on their subsequent experiences, and whether or not they grow up to be instigators cannot be predicted. Nonetheless, there are active provocateurs of suicide, and when we do encounter such a person, it seems quite probable that we can expect to find an inner world that is devoid of life. Also, we can expect that it would be very hard to ever create sufficient safety for them, even within the therapy setting, to allow grief to begin so that their need for omnipotent control can be relinquished.

CHAPTER 4

Passive Instigators

Walking By on the Other Side

A POISON TREE

I was angry with my friend:
I told my wrath, my wrath did end.
I was angry with my foe:
I told it not, my wrath did grow.

And I water'd it in fears,
Night and morning with my tears;
And I sunned it with smiles,
And with soft deceitful wiles.

And it grew both day and night,
Till it bore an apple bright;
And my foe beheld it shine,
And he knew that it was mine,

And into my garden stole
When the night had veil'd the pole:
In the morning glad I see
My foe outstretch'd beneath the tree.

William Blake

In the poem above, Blake draws the picture of the passive instigator. Seduced by charm and deceit, the enemy-victim grabs for the poison, tricked by the promised sweetness and his own desperate need.

It is relatively easy to recognize the active instigators of suicide: they deliberately and openly incite someone else to kill themselves. They hate the very existence of their unfortunate victims and drive them from life itself. These are the *active* instigators, human forces outside the victim-to-be who aggressively stimulate the suicidal actions. Tommy's father, Katy's mother and Meles fit this pattern. Misdirected anger lies within every instigator.

There are other instigators who are more difficult to identify—and therefore more dangerous: their feelings are hidden. These are the *passive* instigators who share many traits with the active instigators, but with a significant exception: they do not let the depth of their hostility or fears show openly, not to the victim, not to anyone else, not even to themselves. If you suggest, ever so diplomatically of course, that they might wish harm to a friend, they become offended, disclaiming their anger. To disguise their hostility from themselves, they may even present a defensive stance of "doing good." Remember Hero, first singing her love for Leander, then letting the light of her attachment to him blow out, leaving him to die in the cold embrace of the black waves.

Most of us at some time or another have had the feeling that life would be easier without this one or that one who is such a thorn on our path. So we lose a phone number, claim a previous important engagement, pass off their little pin pricks with a shrug, or do whatever it takes within our moral boundaries to convince them to leave us alone. We just might scream, "Drop dead!" This is an impulsive reaction to a present pain. It does not necessarily represent deeper, more chronic feelings.

The instigator-suicide interaction is shaped and toned by players, their characters, their ideals and their fates. A typical drama emerges: a scenario marked by yearning and manipulation, by love, rejection and death. In their formative years, something has twisted their moral or social development bringing about the lack of a cohesive self-identity that is marked by persistent dissatisfaction in social relationships. Embitterment and rancor pervade their existence as they unknowingly seek to gratify a revengeful urge that has resulted from inner traumatization and stigmatization. Their previous injuries leave these instigators with unremitting fears of death, with physical or emotional stigma and anxiety about future abandonment and loss.

These persons become dominated by the need to preserve the barricades they throw up against overwhelming anxiety and their fears for life itself. To escape, they seek attachments with others in hope of undoing their disappointments and trauma. Ironically, the instigators mar these attachments by displacing their anxiety and hostility onto those who seek their love, the very people whose love they have invited. Their suffering leaves them little room for recovery, except, that is, by taking blind revenge on someone who is innocent of doing them any harm. Under cover of their attachments, these passive instigators are out for revenge.

The passive instigator does not consciously look for a victim. The bonding takes place when the unconscious drives of the instigator resonate with certain dynamic forces dormant within the potential victim.

Freud gave very little attention to the role of others in fomenting suicide.[1] In 1921 he wrote briefly about a young man who was tormenting his mistress. He concluded that the young man was trying unconsciously to drive her to suicide in order to get revenge. Why? The man had himself attempted suicide several years before when a different woman rejected him. Freud correctly saw that his patient was traumatized by the loss of his first love and that, to revenge himself against her, he turned his aggression toward another woman. However, instigation was not the focus of Freud's attention. He was more interested in the man's early identifications with his parents.

Misdirected anger lies within every instigator, and in some cases the hostility may grow into a homicidal drive. In a fleeting image or an angry moment, passive instigators are sometimes vaguely aware of their desire to make the victim leave, but they would usually be loathe to admit they really and truly want somebody to die, much less murder themselves.

Chained deep down inside the passive instigator there hides a revengeful death scheme. Eventually it escapes, perhaps in the form of Blake's "apple bright," and lies shining and tempting for the victim to steal.

Our leadoff passive instigator is from a rather tragic case history.

JANE AND BOB

Jane and Bob had originally come for counseling to discuss a single problem: Jane wanted to attend graduate school and Bob ardently opposed it. At Jane's insistence, Bob agreed to counseling. Both claimed their marriage was satisfactory but there was one problem that they could not settle. It appeared that Bob was concerned that Jane might become too independent and not rely on him anymore. He needed the assurance that she was there, at home, for him. They agreed that in the few conflicts during their marriage Bob always surrendered and gave in to Jane. For after all, Bob reported, Jane was the person who was in charge of their home. Jane's major complaint was that Bob never wanted to travel, which she considered important for her life. This was the one instance in which Bob maintained some control. Jane confessed that she had thought at times of a divorce because he was a weak man who never took initiative in their home life or in his work. She had never taken any steps toward a divorce because she recognized he was devoted to her and to their family.

When they were first seen in counseling, Jane and Bob were in their early fifties and had been married over twenty years. Their two children were married and self-supporting. Jane kept her trim figure with regular workouts at the local gym and still had the youthful look and the perky blue eyes that Bob had found so irresistible. But quite a few inches of waistline had crept up on Bob, and his brownish hair was surrendering its ground rapidly. Their friends considered them an attractive couple. Then came a critical time in their lives. In therapy they seemed to resolve their conflicts and discontinued further treatment.

Two years later, Jane returned for therapy, sobbing uncontrollably and moaning that she had killed her husband. She loved him so much, she could not live without him. She told this story: She had entered graduate school. Then other problems began, especially for Bob and his employment. For twelve years, Bob had held a very satisfying mid-management position at a local computer company, but a larger corporation was swallowing up the company. Suspecting he would soon be out of a job, Bob lapsed into deep despondency. He spent some time checking out his life insurance, health insurance, retirement plans and his will. He put documents and notes on his desk so that Jane could easily see what he was doing, if she cared to look. He did not talk with her about the substance of these papers, or his reasons for working on them.

In spite of several signs that he was quite depressed, Jane did not ask him about his sudden interest in their legal and financial matters, preferring to think it was merely one of his obsessive preoccupations. Because he was either irritable or withdrawn into silence, she avoided him. When he tried to talk about his fears of losing his job, she dutifully promised him he would not be fired. Everything would be all right. He should not worry. In other words, she patronized him and dismissed his concerns as unfounded.

One evening Jane went to her class and afterward to a café for coffee. She returned home about 11:00 p.m. When she parked her car in the driveway, she noticed a light in the garage, but did not think much about it. Bob was not in the house. At first she thought he had taken a walk, as he did at times. She remembered becoming impatient and angry that he did not come home when he knew she would be there. Jane said she then read some of her lessons. At midnight, she remembered the light in the garage and decided to see if he was in the garage, perhaps preoccupied in some project. She found him in the car, its motor running, his head slumped down, his breath coming in soft wheezes. She turned off the motor and tried to talk to him. He did not respond. Later she said she was in shock and did not know what else to do. A good ten minutes went by, with no frantic 911 calls, no mouth-to-mouth resuscitation, no night-rending screams to the neighbors for help. With Bob still refusing to open his eyes, she did at last phone his brother for advice. He told her to call for an ambulance that very instant. At that, she called, but Bob died on the way to the hospital. She had called too late. Or had she?

It is apparent that Bob was the dependent person, the one who desperately needed assurance of her love. Jane's desire to attend graduate school was a threat to him; he correctly sensed her independence as a sign of rejection, especially if she no longer needed his financial support. The possible loss of his job had reinforced that idea and intensified his feelings of rejection.

It is also clear that Jane, on the other hand, seemed to have been giving signals of rejection to Bob throughout their marriage. She was critical of his passivity and demeaned him to me as her therapist and, I suspect, to their friends as well. When Bob sensed that he was losing his job as well as her love, he killed himself. But he carried it out in such a manner that he could have been rescued by Jane and his life might have been saved.

Jane claimed she was so shocked that she could not move when she saw him in the car. She just stared at him with his head slumped down between his shoulders. She said that when she "came to," she called his brother. The shock did not spur her to action; it did not energize an effort to save him. Following Bob's suicide, Jane's life was in turmoil. She stopped attending classes at the university, and claimed she could not study or work. She returned for therapy a grief-stricken, guilt-smitten woman.

Later in therapy she would discuss her frequent anger with Bob and how often she wished he would just disappear from her life. The shock of finding him almost dead was at least in part the shock of having her wishes fulfilled.

As her story unfolded, it became possible to identify some threads of her history that suggest the forces at play in her life with Bob. The one incident that seems to clarify some unconscious hostility came with this memory: One day when she was nine, a friend invited her to a birthday party. Her father readily gave her permission to go, but to fill the time before she was to leave, her father told her to help her older sister wash the dishes. Instead, she went outside to play. Though she was his favorite daughter (of that she was certain), he grounded her. "No party? Not fair! Not fair!" rang out—but only in her mind. The next day, her father committed suicide.

Her father's death left her with the dogged voices of guilt and fury deep inside her. The guilt said she killed him because she had disobeyed him, and been angry with him over his punishment. The fury screamed in reply that he deserved to die for being really, really mean. Later she watched her husband drifting away from her in his depression. He was not providing the absolution she wanted. She projected the guilt and anger against her father onto her husband; he, in his dependency, accepted this guilt as deserved. I can speculate that Bob's depression probably brought memories of her father's depression before he killed himself. Bob's depression, then, so like her father's, could account for some of her inability to act. She could do nothing as a child; she did not know what to do as an adult.

Passive instigators like Jane are often ruled by unresolved feelings rooted in earlier trauma. Not recognizing the implacable thrust of their wounds, Jane and instigators like her dismiss their memories, never understanding the impact that the horrendous shocks lying dormant in their unconscious can have on their later lives.

Jane never truly grieved for her father. She felt betrayed by his death, but the betrayal also left her with a compulsion to be the one in control. She could not risk fully trusting again. By choosing a husband she could dominate, she might escape her fears of more punishment and loss of love. Those fears also propelled her to restage her father's suicide in the neglectful rejection of Bob.

The following story, from an unlikely source, demonstrates how an apparently innocuous event can resurrect a damaged self-image and vividly describes the inner turmoil of a passive instigator.

THE FALL

At first, we may think that the lead character of Albert Camus' *The Fall*[2] is merely an innocent onlooker when an attractive young woman jumps into the winter-blackened waters of the Seine. But Clamence is no minor character. In his subsequent morbid reactions to this apparently random encounter, he fully enacts the role of an external passive instigator, showing the vulnerability of his defenses against his own death drive. Somewhat reminiscent of Coleridge's Ancient Mariner, Camus' doomed hero tells his own story, over several days, to a fellow drinker he meets in an Amsterdam bar. Clamence is ill and cannot talk for long periods at a time. He becomes ever weaker until he cannot leave his bed and can hardly talk. It is obvious that in a day or so he will be taking his own fall.

Clamence had been a brilliant criminal defense attorney in Paris, with a passion for defending the weak, especially widows and orphans. He wore his heart on his sleeve. The slightest hint of distress would mobilize him into vigorous and expert action on a victim's behalf. Above reproach in his professional life, he held the respect of his peers and judges alike. He was an avid do-gooder even while walking the streets of the city. Seeing a blind person about to cross the street, he would hurry to help, even shoving a closer helper out of the way. He readily gave directions to those lost along their way, would help push a stranded car, would buy poppies from Salvation Army vendors, would give money for tattered flowers to an old peddler, would extend alms to beggars, would give up his seat in the theater. To all appearances, he was a generous, helpful man, in harmony with his life.

This icon of virtue was walking home one cold, rain-swept November night, crossing a bridge over the Seine. It was very late, but even with the rain soaking the darkness he felt quite animated. In a moment's idle glance, he noticed a young woman, slim, attractive, dressed in black, leaning over the railing, staring at the inky stream below. Her image disrupted his pleasant mood, it "stirred" him, and she aroused his anxiety. He hesitated, even stopped momentarily. But going directly against his consciously established pattern, he made a crucial decision: he passed her by, distancing himself from her obvious anguish and her danger. A mere fifty yards further on, he "heard the sound—which despite the distance, seemed dreadfully loud in the midnight silence—a body striking the water." He stopped short, but did not turn back.

> "I heard a cry," he says, "repeated several times, which was going downstream; then it suddenly ceased. The silence that followed, as the night

suddenly stood still, seemed interminable. I wanted to run and yet didn't move. I was trembling, I believe from cold and shock. I told myself I had to be quick and I felt an irresistible weakness steal over me. I have forgotten, what I thought then . . . slowly under the rain, I went away. I informed no one."[3]

Clamence becomes utterly miserable. His first reaction is to think that he too ought to commit suicide and thereby punish his friends just as he is feeling punished. When he realizes he does not have any friends, he becomes obsessed with self-observations. He discovers that his former generosity and altruism have merely served to make him feel "above" all others, in the same way that he preferred mountains to valleys, balconies to theater floors, the bus to subways. As Clamence said: "I was always bursting with vanity. I, I, I is the refrain of my whole life which could be heard in everything I said . . . I recognized no equals. . . . When I was concerned with others, I was so out of pure condescension and all the credit went to me."[4]

He had empathy with no one, only a gratification of his sense of power. He had lived in a tower of narcissism, countering his own fears of death through a reaction formation, that for him meant giving outrageously to others instead of quietly hating them or acting out aggressively against them. He said, "Power . . . settles everything."[5]

Camus gives no clue as to the woman's motivation for suicide. But after hearing those cries from the waters below, Clamence's guilt over his inactivity when she was killing herself rules his life. Images of death burst into his daily life, compelling him to face his desires for others to die. For instance, he was a bachelor who bragged that he was always successful with women. Many women. He had desired to be loved, or so he thought. But it had become plain to him that as soon as he gained a woman's affection, "the ideal solution would have been the *death of the person* I was interested in" [italics added].[6]

To nullify something means to make it of no value or consequence, such as a law that has been nullified and thus can no longer be upheld. In effect, Clamence completely nullified the very existence of those he helped, in much the same way that he nullified any genuine attachment to his sexual partners or to the woman on the bridge. These people meant nothing to him except in the moment that they added to his sense of power and pride. So he walked by the woman in black, shrinking her entire being to nothingness. He would have said that she was a stranger to him—but she certainly became no stranger to his later inner life.

In this chance encounter, the woman touched a part of him that he had kept well disguised behind his masks of altruism and generosity. When she died, he could no longer hide from himself. His once buried feelings took center stage with a vengeance. From the moment he abandoned the woman on the bridge, grief and guilt ruled his life because of his passive instigation to her suicide. His life lost all meaning, and he was compelled to acknowledge his homicidal desires for others to die. When she fell, he fell.

No longer harmonious, his life was "out of tune." He lost his legal practice through eruptions of anger in the courthouse against his clients, against the judicial system and against the judges. He fostered distrust of his colleagues and of others. Increasingly paranoid, he felt he had enemies and that everyone was laughing at him. He even wrote a pamphlet exposing how the oppressed inflict the pain of conflict on decent people—quite the opposite of his former opinions. His anger seemed uncontrollable. He lived "in a fog." This suggests that he remained so disturbed by ignoring the woman on the bridge that reality became dim and unreal to him: he was dissociated.

Increasingly alcoholic, he moved to Amsterdam, where he lived in a single, messy room and held forth nightly at a bar in a gin-soaked haze, dispensing legal advice to one and all. Obsessions and phobias such as double-checking the bolt on his door and fearing to cross bridges now controlled his actions. An unwilling host to hallucinations, he heard people laughing at him, saw corpses floating in the waters below and heard screams out of the dark. Obviously he suffered a post-traumatic reaction to the passive approval of her suicide.

The inner turmoil that is described in this story represents the inner world of an adult who finds himself an instigator. Jane's reactions were just as vivid, if not so aptly described as in Camus' story. Traumatic experiences can break through the defensive barriers of the unconscious and renew forgotten memories. Camus' hero said that he "found his memory." One patient told me that memories of her abusive childhood returned in full force when her husband struck their teenage daughter. She recalled horrendous details of her mother's physical abuse during her early childhood. The dissociation that blunts the memories of a traumatic incident may be enlivened, permitting a forceful return of memories.

In therapy, we often help the patient experience a gradual return of the repressed memories, and we hope to do so in a careful manner that will not disrupt the patient's life. Even so, with the return of the repressed memories comes some increasing inner chaos for patient. Thoughts and images may besiege the person. In this story the image of death haunted Clamence when he went to sleep and when he awoke in the morning. With Jane, the picture of her husband dying in the car had nightmare qualities for her, even in her waking life. An encounter with the inner self forces one to face the superficiality of existence when it is hidden behind so many defenses, functional or altruistic. In the story, anger emerges and replaces the more characteristic altruism, and Camus' hero had thoughts about "jostling the blind man on the street; and from the secret unexpected joy this gave me, I recognized how much a part of my soul loathed them."[7] This forced encounter with the self may be disastrous. It was for Jane. In *The Fall*, Clamence attempted to quiet the inner chaos with alcoholism, but that led to a dissolute life.

Jane was a passive instigator. Only somewhat aware of Jane's continual rejection, Bob was keenly sensitive to her moods and wishes. He succumbed to her in their arguments, obviously not wanting to face the rejection that came with disagreeing with her. When Bob died, Jane had to come to terms with her negative attachment to and rejection of him and with her passive wishes to be rid of him. She had not divorced him because he gave her too much. She could rely on him, almost. But the love she offered was the "apple bright" that never came to fruition for Bob. He could not quiet her inner turmoil. Bob was always trying to please but could never quite satisfy her. Her neediness proved too much for him to endure in life.

The dynamics of suicides such as this are common enough. At first the suicides seem unexplainable, but an investigation of the relationships and the interactions may well reveal the role of the survivor, that is, of the instigator.

Passive instigators to suicide are those individuals who first of all are dealing with the stigma and trauma of their own lives. Consciously or unconsciously they need to reenact scenes of loss, abandonment or death, in futile attempts to undo their sting. The woman on the bridge corresponded to a significant woman in Clamence's life. Jane unconsciously put Bob at center stage to play the father who had rejected her and had died the next day. In her anger at Daddy, she revoked her attachment to Bob; then given her chance, she left him (or was it Daddy?) to his carbon monoxide. She passed by and her tree "bore an apple bright."

Unlike the Good Samaritan, Clamence and Jane passed by on the other side. Their stories show how readily certain individuals can become programmed by their internal, unrecognized conflicts. They may not be totally heartless people. They have suffered, too. But the stories vividly exhibit the necessity of exploring one's uncharted depths, especially the ones marked, "There be monsters here."

The positive attachment bond is a powerful affectional tie that an individual has with someone who offers reciprocal security and affection.[8] It can be a parent-child bond or a long-lasting relationship as in a good marriage, in which two partners can give and receive affection, closeness and emotional gratification and assurances of comfort and security.

The quality of attachment, however, is not always positive. When early bonding has elicited anxiety, disappointment, grief, anger or a myriad of other bad feelings, the unconscious expectations for future attachments will reflect the earlier negative experience. Much as a person may not consciously desire these negative attachments, they are often repeated.

In analyzing the personalities of instigators, I discovered that they do become attached to their victims. Unfortunately, their unconscious expectations from others are so warped and unrealistic that no one could possibly satisfy them. In time, the bond becomes insecure and loaded with anxiety, and the victim-to-be is colored by and identified with whoever originally damaged the instigator.

Malevolent attachment. This is a pathological relationship between two people, one of whom may be socially or biologically entitled to expect security and love from the other. For example, a child will instinctively expect protection and nurturing from a parent. Likewise, spouses or partners may assume they can rely on each other for support. However, the malevolent person actively rejects the other with expressions of hostility, anger, deprivation or withdrawal. The malevolent one resists any overt or silent appeals for approval coming from the dependent one. There is often a conscious, spoken wish for evil to befall the person even for his death. Sentiments like "I wish you were dead" or "you are a nail in my coffin" characterize these pathological attachments.

Tommy's father in Chapter 1 and Katy's mother in Chapter 2 provide examples of the malevolent attachment. Both parents expressed such hostility toward their children that they could only satisfy their parents' wishes by suicidal actions.

Negative attachment. The negative attachment refers to the relationship between two people in which the negative one withholds positive feelings from the other, even though mutually positive feelings had been present earlier and expressed in actions or words. The negative one spurns the other person's need for understanding and spontaneous support. The negative attachment may be expressed as simply as, "I don't love you."

An example of a negative attachment may be found in parent-adolescent relationships in which the parent (or adolescent) is actively rejecting or hostile during this critical developmental period when adolescents so desperately need the support of caring, concerned parents for their well being. Likewise, a competitive sibling or a spouse may withhold love even while professing to care.

Both persons may remain in the relationship indefinitely, seeking the love they both desire. When a more positive attachment is not forthcoming, the obvious hostility may generate so much desperation that the rejected person is driven to a suicidal attempt. The threats of suicide by the rejected person are often misinterpreted as attention-seeking actions and consequently ignored or even laughed about. But they are a plea for help which, if not given, will often lead to a successful suicide.

Instigators in our cases of negative attachments suffered from deficits in interpersonal relationships that stemmed from chronic, often unconscious, fears of rejection, fears that they turn upon the other person. It is a dark aspect of their shattered self-worth that incites misplaced revenge against the potential suicide victim, the one who has blindly relied upon the attachment long after it has become poisonous.

Nullified attachment. To nullify is to act (or feel) as if the other person did not exist. In this relationship, attachments are denied or aborted, made null and void. The nullifier acts as if the other has no value or consequence. Nullification can also occur when the nullifier simply ignores or denies the existence of the other. Note that to nullify is more than the casual social snub, although at times this act may fit the pattern. The nullification is a conscious, self-righteous, judgmental and hostile action; at other times it may be less conscious, less overtly hostile but similarly justified.

Circumstances may be such that this person may never be compelled to face his innermost hostile and grief-loaded feelings and may continue his life in a self-satisfied style although bitterness towards others outside his approved circle persists. He can often justify or rationalize his actions and feelings until that time when his behavior against another so forcefully contradicts his self-image that his defenses disintegrate. The aftereffects then provoke such inner turmoil that turmoil pervades his life because he must now encounter within himself his own destructive, hideous feelings and actions.

To nullify a relationship may have serious and deleterious consequences for both. The effects of being the recipient of a nullified relationship may be disastrous for that person if he has such little inner strength that he cannot assert his own right to live. If earlier rejections have been traumatizing, any additional rejection suggests that suicide is the only option. Another banished person with more inner strength may not be so thoroughly devastated. Rather, he may plod on in anger or revenge or with a determination to prove himself, to himself.

When my husband's father stated that he never wanted to see my husband again, his father did, in effect, nullify any attachment to him. While my husband was deeply anguished by the banishment from his father, he could continue with his life and his plans for life because of other sustaining attachments. His father apparently never appeased the rancor within himself.

The effects of denying another's existence were seen in the story of Timagoras and Meles in Chapter 2. Meles was so devastated by his own act of nullifying the existence of Timagoras, that he, too, killed himself. There is another example in Camus' novel, *The Fall*. The hero, Quentin, nullifies the existence of a person about to commit suicide by ignoring her. Afterward, he suffers such intense anxiety that his life is completely changed, for he is forced to admit to his own murderous impulses.

Fantasized attachment. A fantasized attachment occurs when one person holds an internal image of an ideal person and then relates to another as if he were the reification of the ideal. When the fantasized projections are accepted, an intimate, intense relationship develops. In this relationship, the person who projects the idealized image attempts to fashion the feelings, thoughts and behavior of the other in order to gratify his own narcissistic, self-aggrandizing needs. Only those behaviors and feelings that fulfill the projections are accepted; other behaviors are countered with denial, hostility, dismissal or retribution. The projections may be those of an idealized or of a demonized person, like that of the perfect loving mother-wife or the evil abusing mother-wife. These fantasized images provide a defensive wall against painful memories of past spoiled attachments.

Initially, the partner may be pleased by the idealization and attempt to live up to the expectations of the other, like a child trying to win parental approval. But it is a make-believe relationship: one person writes the script, the other plays the role. It may be the "hero on a white horse" that comes to the rescue of the heroine as many potential brides may yearn for or the Shirley Temple doll the parent seeks in the child.

Unfortunately, attempts to gratify the projector will soon pall, and the partner will be unable to fulfill the role satisfactorily because the expectations become ever more demanding and unreal. And also because the idealizations are a defensive maneuver against inner anxieties and griefs of the projecting person. The partner role player will also want some acknowledgment for his own feelings. It is an unreal relationship, denying the reality of both participants.

This attachment pattern maligns the integrity of both, the one who acts on his projections and the other who must conform or risk losing the relationship. Clearly, the sense of self is weak and undeveloped in the creator of an idealized partner because his projections conceal deep pools of despair. Hence any attempt to find the remedy for deeply embedded inadequacies and disappointments in this way is futile. The story of Hanna vividly pictures the effects of a mother's rigid projections upon her daughter.

Ambivalent attachment. This attachment pattern is often described as a love-hate relationship. However, the ambivalence is not simply the feeling of "he loves me, he loves me not." The ambivalent attachment involves an intense need to merge with another. In this pattern when the person feels "like one" with the other, the ambivalent one has a comfortable sense of well being. That is, when the ambivalent one's existence merges with the other's in significant feelings and actions, such a person feels content and secure in the relationship. There is a heightened intimacy and dependency in this attachment pattern and any physical or emotional separation is strongly protested. The person requires proximity to the other although the closeness shrouds a subtle hostility. This pattern often entails a jealous clinging.

This quality of attachment begins in infancy when the infant is forced to develop oversensitivity to an anxious, sometimes rejecting mother. The infant learns to respond to the mother's feelings in order to enjoy any tidbit of comfort or warmth; the infant's feelings are not responded to by the mother and eventually, repressed in the infant himself. Incorporating someone else's feelings and actions as one's own demands an abject surrender of one's self-integrity.

Then when the partner, who may feel suffocated by such a clinging person, strives for some measure of separateness, the relationship becomes strained and anxiety-loaded. Often enough, both may have outbursts of anger, resentment and abuse.

There is frequently circularity within this attachment pattern, with the intimacy of the relationship evoking anxiety in both. Old fears of rejection are awakened in one and a sense of being suffocated pervades the other. An increasing emotional distance between the persons ensues; then they begin seeking a new closeness through merging once again. It is an on-again, off-again relationship.

The social self is deeply impoverished in this attachment pattern because the members can find a sense of self only to the degree that their feelings, wishes, and actions reflect a unity. In truth, both partners find some temporary gratification in this attachment pattern. However, any movement toward autonomous or independent action severs the bond. There is a thoughtful picture of the ambivalent attachment pattern in Arthur Miller's play, *After the Fall* in Chapter 6.

Self-attachment. This attachment pattern is the obverse of the ambivalent attachment. In the ambivalent relationship, the bonding results from the subjugation of one person's feelings to those of the other. The self-attached person carries around such a crippling anxiety that it can be relieved only in the bonding with another person who reinforces the self-attached person's aggrandized self-image. There is no integrity afforded to the other except while the needs of the self-attached person are being met. The self-attached person is convinced that his feelings and actions are the correct ones. Other persons lose value except as they substantiate his ideas and actions. In one type of this narcissistic picture, the person may become angry, even destructively aggressive when faced with any contradictions. Another self-attached person is more sensitive, more easily offended and very vulnerable to rejection.[9] Narcissus might have loved Echo, as she hoped, but his fascination with himself prevented a relationship.

We shall see how those with narcissistic attachments may take a very passive or a quite hostile stance toward others. In either case, the self-attachment pattern deprives anyone else of any sense of autonomy or individuality—except while fulfilling the needs of a Narcissus.

These are pathological attachment patterns because the security of existence and the warmth of reciprocal love are absent. I believe there are other patterns that are even more destructive to life, such as the following.

Usurped attachment. In this kind of bonding, charismatic leaders fraudulently impersonate the kind of parental figures with whom many people had desperately needed an attachment. The leaders induce others to adore them, to give them all their assets, and to abandon more meaningful relationships in order to share in the warm glow of the leader's love as he or she leads them to eternal bliss by way of communal suicide. The Jonestown and Heaven's Gate members are examples.

Exploitative attachment. This attachment is the instrument of people such as terrorists who employ any stratagem, fair means or foul, to enmesh others into a bond so strong that they will destroy their own lives in order to fulfill their exploiters' insatiable hungers for economic, political, military or religious power. The siren call of this attachment is especially strong to young adults, with their sense of cognitive omnipotence (knowing it all) and their altruistic strivings (wanting to save the world).

I hope that identifying and distinguishing the different types of instigator attachments will provide some understanding of the instigator-victim interactions and greater understanding will help avoid some of the terrible outcomes seen in these chapters.

CHAPTER 5

Passive Instigators II

But I Was Doing the Best I Could

> To Mom and Dad,
> I know your life
> will be easier without me.
> I love you,
> Sonny

That evening, fifteen-year-old Sonny said a special good night to his mother and father, kissing them both on the cheek. Then he did something extraordinary. He went to his younger sister Kay and then his little brother Ron to bid them good night, telling them to be happy and to be good to Mom and Dad. Later his parents heard loud music coming from his room, which was unusual, but ignoring it, they soon went to bed themselves. When his mother called him for school the next morning, he did not respond. At length, angered by his over-sleeping, she went into his room. There he was, swaying gently in the morning air below a light fixture, his favorite chair kicked over, the note carefully smoothed out on his dresser.

Sonny's self-extinction is not rare. After homicides and accidents, suicide is the third leading cause of violent death for adolescents, with one such wrenching loss about every two hours. Sometimes, as with Sonny, no one can answer the question left murmuring in the shadows, "Why?" With no ready answer, too often parents, brothers and sisters, friends at school, teachers, church acquaintances and neighbors become infected with the guilt and sadness the victims leave behind.

For adolescents and parents alike, this is a time when both should be exploring new and broadening avenues of love for each other. Many parents dread the teen years of their children, fearing they won't be able to protect them from the thrills—and dangers—of alcoholism, drugs, sexuality and rebellion. For their part, even while striving to retain their attachment with their parents, the youngsters are launching their sometimes stormy crusades to occupy and explore their own developing sense of themselves, their identity and independence. In the ensuing battles, the unintended casualties on both sides may be love and respect for each other.

Especially if the parents succumb to an ambivalent attitude toward the adolescent, a love-hate relationship develops that can irrevocably mar the attachment that the young person has been relying on and hopes to preserve. But when the parents complain to high heaven about the difficulties the adolescent brings to them, or when deep down, Mom or Dad wants them out of their lives, sensitive adolescents may just grant their parent's wishes, surely in despair, perhaps in revenge.

When an adolescent attempts or succeeds at suicide, there is often a tendency to place the responsibility upon a "depressed adolescent" or upon a "dysfunctional family." But the simplistic label *dysfunctional* may discourage the critical deeper look at the details of the "dysfunction," necessary for true understanding. To give an example of one parent's attitude toward her teenage son, a professional woman with whom I met told me that many a time she had told her son, "When you're eighteen, you're out the door." He left her home even before eighteen. His "door" was suicide. In a different scenario, the youngster may reject the parents' values in an angry rebellion. Uncomfortable as this can be, it obviously is a healthier reaction than suicide and the misery it causes all around, because it openly expresses feelings and takes the adolescent one step toward autonomy and adulthood, assuming the rebellion is not seriously antisocial or physically damaging to anyone.

The parents' role in the suicides of adolescents has come under some scrutiny. One psychologist, R. E. Gould, wrote, "For many reasons the parent[s] may wish the child did not exist . . . [and] basically feel they would be happier without children."[1] Joseph C. Sabbath discussed the "expendable child," which in his theory "presumes a parental wish, conscious or unconscious, spoken or unspoken, that the child interprets as their [parental] desire to be rid of him, for him to die."[2] He postulated that the problems of the parent-child relationship reach a critical point during adolescence, often highlighting the parents' unresolved conflicts with their own parents from their own adolescence. And so a corrosive and escalating attack and counterattack set in. The parents see the adolescent threatening their personal and marital stability—not to mention their public reputation. The adolescent feels hated and persecuted, unloved at every turn. Suicide may be just around the corner.

In my work I have tried to look behind the immediate parent-child relationship and focus on what brings parents to the point of instigating their children's suicides. The parents of Sonny quite unintentionally (they thought) and apparently with no words at all displaced onto their young son their long-standing conscious and unconscious despair about the course of their own lives.

Earlier, with their marriage unsatisfying and home strife-ridden, Sonny's mother and father had begun family counseling. At forty, Sonny's mother, Amy, was short, stocky and clumsy, with no sense of style, her hair cut straight and close to her head. Her face was scarred and her left arm had been permanently disabled. An attorney, she was garrulous, possessed of a voice that was strident and loud. Even after Sonny's death, she was still angry and confrontational. Albert, the father, was stout and an inch shorter than his wife. A research physicist at a national atomic laboratory, he, too, was quite verbose, though not so abrasive.

When I first met them, Amy immediately complained: "The children are always arguing or fighting. I can't manage them. I think the school should help us out more." She spoke rapidly, without pause, as she listed their problems: Sonny's long hair; Kay's age (12, overweight), endless temper tantrums and sassy back-talk; Ron's age (8, appealing) and seeming refusal to learn in spite of special help at school. Amy complained, "Shameful! I always had good grades, even though my life was miserable!" Finally, the unending barrage of arguments and fights topped her list of unhappiness. Relaxing a bit, she reported that only Sonny was doing well in school. I saw him as a tall, lanky boy, who seemed unadjusted to his new height, loping along like an Ichabod Crane, his clothes flapping carelessly about him. A high-school sophomore, Sonny was bright enough to be taking college math classes. Today, he would surely be called a nerd.

When I asked the parents how they got along with each other, Amy quickly stepped in, "Sometimes when the children are in bed or in their rooms, Albert and I argue with each other about money or sex." Albert added, "Of course, the children don't hear us." Or so Amy and

Albert chose to believe. They were probably wrong. With clashing opinions on just about everything, the whole family stewed: parent vs. parent, parents vs. children, child vs. child. Nowhere in the house was there ever any peace or calm.

In childhood Sonny had few friends, and now in high school he had none at all. To me he appeared a very sensitive boy, keenly aware of his parents' discordant moods. He reported that sometimes he tried to bring some resolution to the family dissension, but over the years he realized he could make no peace when any two or more of them were in the same room at the same time. With no interest in his sister's or brother's television programs or their games, he ignored them as much as he could. At last he began doing his chores quietly and easing away to read in his bedroom.

Even after Sonny hanged himself, Amy still complained about him. She bitterly recalled that when he was little, he was always in her way, clinging to her skirt until she pushed him away. After school, she would have to chase him out of the kitchen so she could get dinner. At about twelve, he started whining that he was not happy. She told him that everyone was unhappy at times and to get over it. Once he said he could not stand their arguing and wished they would stop it. Nothing changed. So he would just hide in his room, reading or listening to music.

Amy said Sonny seemed really down when he did not find friends in high school, but she simply told him everyone had problems at that age. Then, as if to check herself, she added that he was a good boy, a very sensitive boy, always seeming to know when there was trouble at home. "Sonny never really gave us any problems—no drugs, no drinking, very devoted to the church."

It is tempting to concentrate on Sonny, his gangly walk, his lifelong despair and his longing for companionship and love, but that would block us from looking at the forces pushing him to suicide. The ambivalence of his mother about Sonny and the other children was clear. She was overwhelmed by the responsibilities of both her profession and her parenting, and she blamed the children for her predicament. Far more than Albert, she balked at expressing any warmth toward them.

After Sonny's suicide, neither Amy nor Alfred extended their arms to the other in loving empathy or remorse over losing their son. Neither could understand why Sonny had taken his life. They were not at all introspective, and in spite of his note to them, they did not examine their own roles in his death. Instead, they said, "We're shocked, just shocked! How could Sonny do this to us!" Ron and Kay seemed stunned into quietness.

At the time, I had the impression that Amy was not as surprised as she claimed. Yet I doubt she was being dishonest with me. I suspect she was being dishonest with herself, as she had been all her life. She had avoided confronting her pervading dread of loss and the continuing trauma of her physical injury. Because she never recognized and grappled with her own feelings, they remained like inner cancers, exuding anger, guilt and control. Although faced with Sonny's suicide, she continued her lifelong pattern of denial, never owning up to any part in the family's tragedy. She quickly discontinued therapy, which would naturally have focused on her own feelings.

Amy and Albert stoutly denied that either had ever wished for his death, silently or aloud. Neither had said, at least not in Sonny's hearing, that they would be better off if he were dead, as had Tommy's father. Both readily admitted, however, that Sonny had arrived at an unfortunate time in their lives. Under the surface, though, the seeds of death and fear for their own lives had been sown deeply within them long before. Briefly, here is the story behind these unhappy and unwitting instigators of their son's suicide.

Amy was in her second year of law school and determined to become an attorney. With Albert, she was enjoying her first romance, but she certainly did not want any permanent commitment. To her dismay she discovered that her affair with Albert had left her pregnant. Unmarried and members of a strict religion, they quickly married to avoid the shame of her pregnancy. From the very first, Amy resented the child that was coming. Simply squirming in her womb, he disrupted her plans for a professional career, and she would not have it. Upon giving birth, she immediately returned to her studies, leaving the care of Sonny to Albert, who was by then a university professor. Pressed for her reaction to Sonny, Amy recalled that he was "cute"; but there was no warmth in her voice when she talked about her first-born.

I wanted to understand what happened to Amy and Albert before reaching any conclusion about them as parents and then as instigators of Sonny's suicide. Amy's own history was sad. Both of her parents were killed in an automobile accident when she was two years old. She herself was terribly injured in the accident and spent a long recovery time in the hospital. With her left arm permanently damaged and her face scarred, she was taken to live with her grandmother, whom Amy recalled as very old, very poor and very ugly. Sickly and depressed, the grandmother muttered angrily about having to provide for little Amy in her tiny one-room apartment in New York City. Amy remembered being unhappy, unloved and lost, belonging nowhere and to no one. Having lost her anchor to her parents so early in life, Amy grew up reliving her early shock and mutilation, awakening every single day to fresh fears of death and disfigurement. They followed her until late at night, when she lay down to an uneasy sleep.

Her grandmother died when Amy was eight, and she was taken to live with her mother's brother and his family. Here she received adequate care and praise for doing well at school. Even so, she grew up traumatized by the accident and her losses, always afraid that she, too, might be killed. Going to school was painful. She felt stigmatized by her facial scars and her damaged arm. She had few friends because, she claimed—for no reason—other children would not play with her. In high school her social life was even worse. When a boy refused to take her to the junior prom, she was so devastated that she tried to kill herself by taking aspirin.

She managed to survive by developing an awesome determination to get what she deserved from life. Sonny's birth was an accident that was a temporary setback. She never wanted him and rejected him from early pregnancy and throughout his life. The message to Sonny was clearly "I don't want you." It seems to me that she carried within her a pervasive guilt. She had been rejected from early childhood by the death of her parents, and the loss of her grandmother and her disfigurement were weights that she felt she carried because she was not worthy. She grew up with a sense of being unlovable: in her deepest feelings, she had caused the tragic events of her life and was unworthy of love. Sonny bore her projected guilt as long as he could. Deciding he was the source of unhappiness, he chose to leave, by death.

Although Amy's attachment to Sonny would not be called overtly malevolent in the same way that Dr. Jerome's was for Tommy, her feelings for Sonny were certainly negative. She had never wanted him and had never provided the emotional warmth that every child needs.

Albert, too, knew something about loss from his earliest years. He had never known his father, who had left his mother when Albert was three. Growing up in a single-parent family was especially difficult because Albert's mother had to work long hours to support them both. A series of aunts and uncles housed Albert for short periods of time, though his mother occasionally took him home with her on weekends. He remembered stumbling in the way of the adults and often getting spanked or being sent to his room for childish misdeeds. Only one aunt showed him some affection, and he still recalled her with warmth.

When Albert started school, he again lived with his mother, who was still working until late in the day and coming home just in time to give him supper and put him to bed. He was terrified of being alone in the apartment; he would hear noises that made him hide in a closet, sure that someone was breaking in. He had many fantasies of his father being killed in some far-off place and then of himself also being killed. In effect, Albert lost both his parents when his father went away and his mother had to go to work.

Approaching adulthood, Albert dreamed that marriage would finally provide the encompassing bonds of love and the pleasures of harmonious companionship that he had been denied throughout his life. Instead, Amy and Albert were drawn together by their kindred fears and unresolved griefs. Albert's infancy, like Amy's, had infected him with the self-fulfilling conviction that if he accepted any affection, he would be abandoned. Ironically, Albert seemed to have chosen a wife who could not fulfill his dreams of love and who ignored him in favor of her profession.

By the time I saw the family, Albert was a deeply dissatisfied man. His marriage did not bring him the affection and intimacy that he longed for, only a sense of abandonment. When Sonny arrived, like many other fathers, Albert happily imagined Sonny as a graceful athlete on the winner's stand at the Olympics, a Nobel Prize winner or some other glamorous public figure who would have lots of glory to spill over onto his father.

At first, Albert did give routine diaper and bottle care to Sonny, reliving the tender care he received from his own mother. But this limited attachment to Sonny was fragile from the beginning. When Sonny was about three years old, his emergence as a self-possessed little boy ignited Albert's unconscious feelings of being abandoned by his own father and mother at about that age, and so Albert revoked his attachment to his son. Albert then projected onto Sonny the anger he had held toward his father, acting out his anger by taking revenge upon three-year-old Sonny, giving unneeded criticism and punishments.

Albert's status changed around this same time when he was awarded a full professorship at his university. His newly found prestige gave him increased self-respect and the appreciation by his colleagues that he had wanted from his wife and children. This facilitated his withdrawal from emotionally involved parenting. He never did reestablish any closeness with Sonny.

Both parents were now more emotionally invested in their work than in their family or marriage. Both had been deeply shocked and scarred, physically and emotionally, by abandonment and loss. Their grief was never resolved. When they were young, no one had ever helped them understand their losses or comfort them in their grief. Unresolved grief does not fade away. Often, as with Amy and Albert, it resurfaces as anger and frustration and expresses itself through hostility or withdrawal. It makes the scarred person untrusting of love and fearful of commitment. These early traumatic losses remain active issues and fester within the person. For Amy, her useless arm was a constant source of grief, a stigma that she bore without grace. She was a domineering, controlling person who exhibited little outward anxiety. She warded off her fears of dying with preemptive strikes against others. Indeed, she often wanted to be in charge during the therapy hours, advising me, as the therapist, how to proceed: I should focus on the children rather than on her as a parent or a wife.

Although she never spoke of her inner feelings to Sonny, or even recognized them herself, her message was clear: "Get out of my way! I really do not want you." Although Sonny tried to find some way to get closer to her, Amy froze him out. During one therapy session, Sonny said that he really loved his mother. Encouraged to show her physically, he rose from his chair and went over to give his mother a hug, telling her again that he loved her. She patted his back, but said nothing. There was no return of affection. Her attachment to Sonny negated his very presence; she was a passive instigator of his suicide.

Amy and Albert outwardly seemed to be trying to find some security and pleasure in their lives. Still, the emotional baggage they carried from their childhood had never been lightened. Much like the experiences of Paulette and Katy, their experiences with abandonment and death left them guilty as children and angry as adults. Both needed power over their personal lives. They incessantly argued for control within the family, making compromises and accommodations with each other almost impossible.

When the projection of Amy's and Albert's anger at their own parents was misdirected onto their children, the especially compliant and caring Sonny was doomed. The parents were, unwittingly, instigators of his suicide. Passive instigators, to be sure, but Sonny was the expendable child—rejected and bearing their projected guilt as his own guilt for their unhappiness. Their attachment to him was not out-wardly malevolent, but certainly a negative relationship prevailed. "I don't love you" was the unconscious message they sent, and Sonny heard it consciously. Because of his sensitivity to their unspoken fears of death, he became convinced that if only he were out of the way, his parents might find some contentment. He hanged himself, thinking he would make the lives of his mom and dad "easier without me." It didn't work. It never does.

Sonny's death was a catalyst for his parents' divorce, two years later. Albert and Sonny's little brother continued in individual therapy, while Amy and the teenage daughter concluded that they had had nothing to do with Sonny's death and therefore had no personal con-flicts to resolve.

Clinicians have often recognized that parents' misery can easily in-fect an adolescent with faceless, unremitting distress and can become the projected force that incites their child to commit suicide. It seems the height of tragic irony that a parent who would be horrified at the thought of murdering his or her own child can blindly—and unneces-sarily—cause his or her own child to commit murder upon himself.

As an adolescent runs the gauntlet to a healthy life, parents are not the only hazards. Losing a friend, romantic or otherwise, is often an immediate trigger that may impel a young person to suicide. When earlier attachments with parent figures have failed, the choice of a friend rarely is satisfactory, because the adolescents are unconsciously trying to replace the unstable attachment to their parents with an ide-alized, substitute parent. Living with such a fantasy—a parent who gives unconditional love—they run a grave risk of reexperiencing the loss of affection all over again. This failure makes young people deso-late. As we shall see later, Henry James' story of Roderick Hudson is about a friendship between two young men, each unconsciously trying to work through the rejection by his father, each using the other as a proxy father.

In exploring the world of fiction for stories including suicides among adolescents and young adults, I found only a few. Here is one that can give a picture of the inner turmoil in one adolescent.

PAUL'S CASE

In this short story by Willa Cather, Paul was a teenager, "tall for his age and very thin, with high, cramped shoulders and a narrow chest. His

eyes were remarkable for a certain hysterical brilliancy and he continually used them in a conscious, theatrical sort of way, peculiarly offen-
sive in a boy . . . there was a glassy glitter about them."[3] His mother
had died shortly after his birth, and he grew up a motherless child. He
was an enigma to his father, who had two older daughters to raise and
who did not seem able to provide Paul a sense of security or direction
in his life. As a child Paul lived in a world of his imagination, and as a
teenager his fantasies were realized through watching the opera stars
that he saw during his work as an usher in Carnegie Hall. The music
itself seemed to "free some hilarious and potent spirit within him;
something that struggled there like the Genie in the bottle found by
the Arab fisherman."[4] Carried out of his rather sordid, unhappy existence, Paul delighted not only in the music but also in the obvious lav-
ishness of the musicians' lives and style of living.

As ambitious as Paul appeared while ushering for the operas, his
schoolwork suffered. Eventually, he was expelled, mostly for his
haughty, uninvolved attitude. His father put him to work as an errand
boy and forbade him to usher at Carnegie Hall. In spite of his false
bravado, Paul was a deeply frightened lad.

Cather described him as always being tormented by fear, a sort of
apprehensive dread that, in adolescence, had been pulling the muscles
of his body tighter and tighter.

> Until now, he could not remember the time when he had not been dread-
> ing something. Even when he was a little boy, it was always there . . . There
> had always been the shadowed corner, the dark place into which he dared
> not look, but from which something seemed always to be watching him.[5]

Here he was, a teenager lost in a world of a fantasized life of gratification. His father was stern, confused by Paul and disappointed in him. He
praised other young men as models for Paul to follow while denigrating
his own son. Driven to despair over his plight, Paul decided to act out his
fantasies. Stealing a bank deposit from his employers, he set off for New
York City, where he indulged himself by purchasing new clothes, including a hat and shoes. Then he went to Tiffany's for a silver scarf-pin, another store for various traveling bags for his purchases and finally to the
Waldorf Hotel, where he engaged a suite. He lived in high style the next
eight days, even ordering flowers for his rooms and boutonnieres for his
coat. Eventually, news of the boy who had taken the money, which had
been immediately repaid by his father, appeared in the newspapers.

Running out of money, knowing that his days of graceful living were over and feeling that during those eight days he had lived the sort of life he was meant to live, Paul bought a revolver. On second thought, he told himself that was not the way to end his life, so he went to Newark on a train, took a cab out into the country and then walked, stumbling along the train tracks. He remembered everything he had seen on that last, fated morning—every feature of the drivers, of a toothless old woman, the agent, all his fellow passengers—all showing him the ugliness of the world. He lay down by the tracks and fell asleep until awakened by a train coming toward him. When the right moment came, he jumped in front of the engine and left behind all the ugliness of the world, and himself as well.

Paul's father had an attachment to his son that withheld positive feelings toward him; it seemed a negative attachment. Cather portrays Paul as unable to fulfill his father's fantasies for him. Rather, Paul was left alone, to live with his own fantasies, fantasies that were unreal and compensatory for his isolated and empty inner world. The negative attachment is given support in several ways. First, Paul's father was simply bewildered by Paul's behavior. His father had confessed to the school principal how perplexed he was about his son; he wanted Paul to be like other young men in their neighborhood; and he was a rejecting, critical and punitive father, leaving Paul in fear of his rages and punishments.

Paul's fears were real to himself. Arriving home one night after ushering at the opera, he was afraid to enter the house and to encounter his father's wrath, so he crawled into the cellar, terrified of making a noise that would awaken his father. Paul sat on a chair awake all night because he was "horribly afraid of rats" and certain that if his father heard him make any noise, he would come down the stairway and kill him.

Although we could suppose that the premature death of his mother and absence of a warm, secure attachment played a decisive role in Paul's development, as well as in his suicide, Cather offers no evidence for this. Yet, she does offer the picture of a solitary childhood and the emptiness of the absence of love in a child. Paul does not seem as besieged by inner turmoil as by trying to fill an inner barrenness, a treeless horizon.

Rejection takes different forms. Sonny's parents actively rejected and neglected him; in Paul's case, the trauma of no mothering and a rejecting father left him without a secure base for life. The following story of Jennifer tells of a different kind of rejection. It is the story of a girl who was forced into the role of an unreal person in order to mold her to the fantasies of her parents.

JENNIFER

Jennifer's story is particularly sad, because it presents the ripple effects of generational attitudes upon children. This case comes from interviews with the parents of a daughter who had committed suicide. Hanna's only child, Jennifer, had swallowed a huge mixture of medications and had been found dead in a motel about thirty miles from home.

Jennifer's parents were referred to the clinic for grief counseling. A very tall, imposing woman, Hanna spoke forcefully and clearly, most often dominating the counseling sessions. With her perfectly glazed mouth and rimmed glasses, she came across as a cold, analytic woman who kept everything that was personal at a distance. She talked constantly about the famous people she knew, rather than of her grief for her daughter's self-murder. She could not talk about her own feelings except in abstract terms. "Of course, I am devastated!" she would say. Or she spoke defensively: "She had no reason to kill herself! She had everything she wanted." Sometimes she was bitter: "She should have known how much that would hurt me. Why would she want to hurt me like that?" While these statements indicated some depth of hurt and devastation, she exhibited very little genuine grief. In essence, she seemed disgusted that Jennifer would kill herself. Jennifer should have known that life was hard. After all, Hanna had learned that lesson early in life. Was Jennifer ever angry with her parents? Of course not; she had everything that she wanted, didn't she? But love? Warmth? One wonders.

Jennifer's father, Michael, was rather thin and quiet. He was a university professor with a mild, subdued manner and usually wore tweed jackets that seemed somewhat large for his frame. To the resident counselor, he appeared to be chronically depressed. Unlike Hanna, he seemed genuinely aggrieved by Jennifer's death. When asked about his relationship with Jennifer, he responded that when she was a child, he was always busy—preparing lectures, reading papers and writing—essential activities for him to gain tenure in the university. He had wanted children but had given over all responsibility for Jennifer's care to Hanna. He could recall a few times that he read a story to Jennifer, but he was not interested in the activities or games of children, especially those of girls, for they seemed tedious and frilly.

Although he claimed he was proud of her, he didn't think he had ever told her so. Throughout her childhood he followed her development "with interest" and looked forward to knowing her better as she grew intellectually and became able to talk with him as an adult.

A university student majoring in economics, Jennifer seemed to have a successful career ahead of her, especially as a high-school teacher. Or so Hanna had decided. She described Jennifer as a healthy, well-adjusted girl who was devoted to her home and her parents, a quiet girl, never giving them any trouble during adolescence. Hanna insisted that Jennifer was always happy. Hanna did remember, however, that when Jennifer was about two years of age, she and Michael had to bandage her hands, and even her arms at times, to keep her from biting herself. As a child, Jennifer had problems sleeping, and was deathly afraid of the dark. Hanna just let her cry herself to sleep. She did go so far as to put a night light in her bedroom, which seemed to help somewhat.

In high school, Jennifer wanted to have her arms tattooed, but Hanna strongly forbade that. Jennifer was seeking some mark, some identity for herself. Jennifer cut her arm once with a razor, but Hanna felt that was only an insignificant adolescent rebellion. Jennifer took high honors in academic work but made few friends. Since Hanna forbade her to date, Jennifer missed out on most of the school's social activities. In college, she found it almost impossible to make friends. Jennifer did date one boy, who soon left her. He had, however, stirred up Jennifer's sexual feelings—a forbidden, frightening reaction for her, since she had been taught to control all her feelings.

Again, it is necessary to look more deeply at the depression and despair that left Jennifer with no path in life except to death in a motel room. The family relationships and especially the family projections that lay behind her suicide seem decisive factors in Jennifer's suicide.

Hanna was a reserved, unemotional person. Her parents had been very wealthy and she had been reared by nannies. Living in a home behind iron gates, she and her sister had never been permitted to play with the other children who lived near them—they were not good enough for her. As Hanna's parents pointed out, she and her sister had a playroom in the house with all the toys that they could desire. Hanna's mother was busy with her social responsibilities and was not interested in having fun with her little girls. Hanna saw her father only when he was not traveling, and then not for very long because she and her sister were with their parents only one hour per day at tea time, sometimes not even that much. For these occasions, the nanny would dress her and her sister in cute, frilly dresses and present them to their parents, as if to royalty at court. Hanna learned not to rush toward her mother or father, not to cry and not to complain. To them, she was a pretty doll who curtsied at teatime. She could not remember being hugged by her parents, not ever. As she proudly claimed, they were not an emotional family. She did well in school, private schools of course, and was tutored whenever a subject, such as algebra, was too difficult.

Hanna never had a secure, warm attachment to either of her parents. Instead she formed a fantasized attachment to them, imagining them as loving and giving. In her childhood playacting, she remembered that she took the roles of loving parents, especially of the mother she longed for. Speaking with me, Hanna defended her parents as wonderful, but the parents she defended were only the ones she had imagined—and she continued to hold this idealization of her parents throughout the counseling sessions, refusing any interpretation that she needed more from them. In reality, however, she had been compelled to act as a robot in their presence, saying, "Yes, ma'am," "No, ma'am," "Yes, sir," "No, sir." Hanna remembered that once when her mother asked if she were happy, she responded, "No, ma'am." Upon hearing this, her mother said, "Impossible!" and sent her away. She never again revealed her feelings to her mother.

In effect, both her parents had emotionally abandoned Hanna. Neither provided her with warmth, love or security. She remembered that her father played checkers with her one time when she was about ten years old and she was very proud of that. Her father committed suicide when she was eleven, but not until many years later was she told how he actually died. His death was a terrible loss to her; even her dream of a more loving relationship sometime in the future was shattered. His death only multiplied the fantasies of him as the perfect father she had hopelessly longed for. His death made her mother seem more distant and even colder.

The attachment that Hanna's mother had with her was a nullified attachment. To her mother, Hanna had never become more than a doll, a robot. For her part, Hanna's attachment to her mother was to an imagined, unreal mother. Firmly convinced, and in strong denial of any anger against her parents, she avowed that she had the best of upbringings. Therefore, Hanna had treated Jennifer in much the same way. As she stated quite accurately, they were not a family who expressed a lot of feeling. "But of course Jennifer must have known that she was loved!"

The attachment that Hanna had with her own daughter, Jennifer, was also a nullified attachment. Hanna fantasized that Jennifer was the idealized child that she, Hanna, was supposed to have been. Jennifer, too, was a doll. It was an attachment that prevented Jennifer from growing into a real person and fulfilling her own potential for love and creativity. There was no warmth showered upon her. Hanna's demands that she squelch any emotional expression were too much for Jennifer. Through her suicide she obeyed her mother's command that she kill her feelings.

Such a fantasized attachment masks the underlying hostility. It copes with a hostile world by inventing one that gratifies the need for love without setting free the aggression lurking underground. Hanna needed Jennifer to be the perfect child that she, Hanna, could never be because she was unhappy. Jennifer, feeling her mother's rejection of her and sensing her mother's hostile reaction to her feelings, thought she had no escape but to get out of her mother's life—and give up her own. The dynamics are similar to those of Tommy's father, who wanted Tommy out of his life. With Jennifer's mother, though, the wish was unconscious. Hanna's wish to be rid of Jennifer was a projection of Hanna's early, unacknowledged hostility toward her own parents, plus perhaps the sense that she herself should not exist. Later, Hanna unwittingly projected that guilt onto her own daughter. These are the tragic outcomes of generational problems thrust inadvertently upon unsuspecting children.

Interestingly enough, Hanna never admitted to Jennifer's unhappiness and despair to herself or others. She repeated the defense she had learned from her mother upon her father's death. Years later Hanna would tell her friends that Jennifer had died of a brain tumor. This type of denial and the absence of introspection perpetuated the destructive, cross-generational cycle. Through Hanna's inability to face her own feelings and her own past, Jennifer was unconsciously impelled to make real her mother's (and perhaps father's) living death.

Jennifer's case shows how unaware parents may be of their children's misery. The projections of Jennifer's parents were that she was the happy, ideal fantasized child. A "good" girl, she was supposed to fulfill Hanna's fantasy and Michael's expectations. Jennifer, like her mother, was never free to express her dismay, her anger or her frustrations with her mother or her father. Of course, her early distress was shown by biting herself and then by the self-mutilation during her adolescence. These were red flares in the night, desperate signals for help. Since Jennifer could not satisfy Hanna's and Michael's fantasies, her cries were suppressed, even extinguished and ignored, until she finally put an end to them by her suicide.

In these accounts, our attention has been on the difficulties that parents bring, often enough without awareness, to the family scene. A traumatized and stigmatized parent can engender an adolescent's self-destructive feelings, often enough through the parent's projections onto the child of their own guilt. Because of their unresolved conflicts, such a parent may become the instigators of the child's suicide. Signs of family dysfunction suggest that the conflicts of the parents are intruding into the life of the child or adolescent—even when the parents seem to be trying to "do their best." The depression, rebellion and/or withdrawal of the adolescent signal loudly and clearly that the attachment with the parent is on a path marked Danger.

Adolescence is a kind of odyssey toward independence which passes through the unquiet waters of heightened sensitivity and increased emotional awareness, the shoals and tricky tides of burgeoning sexual and aggressive feelings. Growth toward independence is often frightening for the teenager and is actually accompanied by an increased dependence upon parents.

In adolescence, familial attachments are transferred to peers. When the parental attachments are unstable, ambivalent or negative, the transference to peers, rather than being a transition, seeks to fill a void unfilled from childhood. As a result, the friendships are often idealized. In good times, the cliques, the best friends, the heterosexual groupings and the first boyfriend/girlfriend crushes dramatically demonstrate the generalization of bonding from parent to friend. When these normal attachment strivings are over-loaded with the ungratified longing for a secure attachment, despair follows. When these idealized friendships fall apart, as they often must, the grief of the earlier insecure attachments is compounded. The frequency of suicides among adolescents reflects their inability to handle the grief. The failure of new attachments can cause hopelessness to set in. This hopelessness is, in itself, a return to the grief of the infant who has lost or has had no security with a loving parental person.

Jack Novick thought that "The sequence leading to the suicide act is precipitated in all cases by external events which impose on the adolescents the responsibility of taking a step that represents to them the breaking of the tie to the mother."[6] I propose that the external event is in almost all cases the loss of an idealized attachment that is compounded by the earlier grief arising from insecure attachments to a parent.

Difficulties in parental attachments to their teenagers are often exacerbated during adolescence. Attachment processes, at best, are fluid and unstable during the teenage years because of the developmental changes inherent in that period—physical, emotional, social and intellectual. Parents themselves are often under stress, as their adolescent becomes a different person than the child he or she was. As the adolescent becomes physically different, he or she may pass through degrees of awkwardness as well as changes in his or her response to parents. The parents, in empathy with their child, often may feel unsure or awkward in knowing how to respond to their child. There are new rules, a new order in the house, different expectations of parents, all serving to cause the parents to step cautiously. The caretaking bonds so necessary in childhood must be redefined with the parents as the adolescent strives for adult autonomy.

When the parents try to prolong the restraints of childhood on the adolescent, conflicts are guaranteed, unless the adolescent submits in a regressive manner, an unhealthy reaction for the adolescent. When the parents carry unresolved problems from their own adolescent years, their projections may severely damage the emerging adult. The first step in helping the dysfunctional parents is to guide them to an awareness of their unconscious projections. With the parents' insight into their own long-lasting conflicts, freedom for the family can begin and love can be released.

CHAPTER 6

Ambivalence and Instigators

He Loves Me; She Loves Me Not

A suicide kills two, Maggie.

Arthur Miller

It has become more and more apparent that the choices of relationships made by instigators are determined by the emotional and physical traumas that events of their lives imposed upon them. Probably very few people escape some hurts from childhood, but traumas may be crippling to life itself. Potential traumas are many: physical abuse, physical deprivations, the life-wracking wounds from fire, gunshots, stabbings, vehicle crashes, train wrecks and other catastrophes too many to enumerate, that send people to the ER, the trauma center or the morgue. Such assaults on the body, not to mention sexual abuse, neglect and sadism in its many forms, have severe psychological as well as physical consequences. The personality that emerges from the scars is much like a tree that grows around a limb that has been cut off or a tree bent by persistent wind from an upright growth to a grotesque angle. While the scars seem forgotten, they often remain to become infectious and pernicious. As with the clinical cases discussed below, the damaged tree may also fall on someone who is merely pausing to admire an autumn leaf.

Passive instigators are ambivalent about living. They have survived through psychological traumas that were not necessarily sudden or instantaneous events. Their trauma often resides more in a persistent early negation of their feelings and of their life. They are more like the tree whose trunk is bent by constant winds than the tree with an amputated limb. These instigators long for love, but love opens the scars of trauma, of rejection and of fears of death. The relationship between Eros and Anteros reigns supreme. Revenge rules the day.

Ambivalence has its source in early child-parent interactions.[1] It arises from an infant's emotional adaptation to the parents' inability to provide consistent caring for the child. Never knowing whether its mother will be loving or rejecting, giving or hurting, the child becomes overly sensitive to the smallest cues of mother's feelings and may react with anger and violence to the on-again, off-again care. The mother does not experience the normal mothering reaction of merging with the infant's feelings. Instead, she remains encased in her own feelings. If the child is to receive any warmth, the child must be sensitive to the mother and merge with her emotional state. The child's search for love is filled with anxiety. Will she love me or hate me?

Children who have received such ambivalent parenting are more likely to victimize playmates, torture pets and be more hostile and aggressive than are securely parented children.[2] In this respect, they may already have become instigators, in the mold of Mary and Paulette (see Chapter 3). As adults, these persons tend to have possessive, jealous and irrational attachments.

These instigators need to "own" their partners. They are often obsessed with closeness and dependency. Because there is little foundation for trust, the merging is contrived. As long as the instigator can merge with the partner, the needs of both are met—the instigator to be totally, lovingly enmeshed, and the potential victim to feel power from the attachment. It sounds good enough. Yet this contrived intimacy in itself provokes the anxieties of abandonment, neglect and death or anger and rejection. Children with ambivalent relationships to their parents have trouble in adulthood tolerating passion or maintaining a commitment to a partner. How could they commit themselves, when abandonment is always in the offing?[3]

Ambivalent instigators go on a manic search for the idealized partner, the all-embracing parent-caretaker with whom they may merge and thus escape their grief and their bitterness. And, in actuality, only someone who is willing to be the recipient of that grief could heal the violent hatred that has been stored within. It seems to me that this can almost only happen in such a situation as psychotherapy, in which the situation inherently grants safe boundaries for both the patient and the therapist. There may be rare relationships that can sustain the grief and endure the psychic pain with the person.

The need of ambivalent instigators is more primitive than introjection; it is an infantile fusion, a rebirth of love and attachment. It should come as no surprise that they are never able to find such a partner, a magical mother who will encompass them. Jeffrey Simpson states that the adult relationships of persons with early ambivalent attachments are usually short-lived.[4] The instigator's dependency on the partner provides the partner a sense of power that helps them deny their own neediness, but it also serves as a crutch which prevents them from addressing the underlying problem.

The partners also seek this relationship. The merging is sweet and temporarily quiets their own insecurities. They flourish when another is dependent upon them because caring gives a sense of meaning to their lives. They overvalue the dependency of the instigators at a cost to their own self-integrity. Because they are accustomed to rejection from their past, each withdrawal becomes more painful, for it threatens, even annihilates, the meaningfulness of their life. The partners return again and again, trying to induce the instigators' dependency upon them. In their futile striving to undo the rejections of the past as well as the present, they risk even more rejection. Eventually, they become passive seekers of rejection, of abandonment and of death.

Ambivalent relationships make for tragic marriages. The relationships become a back-and-forth cycle in which each seeks to be lost in the other, eliciting old and new angers when their effort fails. And it does fail. The honeymoon for these partners is usually short; they can have harmony only as long as they sacrifice their individuality—which is ultimately impossible. The fallout is revengeful violence; it is murder or suicide. The fusion they may briefly enjoy is not the blending of personalities that we see in intimate relationships. Blending implies two separate ingredients, like chocolate and milk, or honey and mustard, which can both be detected in the new drink or sauce. In fusion, the taste of the individual ingredients is gone.

The partners have both projected their own needs and characteristics onto each other, and then in turn identified themselves with the traits they have projected. This psychological dynamic has been termed *projective identification*. This process is bound to fail, for neither person acts within the bounds of self-integrity.

The road these partners take is disastrous. They yearn for secure attachments, but they can neither give nor receive love. Ironically, when love actually is there on occasion, it reinvigorates residual feelings of abandonment and death for the instigators. They do not trust love. Their anxious distrust propels them away from tender feelings; they withdraw emotionally and often physically as well. When the instigator's attachment is withdrawn, the partner no longer has anyone to take care of, and the partner's anxiety is aroused in full. The partner walks as if on eggshells, and pleads, "Don't you love me anymore?" Then the roller coaster begins: the agony of the partner evokes a sense of power in the instigator—the instigator is in control; again the merging is renewed; the merging brings on a resurgence of fears of abandonment and death; the instigator must again withdraw. The partner pleads for a reciprocal sign of love. The ambivalent attachment becomes a constant testing of love for both, much like counting daisy petals: "She loves me, he loves me not." And if this daisy does not give the right answer, they choose another daisy, or three or four more. Back and forth, back and forth. From love to hate, hate to love; from closeness to abandonment; from fusion to separateness; from life to death. Fusion kills the soul of the individual.

With repeated pleadings of the partner for a sign of love, the instigator recoils all the more. While the withdrawal may seem like an arrogant, obstinate refusal, it is really a self-protective stance to keep the violence that lies deep within safely locked away.

MAX AND RITA

Max and Rita requested counseling for their marital problems. An electrical engineer, Max was a tall, muscle-wrapped man of forty-nine who spoke in a bluntly factual and determined manner. Casually dressed in a dark blue shirt and jeans, he came in slowly and forcefully, lumbering along, his legs apart, almost stomping. Rita was a secretary in a local computer industry. Petite, made up after the latest teen magazine covers, she dressed a bit youthfully for a woman in her early forties. Her movements had flair and a touch of seduction. She followed Max in and seated herself with a flounce, flirtatiously smoothing her skirt as she turned toward their male intern counselor. They had said in earlier sessions that they did not want a divorce; rather, they desired help with their marital relationship of seven years. It had disintegrated from the early mutual affection and lovemaking to hostile disinterest and spiteful squabbles which were constantly arising and frustrating them. Pouting, Rita complained, "Maxie still won't tell me he loves me." This is a common enough plea from a person who needs a verbal assurance of love even though there may be many actions that speak of the affection. Her complaints may sound commonplace, but the session I witnessed was to be anything but.

In my forty years of psychological practice, I have supervised the training of many clinical psychology doctoral candidates, postdoctoral interns and psychiatry residents. There were many productive ways in which the trainees and I could learn from our experiences. I could hear audiotapes of the sessions with their patients, listen to their reports of the interactions or review their written reports. Under the best of conditions, and with everyone's consent, I was able to observe their interaction with clinic patients via closed-circuit television. Afterward, the trainees and I could talk about their sessions, exploring what we thought was fruitful and what was not, and why, and how they might proceed from thence forward.

The session I saw was about the sixth such session with Max and Rita. What a familiar story! It presents a common problem of ambivalent attachments in marriage, and shows how feelings left over from earlier experience color everyday life, even when the results thwart the dearest conscious wishes.

Just as she had many times, Rita reiterated that she pleads and almost begs Max just to speak the words. "He won't say he loves me, or hug me the way he used to." Max turned away, his face became sullen. The counselor asked Max what he thought of this. "She knows I love her. Why should I have to say it all the time?"

"How would she know you love her?" the counselor asked.

"Good God!" Max yelled. "We have sex every night!"

"But that's not love, that's just sex!" Rita cried. She continued, "He does not EVER pay attention to ME. He just comes home and watches the television while I get dinner. He just wants me to be his servant. He eats and then goes back to the television and the paper. We never talk anymore. We don't even go for a walk or go to the movies the way we used to. Why can't he just tell me that he loves me?" she demanded.

"I've told you a million times already," Max said. "Anyhow, I'm tired of your threatening to leave me if I don't do exactly what you want! Why don't you just go?"

Rita started to cry and Max turned away in disgust. "She always does that and then expects sympathy from me. . . . I'm tired of playing that game. . . . She cries, we make up, she cries, we make up again and again until the next time she wants something . . . then she threatens to leave."

"If you loved me, you would know what I need. You would be able to say 'I love you' even a million times," Rita responded.

The conversation continued in this fashion, focusing on her need for attention from him and his obstinate refusal to give in to her requests, even in the simplest form of saying that he loved her. She was begging for affection in a childish, whining, not to mention masochistic way. Each time, Max sounded ever more determined not to give in to her desire for verbal reassurance of love.

About twenty minutes into the fifty-minute session, Rita asked to be excused to go to the ladies' room. When she left, the counselor and Max were quiet for a while, waiting for her return. They spoke casually about some of his problems at work.

Five minutes passed. Seven, eight, ten and watching on the television, I grew concerned about her absence. I went to the ladies' room to see whether she was all right. There I found her lying on a narrow bench, blood dripping from a wrist. She held a razor blade in one hand. When she saw me come in, she dropped it and pretended to faint. I called an ambulance to take her to a hospital. She was all right. She had not actually cut herself severely enough to cause a quick death. She had been driven to carry out her threat of suicide and grant his wish for her death, but in a safe place where she could expect someone to find her.

Was Max an instigator simply because he would not say he loved her? Not for that reason alone. Caught in a deeply embedded ambivalence of love and hate, power and submission, he was a passive instigator of her potentially successful suicidal actions. She had chosen "Tell me you love me" as a means of forcing acknowledgment that she existed for him. He, in turn, nullified this call to recognize her existence.

For Max and Rita, their marriage began with the fantasy that they had found the ideal mate who fit perfectly and intimately into their dream of love. This honeymoon phase of marriage is a time when each partner seems submerged in the other, a time when one's life expectations depend on the wishes of the partner and on pleasing the partner. This fantasy disappears when reality sets in—when each person must go about his or her own business—a part of life that frequently does not include the partner. Continued attempts at idealization of what the marriage should be can only lead to an excruciatingly painful destruction of love, for reality sooner or later arrives, forcing both to acknowledge the individuality of the other. The push and pull of ambivalent attachments then mask the intense dependency needs of both.

Max had withdrawn into himself, frightened by the intimacy with Rita and especially by his growing sense of dependency on her. To be dependent was to be helpless; to Max it was a threat to his self-control. He had to avoid this sense of helplessness at any cost, so he withdrew into stubborn silences and resisted her simplest plea for a sign of love. Why? Here is a clue: When he was a toddler of two years, his mother had become bedfast with a serious illness. He remembered being shut out of her room. Now the longing for love and closeness revived the fears of being again shut out as well as rekindling the anger that his mother's rejection elicited.

So here is Max. On one hand, he has identified with his mother. He can now be in control and reject Rita just as his mother had apparently rejected him—or so it seemed to him as a little boy.

On the other hand, he needed and wanted Rita's love. With her love, he had again felt the warmth of being cared about and protected. Yet the very sense of needing her unleashed the fear of losing her as well as the anticipated anger over the possibility that she would leave him, as his mother had. So he pushed Rita to leave, to die, to relive his earlier experience with his mother. The next second, he did not want her to leave him. The on-again, off-again love is only turmoil for him. With Rita's insistence, he came with her for therapy.

Rita, on the other hand, had experienced affection from the act of giving, of "taking care of" others. She had become an expert in sensing what someone else might want. As the oldest of three children, she had gained approval from her mother by being a "good" girl, by masking her own needs and feelings in order to please her mother. And now, she wanted those signs of approval from her husband. Because he was so needing of love when they first met, it seemed like the perfect fit. He needed, she gave. She was needy, he wanted her. Then her very caretaking became threatening to Max, because he projected onto her the hostile rejection that he seemed to receive from his mother. Max's withdrawal was devastating to Rita. She could no longer be "good"; nothing could please him. It was a failure that undermined her deepest sense of herself; giving had provided her meaning for living. Now the sense of being needed was gone. She could now only escape life, as Max suggested, to please him.

Rita, like many others in her position, did have other areas in her life such as employment, where she could have invested efforts to give her life more meaning. Separation from Max would have forced her to find a different source of identity for herself, as divorce often does. She was, of course, an excellent employee working hard to please her employer. Note that the word is *please*, not *succeed*. With persons like Rita, success is often measured by the degree to which one pleases an employer, not by a sense of success in a job well done, although both are often in accord.

Voluntarily in therapy, both Max and Rita wanted to save their marriage. Misunderstandings from the past burdened them in the present, and neither wanted the past to rule their living. This is a common scene. The more Rita sought reassurances of love, the more Max withdrew. The more he withdrew, the more desperate she became. Theirs was not a power struggle. It was a struggle for love. And it was a struggle for freedom from the horrors of the past.

In adulthood, the recurrence of the bitter loneliness of infancy may release the hostility and destructiveness of the young child, but with more strength. To avoid their own self-destructive impulses, the instigators erect defenses against any recurrence of their childhood disappointments, because they are somehow aware that if the bitterness should come back strongly enough, their defenses will crumble. To submit to love is not safe. The ensuing damage to themselves or to a partner or anyone else involved with them may be severe, even fatal. Their survival depends on keeping the defenses strong. Max did not want to separate from Rita, but he had to fend off both his longings for dependency and the strong impulses to attack or destroy her. Rita, for her part, tried to please Max, but when he withdrew emotionally, she lost her sense of identity.

Both continued in psychotherapy, and the relationship between Rita and Max grew more realistic and more caring toward each other. This story had a happy ending, showing that effective, insightful therapy can help fused couples escape the destructive cycle of their interdependency.

AFTER THE FALL

Arthur Miller realized that people, even nations, deny the brutality that is emblematic of the human dilemma.[5] This denial, in his thinking, makes one innocent of insight into the self and into the conditions of the world. This innocence, this lack of awareness of the self, kills; and yet it continues to reign. He has exquisitely portrayed this thesis about ambivalence in his play *After the Fall*.[6] The action takes place in the hopes, thoughts and memories of the main character, Quentin. The play gives us scenes from past struggles as they shaped Quentin's life and hopes for the future, both interwoven with the present.

Quentin, like Clamence in *The Fall*, is a lawyer with an impressive reputation for his work and for his zealousness in looking for the finest threads of guilt in clients and friends. Quentin also feels a kind of free-standing guilt within himself. In his search, his troubled mind at last weaves its way through death to life, through violence to hope, from fusion to true being.

In the play, Quentin is caught in the throes of ambivalence: hatred and love are intermingled. His mother has recently died; his first wife, Louise, was lost through divorce; he has lost his second wife, Maggie, to suicide; and he is now debating about taking a third wife, Holga. His mother had set him up to despise women—and he had hated his mother, too. He had been "special" for her; that is, he was supposed to fulfill his mother's ambitions for herself. She told him many times that the sun rose and shone through him. He was the star of her life. But he remembers her constant harping at him—don't eat too much, wear your garters, practice your writing, don't play with matches (as she slapped his wrist). She wanted the star, not the boy. He also bore the brunt of his father's dislike of him, especially in his teens—why can't you get a haircut, get your shoes shined, why do you have to go to school? I didn't.

His parents' arguments seemed endless to little Quentin. Mother was unhappy. She belittled and hated her uneducated husband. She called him "Idiot." It was true that he could not even read a menu. At her father's insistence, she had given up a scholarship to a university and a romance with a doctor-to-be to marry Quentin's father.

When Quentin was a boy, his mother betrayed him. Because she needed a rest from him, she tricked him into staying with the maid while she, his father, and older brother went off to Atlantic City for a good time. She abandoned him at least that one time. When they re-turned, he ran into the bathroom, turned on the water and was at-tempting, apparently, to drown himself. His mother pleaded with him to open the door. She cried out, "I'll die if you do that! I saw a star when you were born—a light, a light in the world."[7] She called for his father to crash the door.

In his misery, the adult Quentin calls out, "Why is betrayal the only truth that sticks? I adored that woman. It's monstrous I can't mourn her!" Perhaps "Grief is only grief if it kills you." In Miller's play a slaughterhouse in a concentration camp for Jews during World War II is projected onto the stage, and Quentin moans, "Why do I feel an understanding with this slaughter house?" In his mind he strangles Maggie, his wife, and during the action, Maggie becomes his mother. But he cannot mourn his mother, because his murderous hate of her has not died but lies in wait for surrogate targets, such as Maggie, whom he cannot mourn either. He cannot mourn, because mourning will bring the fears of remembering his unbridled anger. Uncovering the love and the grief can only remind him of the violence he felt toward his mother and feels toward Maggie.

A final blow to his search for happiness as an adult comes with remembrance of his mother's words, "I hope you learn how to disappoint people, especially women." This wish arose from a deeply disappointed mother, passing her grief on to her son. And disappoint them he does. Melded with his mother and then with his first wife, Louise, he cries out, "I can't bear to be a separate person." When Louise is leaving him, Quentin says: "I am asking you to explain this to me because this is when I go blind! When you've finally become a separate person, what the hell is there?"[8] Louise has begun psychoanalysis, and is searching for her own identity. Louise tells Quentin, "You don't want *me*" [italics added]. As Quentin reviews all her words in his mind, he is shocked by her phrase, "The way you treat me, I don't exist."[9]

Here, Quentin is doing what his mother wished him to do—he is nullifying the existence of all women except his mother, with whom he was so disappointed. Those resentful words, "You don't want me! What the hell are you doing here?" are repeated by Maggie, his second wife. She, too, feels his nullifying attachment. She states it even more dramatically, asserting that Quentin is ashamed of her. And he is. Yet he can neither give her up to death nor let her live. When she is threatening death, he can nurture his sense of power. His cry to her, "A suicide kills two, Maggie," comes directly from his mother's admonition when he ran to the bathroom, "If you die, I will die too."[10]

Maggie's self-hatred incites Quentin to become her instigator, for she expects to be murdered. Reliving a memory of her own, she recalls that her mother had tried to smother her with a pillow. Maggie defends her mother. She claims that her mother was a very moral person even though her mother tried to kill her once with a pillow on her face "cause I would turn out bad because of—like her sin."[11] Maggie with her expectation of death is driven to prove love is murderous. She has been searching for another instigator, someone with a similar love-hate relationship with her and who, in turn, wants her dead.

Quentin recognizes this and accuses her of trying to make him the one who kills her. Her self-hatred wears him out; his comforting does not relieve her. Her threats of suicide make him even wearier of her. For instance, when she threatens to jump off the dock into deep water, Quentin remembers that her unnatural gasping for breath seemed to him the omen of peace. This was a peace he longs for, yet he loves her. He cries out that something in Maggie is setting him up for murder. Quentin cannot extricate himself from the relationship because of his imprisoning self-love and his need for power—power that he hopes will contain his violence. He wants the same adulation from his wives that he received from his mother—though it was insincere adulation to be sure.

Louise says, "Look Quentin, you want a woman to provide an atmosphere in which there are never any issues, and you'll fly around in a constant bath of praise—I am not a praise machine! I am not a blur and I am not your mother! I am a separate person!"[12] In the search for her emotional health, Louise could only refuse his need to be merged with her.

Because Quentin is hypersensitive to betrayal, Maggie manipulates, blackmails and provokes Quentin with drunkenness, threats of pill popping and promiscuity, even teasing him by telling of an offer of fifty dollars from a cab driver. She tries to kill herself several times but always when Quentin is present to rescue her. It is a test of his love. Love or hate. Hate or love. He loves me . . . he loves me not. It is the daisy test.

When she pours pills into her hands once again, they reach a crisis. He says, "A suicide kills two people Maggie, that's what it's for!" He lets her know that she wants to kill *him*, too. Each time Quentin has saved her, he has become more exasperated until the final time, when he says that he is removing himself from the scene and that perhaps her suicide will lose its point—it will not damage him, too.

But he stays. Maggie tries to give him her deadly pills for safekeeping. He dreads keeping her pills because she will want them back and once he returns them to her, he will be guilty of her death.

They have one last fight over the bottle of pills. He knocks some of them out of her hand, but she swallows many of them. They fight on the floor. Her strength is "wild." In anger and dismay, he tells her to drop the pills, calls her a bitch. And Quentin yells that she will not kill him, he won't let her. He is beside himself and finds himself just where he should not be—near her neck. Instead of removing himself, he tries again to save her from herself. He can only save her with violence. Hot with fury, he suddenly seizes her throat and lifts her. "You won't kill me! You won't kill me!" he screams. The moment of truth comes. Maggie becomes Mother in his strangling hands as he squeezes her throat. Mother, too, had wanted death. Now we understand that the suicidal threats his mother made over the years have poisoned his life. In the play Maggie sinks to the floor, gasping for breath. Horrified, Quentin lets her go. He is shocked by his own murderous impulses, and now knowing that this is in him, he can begin to understand his own love-hate relationship with women.

A woman named Holga has been present throughout the play. She represents hope; she is sanity. Holga knows life and death, and she knows the violence of mankind as well as its generosity. She is the conscience of all, and through love and the recognition of potential violence, she can rescue Quentin—and metaphorically all of us—from the evil within.

―――――――――

The most insidious instigations to suicide are found in these ambivalent attachments. Since the instigators fluctuate between love and hate for the victims, they never give a clear message. These muddy feelings mask the underlying violence fermenting deeply within the instigator. The participants in ambivalent love-hate relationships feed upon each other, both reenacting their past victimization. The instigators are so embedded in the desperate struggle for existence that they achieve a passive kind of power in living. Quentin can maintain his power, not by struggling with Maggie or his mother, but by walking away.

Except with Holga, Quentin passes on the love-hate relationship that his mother gave him to the relationships with other women in his life. As his mother had nullified his existence as a person in his own right, he nullifies the existence of others.

Quentin is an instigator. A passive instigator, to be sure, but an instigator nonetheless. He seeks the deaths of the women in his life, trying to become free of the betrayals and hatreds cast upon him through his mother's influence. Importantly, the women in his life have been seeking an instigator. They want death for themselves. They need Quentin, the instigator. The attachment relationships that Quentin has with these women are not openly malicious until he becomes aware of his own angry, violent, death-dealing desires toward them.

Actually, in his hypersensitivity, he nullifies their right to exist as individuals. Simultaneously, when he needs to be encompassed by them, as he is at those times, he feels loved. This ambivalence is the story behind many attachments—with parents, siblings, partners or even in affiliation with friends.

The passive instigators in ambivalent relationships are among the most dangerous. Through their need to merge, they nullify the integrity of the partner, but they must eventually reject the merging. First, they cannot trust it; there is no security in attachment for them. Their early pattern of love-hate relationship dominates their unconscious expectations of others. Second, closeness and intimacy with another crumbles their defensive structure against the deeply embedded hostile and destructive impulses. Angry interactions become commonplace. Another defense that may be used is withdrawal, either a complete withdrawal through physical separation or a partial withdrawal through emotional separation. The instigator, by the withdrawal, assumes the role of power, the power that the instigator learned from others so early in life—the power to give or to reject. We saw this power in the obstinate withdrawal of Max from Rita, bringing her to the brink of self-destruction.

Third, while the merging is temporarily gratifying and even brings some hope for an idealized attachment, it also reawakens dependency needs which have been long masked under the guise of independence. This kind of independence, however, is not the self-autonomy and individuality that develop from an initial secure attachment. This kind of independence is a defense against helplessness. Finally, the instigator in ambivalent attachments assumes the role of power as learned from early love-hate warfare with mothering persons.

Let us take a closer look at the origins of ambivalence. Basic for living are physical drives for safety and security and psychological drives for attachment, aggression, sexuality and self-enhancement. Eight primary emotions are usually recognized as accompanying these drives. They are: love, fear, anger, sadness, joy, curiosity, disgust and surprise.[13] They enrich the quality of life. Each drive may become coupled with one or more emotions to enhance or to complicate the actions of living. This coupling is dependent upon early experience, so that a kiss (an action) may be given in love or a kiss (action) may be given in anger. For example, a kiss may be a sign of devotion or, as with Judas Iscariot, a sign of betrayal. When a drive for attachment, or for any other need, is coupled with love at one time and then with fear or anger at another, the child and later the adult's inner life are mystified, confused and wavering. Herein is the basis of ambivalence. Is it love or hatred? Is it peace or war?

Let us now turn to a different example of ambivalent love. It tells of a mother-daughter relationship that iced over the warmth that both wanted, even to the third generation.

MISTY

Misty was an accountant who entered into therapy as an adult. She had sharp memories that she had carried with her throughout her life. She was the favorite child of her father; her younger brother did not get nearly the father's adoration that she received. Her mother, Ann, was forever jealous of the intimate, perhaps even sexualized relationship between her husband and their daughter. Misty clearly recalled her father's protection from her mother's wrath and punishments and that he would often excuse Misty from participating in the household chores that her mother had assigned her.

As a child, Misty was eager for her mother's love and tried her best to please her, especially when her father was absent. Alone with her, her mother would not only berate her father but also belittle Misty: "You are not pretty. I don't know why your father thinks you are. I don't know why your father bought you that dress. It looks awful on you. Go put on another one. Don't ever wear that dress to school." Misty remembered the dress in question as pretty, with flowers in blue, her favorite color. "You are so clumsy! You are too fat!" In fact, it was mother who was exceptionally obese. At other times, her mother would tell her that she was the best thing that had ever happened to her, that she was really proud of her good grades and her artistic ability. Of course, her mother claimed that Misty inherited all these good traits from her side of the family. Her mother's ambivalence toward Misty became even more pronounced as Misty got older.

Unfortunately for Misty, her menstrual periods began exceptionally early, at the age of ten. Noticing blood on her pajamas, she ran to her mother. "Mother, I am bleeding!"

Infuriated, her mother yelled at her, "That can't be so! You are lying."

Once again hearing hatred in her mother's voice, Misty picked up the butcher knife to stab herself, screaming, "I know you want me to kill myself!" At that moment, her brother came into the room. She remembers his startled eyes, wide open in terror. Misty dropped the knife and ran from the room. She did not carry out her instigator mother's wishes for her death. Still, her suicidal tendencies continued, and by thirty-two she had made two more attempts. Her marriage was beset by difficulties, partly because her mother continued to harass her and to undercut her achievements. Her husband pressured her to cut the umbilical cord that kept her futilely trying to win her mother's approval. The final crisis came with the realization that her mother was convincing Misty's daughter that Misty was crazy—paranoid or psychotic. These episodes, plus her professional training, brought Misty to therapy. Today, twenty-two years later, I am pleased to report that Misty is a contented mother and a successful accountant.

The ambivalence of Misty's mother toward Misty had its roots in her early life. Ann's mother had been the source of her security but she died when Ann was about two years old. When Ann was five, her father remarried and Ann felt that she had lost his love, too. After her stepbrother was born, Ann felt even more displaced. Multi-traumatized by losses, Misty's mother had learned that to love was to lose. Thus the relationship between mother Ann and Misty was guarded because affection evoked fears of abandonment in Ann. In addition, Ann was jealous of the affection that Misty received from her father because, unconsciously for her, their closeness stirred up the old jealousy of the relationship between Ann's father and her stepmother. Misty's mother had become a passive instigator.

Instigators with ambivalent attachments are beset by dependency versus independency struggles. The sense of self in the ambivalent instigators is weak, finding strength in their relationship with another person. As Quentin called out, "I can't bear to be a separate person," so the instigator seeks a sense of being, by merging with another. The partner is also dependent upon the merging and attempts to prolong it by caretaking. The love-hate dichotomy results from the ultimate, necessary failure of the fusion, leaving both persons ambivalent and mystified about their own feelings.

The ambivalence that dominates the instigator's conscious or unconscious actions and feelings has been absorbed from the mother's denial of love. The instigator has introjected the mother's wish for their death (usually manifest in frustrated, anxious mothering). As we saw with Quentin, his mother did not wish him to love anyone. Of course attachment involves the revival of earlier anger toward an uncaring mother including her death, as Quentin so aptly described in revealing his feelings toward his mother. For these unfortunates, intimacy is unbearable.

Herein lies the forte of psychotherapy and psychoanalysis. One's primary task in therapy is the exploration the self in order to uncover any origins of the anger and grief. This can be an intense process, for the patient must have the ego strength to tolerate the anxiety that dismantling their defenses will demand. Probably one of the most useful techniques is to provide thoughtful explanations that can gradually strengthen the patient's coping skills and substitute for any loss of affective control. This will be especially helpful as the person utilizes the back-and-forth of ambivalence toward the therapist to heal the wounds of life.

The goal of therapy in such instances is to cultivate meaningful knowledge of the self, knowledge that has previously been mystified through ambivalent caretaking.

CHAPTER 7

Self-Attached Instigators

The Jilted Lover

> If not from Phaon I must hope for ease,
> Ah, let me seek it from the raging seas;
> To raging seas unpitied I'll remove;
> And either cease to live or cease to love.

Alexander Pope (from Ovid)

Long ago and far away, there was a white rock stretching out from Levkas (Leucas), one of the Ionean islands off the coast of Greece. It had a temple of Apollo upon it, and according to myth if you leaped or were pushed from the rock you might alter your fate. For example, during the annual festival of Apollo, someone suspected of a crime could be pitched from this rock as a test of guilt. To break the fall, birds were attached to the suspect. If the person survived the plunge, it was proof of innocence, and boats stood by for the rescue. Lovers in the grip of a harsh erotic narcissism could throw themselves from the Leucadian Cliff and find relief from the torments of unrequited love, hoping to prove their love was true.

It is no myth that a very real Greek woman named Sappho was born sometime before 600 B.C., married, had a daughter, lived for about fifty years on and around the island of Lesbos and died some time after 572 B.C.[1] She is described as small and dark, with bright eyes shining with wisdom. Plato called her beautiful for the sweetness of her songs. Of herself she wrote that she did not have a malignant nature but a quiet temper.

She is significant for two reasons. First, according to the best of the world's scholars, critics, mythologists and seekers after beauty in the written word, she wrote the most glorious love poetry from the viewpoint of a woman of these last twenty-five centuries. As Homer was the Poet, Sappho was the Poetess of this classical world. Horace said Sappho could not forget the profounder yearnings of her intense soul that longed after a beauty that has never on earth existed. It was said that of all the poets in the world, of all the illustrious artists of all literatures, Sappho was the one whose every word had a peculiar and unmistakable perfume, a seal of absolute perfection and illimitable grace. Her songs and verse are still inspirational today, but the full effect of her creativity can only be imagined, since only two complete poems and some few of those dazzling fragments of her poetry remain, thanks to those who burned books in the name of morality hundreds of years later.

It is interesting to note that in her day, women in that part of the world were free to learn, to speak, to offer opinions and to be writers. They could gather in groups of their own choosing. Attracted by Sappho's fame, young women from distant places joined her in a society dedicated to study all that related to the arts, especially poetry and music. If they followed her example, they learned about the gods and goddesses, mortal men and women and each other.

Sappho lived in a time when mythology and legend were frequently written and often passed off as history and biography. There is an enormous quantity of literature recounting the busy doings of the gods and goddesses with each other on Mount Olympus and with mortals on Earth. The births, affairs, murders, betrayals, wars, true loves, victims instigated to suicide by false lovers—anything we could imagine a human doing, the gods and goddesses did in styles far beyond Clark Gable and Marilyn Monroe. In our more enlightened age, we believe that the stories were created in the minds of earthly men and women and nurtured by their all-too-human motives, sometimes dark and sometimes glorious.

We also know that real people were posthumously mythologized, accorded superhuman feats and feelings. The whole story of the Trojan War seems to have some historical footing, whether or not it took Ulysses twenty years to get back home, whether or not Penelope waited for him.

Because Sappho was famous as the songstress of love, and because suicide was and still is the most dramatic and tragic ending of a love story, it should not surprise us that in later centuries she was cast as the lead actress in one of the most famous literary, mythological and legendary fantasies of all time. Without knowing anything about it, she was shanghaied into the Lovers' Leap Hall of Fame, there to reign as Queen of Hopeless Love.

This fictitious Sappho falls under the sway of Phaon, the masked man of false beauty. In Greek, Phaon (φάος) means "the glowing one." He may be thought of as the Dorian Gray of antiquity, never aging in public, only in the quietness of his mind. She falls excruciatingly in love with him. He lets her believe that he has the same love for her, her singing and her poetry. Then he dumps her. Without a single parting word, he takes off in the night on a boat bound for Sicily. Sappho is now a victim of unrequited love. Ovid tells us that, her heart crushed, she sang a dirge to Phaon.[2]

> If no woman can be yours unless
> her beauty is thought to be great enough, then
> there is no woman who will be yours.
> But my beauty seemed sufficient when you heard
> Me read my songs; you insisted then
> That those words made me forever beautiful.
> I would sing, I remember, for all
> Lovers remember all, and while I sang you
> Were busy stealing kisses from me.
> You even praised my kisses. I must have pleased
> You in all things but especially when
> We toiled at the task of love.

The abandoned Sappho does the only thing that shattered lovers of legend are supposed to do: she jumps off a cliff, the famous Leucadian Cliff.

Phaon is an antihero. The legend goes that he was an old, ugly, poor boatman of Mitylene, earning a meager living by rowing passengers across a waterway. One night an old lady, a crone, if you please, needed passage in his boat. She had no money. Taking pity on her, he refused any payment for his service and rowed her to the other shore. The old crone, however, was Aphrodite, the goddess of love and beauty. No doubt knowing exactly what she was doing and what he would do, she granted Phaon a wish. His request was for beauty and youth. She gave him a phial of ointment with which he should rub himself every day. With this ointment, he would remain young and dazzling as long as the supply lasted.

Aphrodite was regarded as a vengefully jealous goddess, irresponsible and cruel—inflicting tricks of love. For example, when Eos (Dawn) seduced Ares, Aphrodite made Eos fall in love with Orion. Having offended Aphrodite, Cinyras' daughter was forced into prostitution. Beautiful Psyche, as we shall see, was made to suffer under Aphrodite's jealousy. Other well-known victims were Helen of Troy, Medea and Ariadne. It is quite likely that Aphrodite considered Sappho to be a serious competitor for the throne of the Goddess of Love and made Phaon beautiful precisely in order to bring about her downfall.

Other concocters of myth claim that Aphrodite herself was a victim of love; she knew the despair of abandonment when she no longer could have the love of Adonis and was the first to dive from the heights of the Leucadian Cliff. Be that as it may, with the ointment that Aphrodite gave him, this ugly old man became a beautiful young man. Aphrodite promised that the effect of the ointment would make all women fall in love with him. And they did, including Sappho, just as Aphrodite knew she would. The new Phaon lived with the certainty that when the ointment ran out, he would again be a stumbling old man. But for the moment he was haughty with the arrogance of a new movie star. He wasps a *nouvelle beauté*, a phantom beauty and in love with his newfound face. He was acclaimed wherever he went for his miraculous loveliness.

Six hundred years later, Ovid described Sappho writing a letter to Phaon, telling him that for her there has never been a love such as she has for him.[3] He has a beauty and a face that ambush her eyes. She may not be beautiful enough for him, but could he not consider her genius instead of the beauty which nature denied to her? He could not. She cries, in the letter: "My plea is not that you should love but rather, that you let yourself be loved by me." This is such a common plea for those desperate for love. It is heard throughout the world from jilted lovers, "Just let me love you and then you will love me."

In the meanness of his escape from her, Phaon has left her with little else to hope for; for his sake she has abandoned her poetry and her songs. Desperate to rid herself of her memories of this hopeless love for Phaon, perhaps hoping to reunite with him someday in the shadows of Hades, the legendary Sappho listens to a water nymph who persuades her to hazard the law of the Leucadian Cliff. She is willing to be instigated. Since Phaon has left her, she has little else to live for; she has already forsaken her poetry and her songs.

Torn apart by the loss of her love—a love which must have been the incarnation of her every song of love—she asks the West Wind to carry her up to the Leucadian Cliff. Once there she comes to the temple of Apollo, dressed like a bride in garments as white as snow, wearing a garland of myrtle on her head and carrying a lyre of twenty-one strings that she had fashioned herself. She sings a hymn to Apollo and places her garland on one side of his altar, her harp on the other. She begs Love to spread his wings beneath her lest she fall and die, for if she drowns, her death would bring reproach upon the Leucadian waves. She should die only if her love is false. She marches to the promontory, tucks her garments about her and throws herself off the rock. There are differing versions of her death and burial place, so whether she fell into the breakers or was changed into a swan (as some would have it) will never be known.

There are two messages from this tale. First, this instigator Phaon was actually a marred, disfigured old man with the stigma of ugliness and poverty. Not much more was written about him. Becoming beautiful in an artificial way, he became totally self-involved, a Narcissus. He could have no bonding with a real person, for he was not real. And so we find out again that *narcissism is erotic nothingness*. For how can they love someone when they love only themselves?

Neither Phaon nor Sappho understood the pull of death in their lives. They were both narcissists, each concerned with their own feelings and existence. Anthony Bateman (1999) discusses two types of narcissism first posited by Rosenfeld: the "thick-skinned" and "thin-skinned narcissist."[4] Of paramount importance to the thick-skinned persons is the survival of an *idealized* self, that is, the conviction that their thoughts and feelings are the right ones. They are often obstinate and defensive and put little value on others. Any threat to the boundaries of the self provokes a violence, which is essentially a self-preservational violence. Phaon represents a thick-skinned narcissist, and the adoration of Sappho threatened to break through his defensive mask to his ugliness. Since his life depended on preserving his mask, he either had to get away from her or murder her. In the story, he did both. He sneaked away to Sicily in a boat by night, and Sappho was jilted.

She seems a thin-skinned narcissist, very sensitive, easily hurt and extremely vulnerable to rejection; Phaon's rejection felt like murder to her. It is easy to see that her accomplishments brought her the praise that her narcissism demanded. But then, despite her life's achievements as poet, songstress and teacher, she fixated on the love of Phaon as her reason for living. Phaon's rejection was devastating; it annihilated her image of herself.

Sappho, too, had been traumatized by death. The legends tell of her father's death when she was only six years of age. Phaon abandoned her as her father had spurned her love. She was left with a resurgence of the lostness that had been with her since her father's death. It seems that she was awaiting an invitation to death, looking for an instigator.

Phaon's bond with Sappho was a nullifying bond. In the legend, he loved her singing and even her kisses—but he loved them for the power they gave him over this renowned poet and singer. He needed to prove he could win this lover of love for himself. He wanted to see his reflection in her adoration. Like Clamence in *The Fall* (Chapter 4), who sensed the tragedy in the making of the suicidal woman on the bridge and simply passed by on the other side, Phaon had no empathy with Sappho's feelings. Like Clamence's, Phaon's instigation was passive, but an instigation nevertheless. He knew what would happen to her when he left.

We may point the finger at Phaon as the passive instigator, but what about his creator, treacherous Aphrodite? Driven by her compulsion to be the one and only goddess of love, she created Phaon, the instigator. How ironic! The goddess of love using love to kill off the world's greatest songstress of love, the poetess.

The second message is directly from Sappho. She, the star of Lesbos, had a gift. Symonds (1901) wrote about Sappho and Catullus,[5]

> We meet with richer and more ardent natures for these two are endowed with keener sensibilities, with a sensuality more noble because of its intensity, with emotions more profound, with a deeper faculty of thought that never loses itself in the shallows but simply and exquisitely apprehends the fact of human life.

When she gave up her poetry, Sappho lost her raison d'être, the meaningfulness of her life. She forfeited this beautiful gift—not for real love but for a magical, artificial love. Widely known and well respected, she could not hold onto the gift of living—her singing. Her song was spoiled, and so was her life. It is so often true that the suicide victims narrow their view of life to that of restoring an idealized attachment that can never be. Other thoughts and other persons cease to be for them. The loss of meaning in life is a common plaint of suicide victims. They ask, "What do I have left to live for?" We shall see how others also lose their sense of meaningfulness in life in order to pursue such impossible loves. The Sphinx loses her reason for living when her "death-asking" question is answered, and the Sirens can only commit suicide when their "death-singing" no longer pulls the hapless sailors to their shores. This kind of self-love arises from a neediness of such depth that the oceans of the earth could not fill it. Nor can any person.

We have noticed how ambivalent relationships function when the instigators fuse with the feelings of the partner. It is more than a reading of the partner's mind; it is putting oneself into the partner's shoes in such a way that the instigators lose the sense of themselves. *How you are is how I am*. This is not empathy. Empathy demands the ability to use one's own feelings to feel and resonate with the other person. In *After the Fall*, Quentin stated that he had relied on his mother and then his wife to know what to feel and how to exist. He did not know how to be a separate person.

In these fictional stories are pictures of real life. While it is a temptation to treat them as real people, they can only give us some guidance in thinking about relationships. In the narcissistic relationship, the instigator can relate only to those persons who fuse with his feelings. *"How I am is how you are*. Any other feelings that you may have are alien to me and destroy my existence. Therefore, finally I must destroy you." Since the narcissistic instigator cannot tolerate separateness of the partner, a rage of violence and killing erupts. Often enough this relationship is sadomasochistic, in which the threat of violence of the instigator compels a masochistic compliance from the partner.

In the following story, this self-involvement of the instigator turns the lover into a desperate death-seeker, for narcissism offers no rewards. Narcissism has no love.

SUZANNE AND LESLIE

Suzanne came to therapy nearly destroyed by narcissistic entanglements. Twice deserted by "mean" men, she was well into her fifties and was facing a cold, lonely future. She was without a man, with no mirror to provide a reflection of her beauty. She was European, very attractive and tastefully dressed in the latest of fashion. She could be likeable, even lovable. Quite intelligent, Suzanne deeply resented being only a high-school graduate, so she aggressively belittled those with more academic achievement. Another well-ingrained trait was her lifelong desire to be rich, not necessarily wealthy, but "comfortable." Although a working woman, she carried herself with an air of wealth and its expectations of service.

She described her former husband as an impoverished would-be industrial magnate who had once owned a factory for producing chain store furniture. He had lost his business by not attending to it. A thick-skinned narcissist and self-absorbed to the hilt, he dressed only in the most fashionable of suits and would fly a thousand miles to get his thinning hair styled just so, forgetting that to make his factory profitable he had to make some sales himself. Suzanne had tired of his selfishness and his idleness. She had tried to please him and to live up to his perfectionistic expectations, assuming a careful high-society persona. After thirty years of marriage and the failure of the business, she became exhausted of her robot-like existence and divorced him. Indeed, when I first saw her, she spoke like a robot, primarily using truisms or redundancies to describe her situation.

When she came to me, Suzanne was prowling for a more successful husband. She had screened several candidates, but none was good enough. For instance, she invited a rancher of substantial means to her home for dinner. He arrived dressed rather informally. Sensing her displeasure, he asked if his blue jeans were acceptable. Suzanne let it be known that she preferred more appropriate trousers. She lost him.

After more time on the hunt, Suzanne met Leslie, who passed the means test. Sharing their enjoyment of golf and showy appearances, they seemed suited for each other. Since he had no children as heirs, she was eager to land him. He agreed to marry her. There was one little problem: he was ten years older than she and looked it. To keep her own youthful look, she had already endured the face-lift and body tuck that gave her rather matronly form a sleeker image. Now he must have a face-lift for her.

His surgery was painful, but hugely successful. Primping before the mirror, he grew proud and even conceited. He no longer courted her. With his looks even younger than hers, he began to taunt her. When confronted about some of her needs, he would laugh and say that his first wife could never get what she wanted, so why should he provide a better living for her. He came just one time to therapy with her. In that interview he declared with some pride that he was a stubborn man; he took care of himself first. She would have to live where *he* wanted, use his forty-year-old furniture, and quit *her* job to attend to his whims. Marriage? Why marriage when he was so much better looking than before? Why marriage when other women even younger than she came on to him? He laughed when she asked about their coming wedding plans. (Poor Suzanne had already purchased a wedding dress, a sexy, off-the-shoulder red satin formal.) He no longer took her out for dinners. He no longer called her. When she called him, there was no response or only a cold, "I'm busy."

He was haughty, self-involved and no longer in need of her, a thick-skinned narcissist. She was devastated. She had offered "love for sale," but after his miraculous face-lift (that ointment again!) there was no sale, even though he had courted her for five years and they had planned to marry. It is not certain that he knew the effect of his rejection on her. We do know he broke the false bond. He *negated* any attachment to her. In retrospect it seems that they had always had a sadomasochistic relationship, not a genuine love attachment on either part. He had wanted a trophy. She had wanted money and companionship. Now, she was no longer good enough for him or his money. From the outset, Leslie's attachment to her was one of convenience, easily revoked, leaving no bond. Her devastation and anger over the loss of an idealized relationship forced her almost over the edge to death. She tried but failed to take her own life with an overdose of antidepressants. She came for therapy following that suicidal attempt.

The passive instigation found in the thick-skinned narcissist is deeply rooted in the attachment to an *idealized* self. It is of paramount importance for them to maintain this image to themselves. When that sense of self-image is threatened, the thick-skinned narcissist becomes prone to violence. Anthony Bateman states, "Losing an external object (person) not only leaves this destructive self unmoved but also stimulates a feeling of excitement and triumph as the destructive self is further empowered."[6] In fact, thick-skinned narcissists reject before being rejected, as Phaon and Leslie did. Narcissism bespeaks a narcotic numbness for others. After too long in self-adoration, the narcissist cannot possibly get the same gratification from anyone else. Sappho cries, "If only he would let me love him, he does not need to love me!" But she does not realize that her love is not what Phaon needs; he needs love of *himself*. Like Phaon, Leslie fell in love with his new face. Sappho and Suzanne never had a chance.

Of course, Leslie's narcissism had deep roots. His mother had reared him alone, his father having left her before he was born. As Leslie recalled, he had always hated his mother. First because she was overprotective of him, well into his adolescence. She was always fussing at him, dressing him like Little Lord Fauntleroy, keeping him from play-ing with other boys, not permitting him to join the Boy Scouts and en-forcing other prohibitions. Leslie blamed her for the fact that his father had left. He remembers saying to her in a fit of teenage anger that he could understand why his father had gone. He would have gone, too. The Korean War finally took him away from home and from his mother. While in the service he married a very helpless woman who died after a long illness. He bragged that she had been completely un-der his control.

There is an unusual end to the story of Suzanne and Leslie. They never married. During two years of psychoanalytic therapy Suzanne did gain some perspective on her life and gave up the pursuit of money and men, and of Leslie in particular. Two years later, Leslie called her, desperate to get together. He had become quite ill with the effects of diabetes, lost most of his eyesight, developed difficulties in balance and needed care. He could well have afforded a benign senior citizen facility that would have provided the necessary physical com-fort. He wanted to die at home. You may believe that Suzanne received some satisfaction of revenge by putting him through a good many hoops before restoring any relationship. Then for three years Suzanne attended to some of his needs, mostly running errands to the phar-macy, to the grocery store and of course to the bank. (Phaon should have had it so good.)

Rage and malevolence are at the core of the narcissistic person. Here again are examples of a thick-skinned narcissist in Leslie and a thin-skinned narcissist in Suzanne. It is, however, important to note that there is a fluctuation of roles, as Bateman describes, between the two extremes.[7] It is at the time of switching between these two states of narcissism that persons are most unstable and most likely to commit violence against others or themselves. Thus Suzanne, in her thin-skinned state and in her oversensitivity to Leslie's rejection, attempted suicide. Her life had lost its meaning. Leslie could cling to his thick-skinned defenses only as long as he did not need someone else. Then they changed positions. He was dying and needing her; she was living and did not need him.

Narcissistic or self-oriented individuals maintain their lives mainly through self-preservation defenses; they easily turn into instigators or, failing that, they murder themselves. Narcissus could not hear Echo, not even feel her love; she was doomed to hear her own voice until she turned into a rock. He drowned admiring his reflection and was reincarnated as the lovely flower that we know as the narcissus.

"If you leave me, I will kill myself!" "I will die if you leave me." Over and over again this threat has been used in a futile effort to keep a relationship intact. It is intended to arouse the guilt of the angry person who is leaving. "How can you leave me when I have done so much for you?" "I don't care!" is the response, in action if not in words. It is the threat of losing a love, of being left at the altar, of the loss of face when someone no longer loves. To be jilted is most painful. The *Oxford English Dictionary* defines *jilt* as "to deceive after holding out hopes of love." While losing a lover has hurt many of us, most of us have the ego strength to mourn the loss and then let the person go. It is for the sensitive persons, the thin-skinned, self-absorbed persons who have placed their full reason for living upon receiving the love of one special person, that being jilted leads to the cliff's edge. Jilted lovers do not always commit suicide, but in special circumstances, a suicidal attempt often follows.

This chapter has dealt with the broken heart. The instigation has been deliberate and intended to separate the victim from the world of the living. The instigator wants that person out of life. The next chapter addresses another type of passive instigation—the poisoned gift.

CHAPTER 8

Passive Instigators III

On Looking a Gift Horse in the Mouth

"It's all over! I said when I came here I would give it a chance. It's no use; the thing's a failure! Do with me now what you please. I recommend you to set me up there at the end of the garden and shoot me."

"I feel strongly inclined," said Rowland gravely, "to go and get my revolver."

Henry James, *Roderick Hudson*

I was puzzled by the self-anger of a young man, Norris, a patient, who seemed to have everything he could want. He was an only child, driving a Jaguar his parents had given him, but now unhappy, seeking therapy. He was embittered and depressed and had no interest in living. He gave few cues for his distress. A chance reading of James' novel *Roderick Hudson* provided an opening to understanding the young man's dilemma and his suicidal thoughts.[1] Like Roderick, any of Norris' conflicts seemed to arise from a gift given him by his parents.

Perplexed, I discovered that the word *gift* has not always meant "something voluntarily transferred by one person to another without compensation."[2] As I found, *gift* has surprising meanings, for a gift may be something "given to corrupt."[3] Searching further into the derivation of *gift*, I found that in Dutch the word is *gif*, meaning poison; in German, *gift* also means poison. A gift, then, can be a means to poison another. Many people seem to have experiences of receiving unwanted gifts, which can only be awkwardly accepted or even refused. The complexities of the intentions of the giver and the feelings evoked in the recipient sometimes make both giving and receiving an unpleasant interaction. As we shall see in the following stories, the entrapment of gifts may be fatal.

In this chapter I summarize the beautifully told, tragic story of Roderick Hudson and then look at the case history of Norris to illustrate how the giver of a gift becomes an instigator of suicide.

RODERICK HUDSON

Roderick Hudson, published in 1875 by Henry James, is the story of a baneful friendship between two young men and a gift that proved poisonous. Both men had lost their fathers untimely. Both men's fathers had clearly not been lovable enough for their sons to admire and idealize them, in life or after death. These bereaved young men had naturally loved their fathers but also hated them. Caught between love and hate, their lives were slowed and made directionless by their unresolved griefs. It was as if their griefs had became stuck to their dead fathers as one's hands may adhere to frozen iron banisters in the bitter cold of winter; one dare not loosen one's grip for fear of leaving one's skin on the icy iron.

Most grief-stricken people can pass through mourning and emerge from it, perhaps lonely but also more aware of the value of life. Unresolved grief becomes a transient idleness, and the pain, unending. When one remains grief-stricken and comes to cherish it, then grief becomes chronic and lasting; that is, it becomes paralyzing and chronic, morphing into a pathological idleness. This chronic apathy locks up the person's zest and energy for life. Life becomes unconsciously invested in a cycle of bereavement—loss, sadness, anger, loss followed by more loss, sadness and anger with no recovery from the grief.

The title character is Roderick Hudson, the second son of his parents, the apple of his mother's eye. His father was a "Virginia gentleman," an owner of lands and slaves obtained through his wife's inheritance. The father was a punitive man, cold and alcoholic. When he was drunk, his bony fists and scorching words seemed to sour the house like demons. He was an incessant rake, a business failure who drank and womanized away his and his wife's fortune. He really did nothing productive. He committed suicide when Roderick was thirteen or fourteen by throwing himself into a river, with fragile young Roderick a witness. Roderick's mother, a long-suffering masochist, had hoped that her older son would then support her and her dear Roderick. But the older son joined the army and was killed in battle. Desperate, and with little remaining means, she moved with Roderick to New England into a house she had inherited, her sole remaining possession. There she brought up and pampered her only child. So Roderick was a spoiled teenager who learned about indulgence from his mother and about suicide from his father.

Roderick grew up a very handsome young man, with lots of wavy black hair and a thinly chiseled face, one certainly right for an *artiste*. He became tall, slim and "touchy," easily offended by almost any comment. His voice was unmanly, even plaintive. But he had a talent for sculpting, as evidenced by his incredibly beautiful statue of a graceful young man drinking eagerly from an overflowing gourd held high above his head. Roderick scratched the Greek word for "thirst" on the base of the statue. Roderick called the statue the "poor fellow," for he was always thirsty. And so was Roderick, pampered and never having enough; so was his father, who drank and drank, never quelling his thirst.

But because he was not productive or successful enough to provide a living for himself and his mother, Roderick was apprenticed to a lawyer, where he was kept as a favor to his mother. Even there he did almost nothing, neither studying nor practicing the law. He read perhaps one page of a law book per day, trapped by idleness.

The protagonist, Rowland Mallet, was a rich idler. He was a wealthy young man, terribly distressed about his inner vacuum where he wished for some passion or creative talent, especially passion, to emerge. Rowland's father, Jonas Mallet, was an inveterate, rigid Puritan, "a man with an icy smile and a stony frown." Jonas loathed his son. Shrewd and silent, Jonas could make little Rowland go rigid just by bringing those granite eyes of his to bear on his small son like the sights of a rifle. With that kind of father to love and emulate, Rowland learned very early to frown on himself and to put himself down and soon developed a sensitive and punishing conscience. By the age of ten, Rowland was a frightened, passive boy, his complexion rosy enough for any girl and the measurement of his waist more suitable for a bishop.

When Rowland was fifteen, Rowland's mother became ill, and during her illness revealed to Rowland that during her marriage she had been a singularly unhappy woman, that the marriage had been a frightful error and that the necessity of submitting to her husband made her life a spiritual wasteland. In these moments, Rowland learned that his hatred of his father had been justified. Gradually his mother bestowed on Rowland what love she had managed to preserve, and it made him a gentle man. When she died, he was heartbroken.

Rowland graduated from college and worked in his father's office until he was twenty-five. About this time his father died, leaving Rowland only one-third of his estate with the rest given to charities.

Though he may have felt slighted by his father's will, Rowland inherited sufficient money to take up an idle, unoccupied life. But he did not really know how to live. Rowland realized a "fixed occupation" would be good for him, but he despised the moneymaking mentality of his father. On the other hand, Rowland was not pleasure seeking or carefree enough to be a graceful idler. Directionless, he became immersed in long periods of melancholy.

When the story begins, Rowland is visiting his cousin Cecelia in New England, where Roderick happens to live. Rowland cries to Cecelia,

I am not happy! . . . I am tired of myself, my own thoughts, my own affairs, my own eternal company. True happiness, we are told, consists in getting out of one's self. . . . I want to care for something or for somebody.[4]

Cecelia introduces him to Roderick Hudson, whose artistic promise immediately attracts Rowland. Three days later, wanting to find "at least a reflected usefulness" for his life, and in spite of a vague premonition of future regret, Rowland proposes that he and Roderick go to Rome, where Roderick could learn from the Michaelangelos of the past. Money would be no problem. Rowland will bankroll their expedition, and Roderick's sculpting will make it worthwhile for Rowland.

Here is the poisonous gift. It was not a freely given offer, for Rowland has hidden intentions for the gift; he wants to be fulfilled by another's work. He is not satisfied by the act of giving, but by the unspoken condition of the gift—that his sense of self will be fulfilled through Roderick's talent. Roderick becomes his pawn. Roderick's work will give Rowland a sense of direction and meaning for his life.

Once the two are in Rome, the plan does not work. After actually producing some stunning sculptures and becoming the talk of all Rome, Roderick becomes enchanted by the high European society people around him, by their drinking, gambling and sexual indulgences and especially by Christina Light. She is a beautiful woman who is like a breathing marble sculpture to him. At first she snubs him, but soon she is posing for him. His lovely bust of her brings him several important commissions. He starts them all, but he leaves them incomplete. Rowland feels betrayed. He is angered by Roderick's idleness, but when he confronts him about the unfinished works, Roderick angrily breaks the pieces he has made and refuses to work anymore.

Roderick is in love with Christina, but she challenges his virility. She challenges him to get her a certain blue flower that grows high up on the cliff. The fragile young aesthete Roderick does not have that physical prowess, but he tries. Rowland rescues him, just as he is about to fall. The sensitive Roderick is furious. He says: "I am prepared for failure. . . . The end of my work shall by the end of my life. . . . I am not making vulgar threats of suicide."[5]

The gift backfired. The author lets us know the result—that Roderick has thoughts of suicide. Rowland thinks, "The sense of the matter, roughly expressed was this. If Roderick were really going . . . to 'fizzle out,' one might help him on the way . . . one might smooth the *descensus Averni* (descent into the underworld)."[6]

Rowland is furious and imagines Roderick gracefully and beautifully plunging into a watery grave. Then, images of killing Roderick zoom in and out of his consciousness, but Rowland finds relief from his homicidal urges through meditation in a Franciscan monastery.

Roderick continues to live off the monies of Rowland, traveling to a German spa and then they go to Switzerland. There, the final insult happens. He begs for money to visit Christina, who in the meantime has been married off by her mother to a wealthy old man. Rowland refuses; Roderick then asks Mary, his fiancée, for the money. She and her mother have been brought to Europe by Rowland to see if their presence will help Roderick get back to his sculpting.

Having borrowed the little money that Mary has, Roderick goes off to meet Christina, only to chance upon Rowland along the way. A confrontation follows. Thoroughly enraged by Roderick's shameless behavior, Rowland cries, "It's a perpetual sacrifice to live with a transcendent egotist!"

Roderick, in the insolence of his egotism, accuses Rowland of knowing nothing about love, of having no sensibilities or imagination. He challenges him, wanting to know whether his benefactor has ever been in love. Rowland, wanting to hurt Roderick with the truth, answers that he is in love with Mary Garland.

Roderick, stunned, strikes back, "That is a pity for she doesn't care for you . . . She idolizes me and if she never were to see me again she would idolize my memory."[7] By the end of this bitter interchange, the sculptor acknowledges he "must have seemed hideous" throughout these months and walks off toward the mountains. Sensing something awful will happen, Rowland calls to him, "I should like to go with you." Roderick responds, "I am fit only to be alone. I am damned!" This time, instigator Rowland lets victim Roderick go. Roderick's body is later found lying at the bottom of a ravine.

The idleness of these youths is tightly wrapped up in their intense grief. Truly feeling the grief over the loss of their fathers' love would have prodded them into becoming aware of their hostile, homicidal feelings toward their fathers and would have given them back their energy for life and love. Affection loosens the hidden grief.

Rowland does not package violence with his gift, and the gift could have afforded both of them the fulfillment of their dreams. But wrapped as it is, with the projections of the giver, it can only damage the recipient. There are times when a gift is a curse in disguise, infected from the beginning with hatred and hostility; the hatred Rowland bore toward his father is part of the projections included with the gift. Another projection placed upon the sculptor is that he would provide a vicarious success for the benefactor. Neither projection permits the sculptor to enjoy his creative freedom. In turn, the sculptor has so completely identified with his own father—a playboy who drank and caroused away his wife's money—that he unconsciously acts out his father's life. Then, shocked, he finds himself an image of his father, and commits suicide as his father had already done.

There are times in literature as in life when a gift is more a curse, something given to corrupt. The following is a clinical story of another gift-that-killed.

NORRIS AND HIS PARENTS

I first saw Norris when he was nineteen. A depressed young man, he had been arrested for possession of marijuana, and to avoid prison he was ordered by a judge to have counseling. Norris presented as a mild, dependent young man willing to enter into the therapeutic work. Since he was unemployed, his parents paid for the first year of therapy; after that he took care of his own finances. The first sessions of therapy were centered on his use of drugs and his need to be free from his parents, whom he saw as hovering over him. He felt himself a failure in school and in life. He had no plans or goals for his life. His biggest problem, or so he imagined, was not having enough money. Gradually, he began to discuss the physical abuse inflicted by his father when he was younger, placing much of the blame not on his father but on his mother for her failure to interfere. About the second year into the therapy sessions, the parents retired from their grocery store business and gave Norris a substantial gift. To my surprise, the gift only made matters worse for him. As the weeks went by, Norris claimed this "gift" was ruining him. His anger at his parents became overwhelming.

Norris' father, Fritz, was short tempered, easily upset and vile of speech. Fritz, a large, obese, belligerent man, would roll out of bed every Monday and Thursday morning at 3:30 A.M., cursing each move and reeking from his previous night's beer drinking. Once dressed, he went to the farmers' market for fresh fruits and vegetables to sell in his open-air grocery store. He had very few social inhibitions and readily exploded, sending vindictive splinters against his wife, acquaintances and even customers. In spite of all this, he managed his business skillfully enough to make a good living.

Marie, his wife, also huge and red-eyed, could spew as much foul language as she got from her husband or anyone else. Both were alcoholics. People spoke of them as a little rough but good-hearted. They had no children and never wanted any. Then to their dismay, Marie got pregnant and gave birth to a son, Norris. They hated having this child and made sure there would be no others.

Unlike his parents, at nineteen Norris was lean and agile, about five feet, six inches tall with a babyface and a smile that scampered up like a Smiley toward his wide blue eyes. Even in the face of all that charm, Fritz would sometimes, for no reason he could have named, lash out accusations against Norris of all kinds of moral and physical flaws— and knock him around. Marie might squirm a bit or she might murmur some mild protest, but she never defended Norris and never criticized Fritz. It would only have brought her into his sights and his rage. Then apparently for no reason at all, after one of these high-volume assaults, Fritz would switch from being overly critical and punitive to being overindulgent, granting any of Norris' wishes. No doubt the Jaguar gift came from one of these moods. During Norris' teen years, neither Fritz nor Marie could set him any boundaries, emotionally or physically, as he avoided being home more and more. Fritz and Marie hardly ever knew where he was, and they didn't ask. In a splurge of generosity when Norris turned sixteen, Fritz had given him a red Mustang convertible, much better wheels than any of his jealous classmates drove. In high school Norris experimented with drugs, "showing off," he said, to prove he could take more than his friends could. Expelled from high school for excessive truancy, he never graduated.

After I had seen Norris for some months, the critical gift arrived. Fritz and Marie were well into their sixties and were increasingly anxious about their and Norris' financial future. Without his knowledge, they purchased a good-sized gas station with an auto repair shop for Norris. It was a gift, they said, to be his and his alone. He was to operate it, manage it and keep it for his occupation. The ownership of the gas station was recorded in Norris' name. But, without telling Norris, Fritz and Marie retained title to the real estate.

Norris was surprised and overjoyed. Quite pleased at this show of confidence in him, he ran the business with shrewdness reminiscent of his father's. He coped with the city, county and state licensing requirements with some ease. He learned accounting and employee relations. At one point, he was forced to have some old gasoline storage tanks removed from the ground under his station in order to satisfy certain environmental regulations of the state. This took clever negotiations with state regulators as well as gasoline suppliers and construction workers, but he did it. The business grew. His self-confidence grew, he completed high school and he began studies in the community college.

But Fritz and Marie never quite relinquished their hold on the gift. Like Rowland keeping tabs on Roderick's production of statues, Fritz dropped in often to advise, assist and consult on matters ranging from the brand of toilet paper in the restrooms to preparing income tax returns. At least he called it advising, assisting and consulting. It came down to his obsession to dominate. He could not leave Norris alone with the business: Norris was simply his surrogate. Fritz and Norris often clashed. Rather than retiring and leaving matters to Norris' obviously competent skills, Fritz meddled more and more. He freely helped himself to cash from the registers, not even telling Norris of his withdrawals. Marie, too, would drop by to get some money. At the end of the day, Norris' books seldom balanced. With his profits disappearing even when sales were good, there were slender pickings left for himself. In addition, he endured the public, raging criticisms his father frequently showered on him, even in the presence of customers. In fits of rage, Fritz would hurl things like socket wrenches at Norris, sometimes scoring direct hits. Occasionally Norris could pacify his father on small things by giving in to the temper tantrums, but he found it impossible to submit to his father's compulsion to dominate the business, a business he had been given in good faith, he thought. It was a gift in name only. Like Roderick, the gift bound Norris. It was not a free gift but a gift for the father.

It was more and more obvious that Fritz did not trust his son. With time, there were many confrontations between father and son. Fritz never seemed satisfied with his son's work even though his ventures proved successful, for Norris did not do things exactly as his father would have or wanted him to. Norris despaired of ever being good enough or being loved. In therapy, he talked about the impossibility of ever pleasing his father.

Suffering under his father's continuous control and anger, Norris became less conscientious in maintaining the station; he was erratic in opening and closing times for the station, and lost interest in serving customers well and other necessary business operations. Business began to fail. Norris became increasingly depressed.

With Norris, as with Roderick, the projections that came with the gift had to be refused, even at great cost to himself. Interestingly, I found that some of Norris' approaches to his father were puzzling, as if they were calculated to provoke Fritz to an explosion, the only intimate relationship they had ever had.

Revengeful, the father began to increase the rent for the land, telling Norris that it would make him work harder if he had more bills. Rather than let Norris manage the business, even if it proved that he could not succeed, Fritz became even more meddlesome. In one outburst of anger, Fritz screamed, "I would rather be in Siberia than help you!" This was a turning point—the message was like a jackhammer against Norris' ear, "I do not love you." Then, Norris, unable to pay the rent his father demanded, in an impulsive and revengeful action, closed the business completely. He took a large loss. The gift had now broken the bonds that had chained the father, mother and son to one another. It had proven to be an albatross for Norris.

Norris tried to recover some sense of self with his actions. He was pushed to regress back to the anger of his teenage years in a desperate effort to find some integrity for himself. He was now out in the cold world, betrayed, feeling that his parents had taken back his birthright after promising him that lucrative business for life. He was unhappy, angered and grieved by the betrayal of his father and the false gift. He was even more depressed, but in his anger at his father, he vowed that he would never get another job. This was, according to Norris, a way to get even with his parents, but of course it hurt him even more.

His finances dwindled, and he was soon living in a trailer camp rather than his nice apartment. He was living among people with little money except what they could steal for drugs. Once he tried to overdose deliberately. He slept it off in a couple of days without anyone being aware of it. Although several people who knew him to be a good worker offered him jobs, he refused them all. For him those jobs would be too much like working for Fritz, with all his yelling and treachery. He became a bar hopper, the poor-rich kid who made loud telephone calls from the bar, trying to make his cronies believe he had important business meetings to attend and parents who adored him. As he said to his drinking pals, "I'm their sole heir, right? Everybody have a drink on me. I'm paying!" He lost all his friends, except those who drank with him when he paid.

He tried several times to talk with his parents. They wanted nothing to do with him, except to let him know that his birth was just an accident. They had never wanted children, not even him, with his blue eyes and infectious smile.

He remained in therapy on a weekly basis for about six months but then, against my counsel, he stopped. He was still depressed, still longing for the love of his parents, still angry with his parents for their loaded gift. He was now more openly angry; it was anger against his abuse, including the abuse at the loss of his business, and the anger from the identification with his father. He felt that no one could hurt him anymore. Interestingly enough, although he had built a wall against the dependency that therapy afforded him, Norris continued to telephone me frequently, just to check in.

A year later I learned that Norris had relapsed, and he succeeded in killing himself.

We could easily focus on the tragedy of this young man who was driven to suicide by the barely camouflaged hostility of his parents. It is a real temptation to forget the instigators and look instead at the life they spoiled. But his parents are the center of my concerns. There is little doubt in my mind that his parents generated Norris' death wishes. They themselves had never dealt with their mourning or the loss of love from their parents. So abused, spoiled and indulged as Norris was, he was also victimized by parents who both possessed and dispossessed him. There was nothing he could do that would ever assure him of the unconditional loving attachment—or even security—that he yearned for. When I spoke to Fritz and Marie during Norris' therapy, they were then in their late sixties and were afraid of the road that lay ahead of them. They had not wanted children. They did not want Norris when he was born. Even so, it was obvious that they felt they owned him, that is, that he should bend to their will. From his birth on, their attachment to him was overridden by guilt, as demonstrated by their many excessive gifts. Their final, poisoned, half-gift was the gas station.

Fritz and Marie themselves came from shattered homes where both parents were alcoholic. Marie's father left his family when she was five or six, leaving her mother to scrounge out some kind of bare subsistence living for her three children, making herself as gaunt as a witch. With Norris' arrival, Marie had a safe target for her dormant anger toward males. Her ambivalent attachment to Norris reflected the love she wanted from her father (as well as the love of her own child) and the loss of her father's love who had abandoned her when she was a child.

Fritz' mother died when he was two, leaving the father to care for himself, Fritz and two other children. His father never remarried but had a series of women who lived with him sporadically. His father's drunkenness and fits of anger included routine beatings for Fritz and many a scary night waiting to see what would happen when his father returned from his boozing. Fritz never knew warmth and love. By his own report, when Fritz was eighteen his father threatened to kill him. Fritz soon left home and thereafter was on his own.

Fritz had a malevolent attachment to his own father, and he had a malevolent attachment to his son. Fritz knew all too well that fathers are not supposed to treat their sons with such abuse, so he was sporadically indulgent of Norris, especially after losing his temper. The parents' projections demonized Norris, making it impossible for him ever to be loved by then.

A gift may be given to corrupt. When the gift is intended to gratify or embellish the giver, it will corrupt the recipient as well as the giver. When the gift is intended to enhance the givers' sense of self, it gratifies the givers; they are now "good" and will be loved, but their hostility is masked behind the smiles. The givers seek a symbiotic relationship, one from which they can suckle, find love and give meaning to their lives.

Because of their own neediness, the recipients find a cleverly chosen gift almost impossible to refuse. When it is accepted, the recipients, in effect, sell their soul to have the gift. To regain their integrity, a refusal to participate in the symbiotic gratification of the giver becomes necessary. Usually, these gifts cannot be returned, so the only course of action is to rebel against the expectations of the giver. This rebellion is often ineffective, for the recipient is still under the control of the giver or instigator. It is a fatal attachment for the recipient, loaded as it is with the expectation of submission of the self to the expectations and wishes of the giver. It is a bonded attachment, somewhat akin to slavery.

In these stories, the instigators find a means of containing their inner despair and violence through the medium of a gift that could not be refused. The gifts become a test of lovability of the instigators. Rowland wanted to find some meaning for his life, to relieve the idleness that had paralyzed his thoughts and feelings. Roderick accepted the gift; he gave in, but only temporarily. Norris, too, gave in to his parents' gift, temporarily accepting their bounty until he found that they wanted his submission, to possess him. The price was too high.

These are genuinely malevolent attachments, for while seeming to provide security and benevolence, the gift only covers their usually unconscious, murderous impulses. It is a poisonous gift, because it induces dependency and, worse, submission or death. The recipient tries to keep the gift but reject the bonds of the poisonous symbiosis. When the gift cannot be returned, suicide may seem the only escape. The pawn is all too easily captured.

CHAPTER 9

Provocateur Instigators

From the Outer to the Inner Force

You know what you need to do! Now go do it!

J. Ponten

The active instigators have been the easiest to profile since they are driven by overt, malevolent impulses against the victim. Their intents are clear and often spoken. Unfortunately, it has been easier to identify the underlying dynamics of passive instigators after the fact, that is, after the suicide.

We have found that passive instigators function on differing levels of consciousness. The most readily discernible level is with instigators who are aware of their desire to have an offending person disappear from their lives, but whose ties to the other person are strong enough that they cannot openly break the attachment. These may be negative, ambivalent or self-attachment bonds. In these instances the suicide preserves the instigators' need for a sense of control over their own lives, and the eventual death of the person reinforces the power toward living for the instigator. The tragedy is the suicide victim's unfulfilled wishes of security and love; death follows. Another type of passive instigators is a less conscious bearer of chaos. Unrelenting repression and denial, like razor-fences, have kept their death anxieties at bay. For instance, Max, in his cold, ungiving stance toward his wife, could not admit to entertaining thoughts of wishing Rita's death although his withdrawal from her was sadistic (see Chapter 6). These instigators are actually the most threatening to their partners because, to the partners and to keen observers alike, they may appear to be caring. Underneath the mask, they are struggling to deny their hostility. They fail; their actions speak loudly of their destructive impulses.

Let me restate that "passive instigator" does not describe the person who has a casual, angry wish that another would disappear from one's life. The passive instigator is one with a deeper, persistent infection who has been scarred by fears of death.

Some very striking profiles emerge as we look at the lives of instigators. Early in life, they have all been left damaged and stigmatized, encountering death from severe illness, accident, loss or abandonment. The anxiety born of these fears never surrenders if a healing attachment of security, love and comfort has not helped to assuage their grief. Sorrow reigns like a subterranean dictator in their unconscious lives. The personal, and dynamic, struggle for life itself hides the grief as they cope with the aftermath of traumas. There are strong indications that such events occurring early in life are the foundation for a borderline personality disorder or for a character disorder, dependent upon the age of the child and the severity of the events.[1] Paulette, who is a little older, demonstrates the internal struggle about death, trying over and over to understand death and relieve her grief. But with each attempt, her need to have others die seems to increase, for she finds no refuge, no comfort and no understanding for her grief. She discovers only the power of killing.

The stories in this chapter demonstrate different dynamics of interaction between the instigators and the suicide victims than have been discussed thus far. The instigators accuse the victims of a crime or misdeed, stir their conscience and agitate the anxieties of the suicidal person. Thus they precipitate the self-murder of their victims. In *Der Meister* (The Master) by Joseph Ponten, revenge may also be on the prowl, an Eros-Anteros interaction.[2] In "The Jesuits in G" by E.T.A. Hoffman, the disaster is the fallout from unleashing unresolved mourning.[3]

DER MEISTER (THE MASTER)

One day Gottschalk, a master architect, notices cracks in the main structure of a cathedral dome above the choir area. He had designed and built this magnificent structure himself. The cathedral is his pride, the culmination of his life's professional achievement, a glowing symbol of his talents. He, his wife and his daughter live in the house next to the church. They can look into the cathedral through the stained-glass windows and enjoy its beauty. But now, when he thinks about the horrid cracks spreading through the cathedral dome, he imagines the building collapsing and crushing their house and themselves with it. Yet he does nothing to strengthen the dome of the cathedral, because he does not understand the structural causes of the damage or how to fix it. Further, any acknowledgment of imperfection in the construction of his cathedral will bring criticism and public shame to his reputation and his architectural skills.

He employs an intelligent and perceptive craftsman, Gottfried, a happy-go-lucky, self-taught craftsman who has learned architecture and construction through hard-won experience and work. Gottfried also notices these cracks and explains their cause to his master as well as the repairs necessary to strengthen the building. When Gottfried finds the master obstinately reluctant to do anything to correct the deficiencies of the construction, he writes a report that details the damages and describes the necessary repairs.

He does not give the report to Gottschalk, because he cannot trust him to reveal the design and construction errors or to make the necessary repairs. Gottfried knows full well that this master architect is obsessed with maintaining his fame as a master builder.

Gottschalk is dismayed and angry with his journeyman. He wants the report. Desperate to quash the report, Gottschalk accosts Gottfried. He demands many times that the report be given to him, first requesting, then wheedling and finally angrily demanding and arguing that the report belongs to him as the master. Gottfried is adamant. He wants to save the cathedral from impending destruction. He will not surrender the report.

As time passes, Gottschalk becomes increasingly desperate and anxious lest the journeyman give the report to the authorities. He tries to extort the report from Gottfried. He orders his daughter, a teenage virgin, to seduce Gottfried and persuade him to give her the report. If Gottfried does not give her the report, Gottschalk will have moral grounds based on the seduction of his daughter with which to extort it from Gottfried.

Gottfried will not be seduced. Gottschalk becomes even more desperate and angry. He informs his wife, Berta, that she will make love to the craftsman and come back with the report. Surely, with all her experience in sexual matters, she will know better how to seduce a man. Berta reluctantly submits to her husband's demand and goes to Gottfried, but she is not successful in her attempt to seduce Gottfried either. A man of honor, Gottfried will not have an affair with her or with their daughter. Berta, in revenge and in truth, later tells her husband that if she were twenty years younger, Gottfried would appeal to her.

Gottschalk has completely dishonored his wife and daughter. They have been violated and prostituted, shamed and traumatized by his cruelty. The architect becomes only more angry and frustrated. Learning that the craftsman carries the report concealed against his chest, Gottschalk resolves to have it, even if it means killing the journeyman. After all, his narcissistic pride depends on destroying that report.

He devises a plan to kill or at least to harm the journeyman so he can get the report. One night, with a lantern hanging from his neck to light his way, he climbs the scaffolding to the position where the craftsman will be working during the day. He loosens a beam underneath the scaffolding, so that the unsuspecting craftsman will step on the scaffolding and fall. Unknown to him, Berta watches through the windows of their house.

The next day the craftsman falls forty meters from the scaffolding to his death. The architect eagerly checks the body for the report, but it is not there. The craftsman had already given it to Berta. It seems that Gottfried had not found the skinny daughter of the architect very appealing, but he was attracted to the architect's wife, much as to a mother figure. Berta accepted the document and then hid it in the dome of the cathedral for the next master. Of course, she despises her husband for his dishonor of her and their daughter, and even more for murdering the journeyman.

The architect is in a state of shock. He does not find the report on Gottfried's body. He comes home and enters the dark, shadowy room where his wife, Berta, stands concealed behind the window curtains, staring blankly at the cathedral. Gottschalk mumbles, "He did not have the report; he did not have the report! The women who washed the body did not find anything." Thinking he is alone, he is unrestrained in his dismay. "Did he eat it? Do I have to pump his stomach?"

Berta is dressed all in black, with a mourning veil around her shoulders. She steps out from behind the curtains. Gottschalk is so surprised to see his wife that he starts to shake like an aspen tree in a storm. Berta stands stiffly in the darkness, a shadow figure. She seems to grow in stature. Like Niobe, who cried until she could cry no more after the murder of her children and was turned into stone, Berta now faces Gottschalk coldly, like a block of marble, the only way she can control her grief.

"You let me wait a long time," he says to that stone of his wife, afraid that she had heard him as he came in.

"Did you . . . wait?" he sputters.

"Not for you but for the message you brought me. You killed Gott-fried!"[4]

These words strike like the lightning that splits open the aspen tree. Gottschalk stumbles and falls to his knees, his hands folded, beseeching her pity. But now his wife has the power. She has become his judge and his provocateur. He has prostituted her and her daughter, and he has killed Gottfried. She knows his crimes.

He can only see Berta's eyes shining across the darkening room. The architect feels his will being subjugated by the shadow of his crimes. Just one more time he rises up and cries for mercy. Berta replies, "It is too late; an eye for an eye, Gottschalk for Gottfried."[5] Hearing this statement, he loses his will. *Through the power of the instigator, the will of the victim becomes submissive.*

"I think you know what you have to do. You do know?" She wonders, has she been direct enough with him?

"I . . . I think so."[6]

Berta then tells him to go but to kill himself in a manner that will let his fame as a master architect live on. She appeals to his narcissistic pride, feeding him the illusion that he can do it successfully.

"You know which of the beams would be the easiest to loosen . . . no need to confess . . . I took your confession, all you need to do is atone for yourself. Now take the lantern."[7]

Master Gottschalk lifts the lantern from the shelf, lights it, buttons his coat and puts on his hat. He has the robot-like obedience of a man with a consuming guilty conscience as Camus illustrated in his story, *The Fall.*

He goes out. She watches from the bedroom window, telling him that she can see him. When the light of the lamp goes out in the church, she will cover her face, knowing that he has fallen.

Perhaps with more evidence we might consider Berta to be an active instigator. She does give her husband a direct message—go kill your-self. But although there is some streak of personal revenge in it, Berta is acting more like a representative of social justice. First she judges Gottschalk's crimes, and then she provokes his suicide by activating his fear of public shame, both for betraying his professional integrity and for committing crimes against society.

Gottschalk, trembling with the anxiety of his misdeeds, knows that suicide is the only end for his life. He walks away like a zombie carrying his own death warrant. He will do as she says. He will kill himself;

it is the only acceptable way for him to avoid being weighed in the scales of justice.

Berta is suffering from the betrayal of her husband and the ensuing grief. He has been malicious in his anxious attempts to cover up his ineptitude. Now he has committed murder, carefully planned. Berta, in her grief, can take no more from him. We do not know the quality of Berta's attachment to Gottschalk before these incidents, but whatever it was, she has now negated it, revoked it and shredded it. Gottschalk would not have killed himself if Berta's attachment to him had remained firm, if she had accepted his actions as defensible and his view of Gottfried as valid. But, she could not overlook his actions because her own grief was too intense.

Provocateur instigators are difficult to identify in real life, because their stories are often untold. Their role in another's suicide, however, seems to sidestep yet confirm the social justice system. In their dismay, anger and sense of righteousness, they take upon themselves the role of judge.

"THE JESUITS IN G"

This story also describes a provocateur-instigator. We never learn exactly what has damaged this young man, but whatever it was, it left him quite malevolent. The instigator serves the same purpose as Gottschalk's wife, Berta, but he is more cruelly motivated. He sadistically searches for the dark secrets of another's heart and energizes the conscience of a stranger.

The tale begins with idleness not unlike that of Rowland Mallet in James' story of Roderick Hudson. Like Rowland, a no-talent provocateur dreams of becoming a famous artist, and he is bedeviled by his envy of successful creative people. He is also idle, the true sign of unresolved grieving. Called only "the handyman," he is young and unemployed, presently traveling through a small town, looking for work, relishing his fantasies. Uncouth and obnoxiously curious, he is lacking grace in manner and behavior. His carriage breaks down in a small town and he is forced to remain there for three days while it is being repaired.

Wandering through the town, without much to do, he wants to learn more about art to find out if he, too, could have a future as an artist.

At a Jesuit college, he meets a professor who tells him something about the town. At first, the professor is rather cold in his demeanor, but he warms up to this serious young man's curiosity about art and takes him into a beautiful church. There, up on a scaffolding, a painter is at work, one who clearly possesses both imagination and creativity. Watching him brush over an earlier painting, they hear him moan time and again, "People's faces, people's faces. . . . Oh I am a poor fool!"

The handyman notices an unfinished painting covered up at the side of the altar. He is curious and wants to see the hidden painting. He asks and then demands that the painter tell him about it. Annoyed, the painter tells him that a good little boy does not mess with the screw of the organ while someone is trying to play. In other words, "Please don't interrupt me or interfere with my mood and my attention while I am painting."

The handyman is not easily dismissed. He is a clever and manipulative person and wants to know why the painter moans. Seeing that the painter has to reach out awkwardly for his brushes and then paint in an uncomfortable position, the handyman climbs the scaffolding and starts handing the painter the brushes and cans of paints. They work all night long; the painter seems tireless, lost in his work, talking about it as he applies his strokes. The handyman fakes concern for the painter and asks him some personal questions, but what he really wants to know is the secret hidden behind the moaning. He wants to penetrate the painter's soul. The handyman comments on the unhappiness of the painter, suggesting that something very unfortunate has happened in the painter's life.

The painter responds in a broken voice, "How can you have peace and happiness in your life if you know about a horrible crime?" The painter will talk no more. He grows silent, then leaves the scaffolding.

His malicious curiosity awakened, the handyman becomes like a cat with a mouse, ready to play with his victim in order to satisfy his dark curiosity which, in turn, hides his own secret evils. He wounds by his questions and his questions cover up his own wound, an unnamed grief in the story. There is no doubt that it exists, and that it drives the handyman to become a provocateur-instigator, a "death dealer." In his malice, he seeks the dark secrets of someone else's life.

The professor tells the handyman about a manuscript that the painter's favorite student had written about the painter's suffering. Although hesitant at first, the professor turns over the manuscript. From it, the handyman discovers that the painter had known a princess living near Naples. In a dramatic first meeting, the painter saved her from an assassin by running a knife through the man's neck.

The princess and the painter later married. His wife became one of his models for the altarpiece. But then he became overwhelmed by guilt. In his last truly creative painting, he had painted a picture of Mary, the child and Joseph. He simply could not deal with the fact that he had used his own wife, this earthly mother, as a model for a Holy Mother. Somehow, the painter felt it was an evil misrepresentation. The guilt nearly drove him to madness. The birth of his son made his guilt even worse; the picture became a sacrilege. He cursed both of them. He wished them both dead. In anger, he kicked his wife and she passed out while grabbing his knee.

The handyman becomes obsessed with finding out the truth: did the painter get rid of his wife and child? Did he kill them? The reader knows only that the painter is now without his wife and child. The manuscript does not say for certain that he murdered them.

The professor and the handyman argue about the possibilities. The professor does not believe that the painter is capable of murder and suggests that it is perhaps the guilt of the painter over his sacrilegious picture which makes him just imagine that he has killed his wife and child. The handyman thinks that even though the painter does not admit it directly, he is in fact guilty of the wicked murder of his wife and child. We may be confident that this judgmental statement by the handyman arises from his need to know others as evil.

The one word in the manuscript that points a wobbly finger of guilt at the painter is *vergebens*, that is, "in vain." However, in this sentence, the intended meaning of the expression is not clear. As reported in the manuscript, the painter said, "I look upon her dead face *in vain* and it is here that my outrage and wickedness began. You have stolen my life, my wanton wife. I yelled at her and kicked her with my foot; she grabbed my knee and passed out."

There is no certainty that the painter killed his wife or his child. All that is reported is their argument and that later she and their son were gone. The handyman becomes even more curious, obsessed with the idea of murder. Now the professor encourages the efforts of the handyman. He is curious, too.

Again the handyman helps the painter. He climbs up the scaffolding and quietly starts to hand the cans of paint to the painter. The painter is surprised at his help, but the handyman just responds that he is the painter's handyman. The painter smiles. The professor listens from below.

In this narrative, *handyman* is a code word for instigator. A handyman is "one who is inventive or ingenious in repair work." And this handyman is ingenious in his working around the defenses of the painter. One might postulate that he was acting in a manner similar to psychotherapists as they help the patient search for truth within themselves. We can begin to see the cooperation between the outer instigator (the handyman) and the inner instigator (hidden within the painter). The outer instigator awakens the hidden grief of the inner instigator, which then pushes his victim on toward suicide.

Now, as a trick, the instigator-handyman starts talking to the painter about the painter's life as if he knew every detail of it. In fact, the handyman is simply bluffing, because all he really knows is what is in the manuscript. Once more faking a sincere interest in the painter, he quietly works his way to the climax, then screams out in a merciless rage, "You killed your wife and child!"

The painter throws up his hands, his face twisted in shock. He exclaims, "I am innocent of the blood of my wife and my son! But certainly, I am not innocent of the blood of the assassin from whom I saved my wife." The painter then cries, "Another outburst like that and we are both going off the scaffolding, smashing our heads on the stone floor of the church!"

The handyman sidetracks the painter just long enough to slip away, while below the professor laughs at the handyman's cruelty.

Six months later, the handyman returns to the town. The professor informs him that, as a result of his cruel confrontation, the painter completed the altarpiece and everyone is impressed. Even the figure of Elizabeth, mother of John, has been finished. Besides the mother and child, there stands the figure of one who prays, the radiant artist. The professor also reports that two days after the painting was finished, they found the painter's walking stick and hat lying by an old river. There must have been a suicide.

The handyman is not an instigator in our usual sense. Rather, he prods the painter's conscience, which reawakens his inner judge. The painter accepts the accusation of guilt that the handyman places upon him only because he already has the stigma of killing someone, even though in an honorable action. The hidden grief of the painter is back in full force. He has lost his wife and child. His defenses are gone. With the resurgence of his grief, his creativity is restored and his ability to love returns. He is free to complete his work—and free to take his own life.

The painter lived with unfathomed grief when he was moaning,

"People's faces, people's faces." It could well be that the painter's grief was the inner instigator of his suicide. That seems so, but the grief needed a provocateur, the handyman.

Provocateurs have an uneasy awareness of the evil within themselves that they project onto their victims. It is not an attachment to the suicide victims per se, but to that malicious part of themselves that the suicide victim represents. The provocateurs seek fellow citizens; they resonate with the hint of evil within others. They seek their own power through the power to make others confess evil; others are as bad as they are! Penetrating the other person's defenses in this prying, sadistic manner breaks down the repressive barriers of the suicidal persons and incites them to a violent reaction. The instigators in these stories are like bounty hunters enforcing social contracts with fellow human beings, even if they themselves hide guilt. They excavate the victims' buried denial and repression in order to prove others as vile as they are.

Illustrations of such vigilantes of social justice are not hard to find, but one can only ask questions about possible provocateur-instigators. For instance, Admiral Jeremy Michael Boorda, the first enlisted sailor in the history of the U.S. Navy to move up the ranks and achieve the highest one of Admiral, killed himself.[8] He was praised by President Clinton as a man of "extraordinary energy, dedication and good humor." He had received many commendations and awards for his service in Vietnam, and among the medals that he wore was the "V" medal given for combat service in Vietnam. He probably deserved the medal, but his formal citations did not include the combat "V." At the time of his death he was scheduled for a meeting the next day with President Clinton and other members of the Joint Chiefs of Staff to discuss an initiative on seeking a permanent worldwide ban on land mines.

Admiral Boorda had agreed to an interview with the bureau chief of *Newsweek* at 2:30 on the day of his death. About noon he found out that the interview was to focus on questions about his Vietnam combat medals. The implication was that *Newsweek* was investigating whether Boorda had actually been awarded all his medals, especially the "V" decoration.

Evidently Boorda, sensing that his false wearing of the "V" might be revealed, left his lunch in the office, saying he was going home to eat.

He was found dead at 2:05 p.m. in an area near his office at the Washington Navy Yard.

The implication seems to be that the fear of becoming dishonored, the shame of wearing an unearned medal and the grief over being exposed were more than he could live with. Yet I would like to raise this question: Were the reporters the provocateurs of his suicide? To me, the story as reported strongly suggests that his denial had been effective for him—until he was to be exposed, much like the victims in the stories by Hoffman and Ponten. Perhaps it was not his own guilt of wearing the "V" medal that brought about his suicide, but the fear of being exposed. It took the provocation by the reporters to make him fear his misdeed and then to prefer suicide to public scorn. Their provocation on that particular day was perhaps a matter of chance, but once anyone in the journalism community knew about it, the questions would surely have been raised sooner or later.

The same dynamics appear to be at work in the suicides of some of the priests who have been exposed as child molesters. For instance, as reported in the *Santa Barbara News Press* in the spring of 2002, Father Donald A. Rooney of Parma, Ohio, took his own life.[9] Only after the *News* reporters' exposure of his pedophilic actions and those of other priests alerted the public to their crimes did the self-inflicted death become Rooney's choice.

The role of a provocateur is similar to one who sabotages the life of another. The personal motives of the instigator may be many, and these stories only begin to provide an understanding. What does seem clear is that there are sometimes memories or actions that remain hidden until someone pushes to reveal the secret. It seems the shame of being exposed or the guilt over the exposure is so devastating that some persons prefer to kill themselves rather than face the social consequences.

To break through repressed memories is to recall earlier unhappy feelings or traumatic experiences that have shaped our lives. This process is only to be undertaken with the help of a skillful psychotherapist who can lead this release from deep psychic pains and to a recovery of a healthier sense of self. The positive attachment and trust that develop between the therapist and the patient provide the necessary dynamic interaction that permits these repressed experiences to be relieved safely.

CHAPTER 10

Heroic Provocateurs

Riddles and Rhymes, Music and Massacre

Some suicides seem to be preordained, self-administered executions; that is, when the provocateurs fulfill certain requirements, the criminals have no choice but to kill themselves. The stories of Ulysses and Oedipus illustrate this scenario: they did something clever to cause the serial killers Sphinx and the Sirens to do what Fate said they had to do.

ULYSSES AND THE SIRENS

The Sirens were enchantresses on the island of Anthemoëssa, a land of flowers.[1] Singing and playing irresistible melodies on unusual instruments, they so enflamed sailors that they would leap from their ship and swim to the Sirens and this Promised Land. Their songs offered knowledge and wisdom, would foretell their future and quicken their spirit; it was knowledge with a strong sexual invitation.[2] On arrival at this Promised Land, the sailors were either smashed on the rocks lining the shores or devoured alive by the Sirens, whose feet rested on ground white with the crumbling bones of dead seafarers. From these bones, the Sirens fashioned their musical instruments.

Their name, Sirens, comes from *seira*, meaning chain. In Greek their name is *seireios*, which also means hot and scorching, like the star Sirius. Thus the sailors were emotionally chained to the Sirens with an unbreakable bond. As we have already seen, such bonds are difficult to break, especially if the attachment is negative, ambivalent, malicious or nullifying. The idea of bonding becomes even more intriguing when we consider the attachment to folk heroes like Marilyn Monroe or Elvis Presley, whose power to enchant continues even today, long after their deaths. For instance, there are many impersonators of Presley and many who claim that he really is not dead at all. The fantasized chains these folk heroes offer seem almost unbreakable, as were the attachment powers of the Sirens. However, living under the spell of folk heroes may fascinate but, to my knowledge, has not yet killed anyone.

The seafarers' encounters with the Sirens show vividly how closely the suicide and the instigator entwine each other. The attachment held out by the Sirens is based on a singing-listening connection: those who come to listen are bonded to them, whereupon these death-singers lead their listeners to their demise. Since the Sirens are omniscient, they know they are doomed to die as soon as someone resists their music. But they cannot help themselves; they cannot abstain from singing.

One story of the Sirens' origins is that they were challenged to a singing contest against the Muses. They lost. As losers, they were condemned to this lonely island where they must sing out of narcissistic isolation. Their physical appearance remains a question. They were either all women, or women above the thighs and birds below, or women with winged feet. One of their functions was to escort souls into the realms of death; that is, the death-singing was their existential purpose.

Ulysses and his men were homeward bound after the expedition that had won them much glory in the conquest of Troy. After twenty years of traveling and surviving many near-fatal adventures, Ulysses was finally nearing his home in Ithaca, but first he had to sail by the island of the Sirens. He had been warned in the strongest terms about their singing, warnings that made him want all the more to feel the rapture of their singing for himself. He accepted the challenge to hear the music and at the same time rid the seas of a major hazard to navigation. To protect his sailors, he put wax in their ears, then ordered them to bind his hands and feet to the mast. If he implored them to unfasten him, they were to secure him with yet more chains. He did hear the songs of the Sirens, and he did sail by the island unharmed. With this failure of their life's existential purpose, the Sirens could sing no more; their song had lost its power. The Sirens plunged into the sea and were turned into very unmusical rocks.

Ulysses had been enchanted but not bewitched, captivated but not captured. He was dazzled but not deranged.

Ulysses fits our picture of an instigator who has been carrying his own stigma and fear of death. When he was born, the wet-nurse laid him on the knee of his maternal grandfather, the master thief Autolykos. Right there, lying on his knee, his grandfather gave him the stigmatic name Ulysses, "son of wrath," "son of a hater," "victim of hate" or simply, "the hated one." He also bore an early death trauma. Once as a young boy when he was hunting a wild boar, the animal wheeled around and attacked him. It was a death-threatening attack. He escaped, but not without a long gash on one thigh. The scar on his thigh, his fear of death and his need to challenge death stayed with him the rest of his life. It is by this scar that his old wet-nurse recognized him when she washed his feet after his return home to Ithaca disguised as a beggar to find out what had been happening in his kingdom.

Ulysses was known to be wily. Among his many sobriquets were "Ulysses of many devices" and "crafty." His craftiness helped him defeat his enemies and avoid his own death drive in each of the challenges on his long journey home. He outwitted the Cyclops, defeated Circe, saved his men from the lotus-eaters and connived that Hector's little son, Astyanax (meaning "Protector of the City"), be killed because Ulysses feared Astyanax would seek revenge for Troy. After the Trojan War, the sword of Achilles was awarded to Ulysses, rather than to Ajax, who had the rightful claim. Ajax was so insanely offended that he hurled himself onto the point of his sword. Was Ulysses the instigator here, too? Clearly, many instigators are ingenious manipulators, cleverly hanging onto their own lives at the cost of others. In clinical terms, they might fit a diagnosis of psychopathy.

Since Ulysses forced the Sirens to kill themselves, I consider him to be a provocateur-instigator. He may also be called a heroic instigator, one who risked his life to rid the ocean of the Sirens. Before I say any more about heroic instigators, let me offer another hero from mythology, Oedipus.

OEDIPUS AND THE SPHINX

Although theory has flown far away from the original postulates of Freud, the stories of Oedipus remain the underpinnings for much of current thinking and research. For many of us, Oedipus is a mythical hero, perhaps an antihero, not because of his awesome and tragic life story, but largely because Freud identified him as embodying critical aspects of human psychological development. One significant episode was played out when Oedipus became the instigator of the Sphinx.[3]

When Oedipus was born, his father and mother, King Laius and Queen Jocasta, succumbed to a prophecy that Oedipus would some-day kill his father and marry his mother. To prevent that from happening, they had his feet pinned together. Then they ordered a servant to take him out into the woods and leave him there. The servant took pity on this abused baby and gave him to Polybus, the king of Corinth and his wife, Merope. Because of the damage to his feet he was given the name *Oedipus*, which means swollen foot. Thus from his infancy he was abused and abandoned by his parents. He fully qualifies as a stig-matized, traumatized hero.

Thebes, an important city in Greece, was suffering under the domi-nation of the Sphinx, sent by Hera to punish King Laius for a crime that had been ignored by the Thebans: he had raped Chrysippus, the son of Pelops. With the face and breast of a woman, the body, feet and tail of a lion and the wings of a bird, the Sphinx was treacherous, evil and merciless. She was laying waste the fields of Thebes, predomi-nantly an agricultural community. In addition, she sat on Mount Phikion at the entry to Thebes, devouring everyone, whole and raw, who could not answer her famous riddle: "What has one voice, and is four-footed, two-footed, and three-footed?"

Everyone knew that she could not survive a correct answer. But no one could think of it. The brave ones who tried, even a son of Creon, one of Thebes' rulers, wound up as Sphinx meat. The whole meaning-fulness of her existence resided in this question-and-answer game. The right answer would rob her of her power, bringing about her death. Oedipus, a self-exiled young man, a wanderer, knew the an-swer from his own experiences. He had crawled on all fours as an in-fant, walked on two feet as a man and then would walk on three feet in old age with his cane. He challenged her. She asked the riddle. He an-swered, "A man." When he gave this answer, she jumped onto the rocks, or into the sea, and killed herself, giving us a new sobriquet for Oedipus—the hero.

Knowing her crimes and her fate, Oedipus provoked her suicide. It is consistent with my concept of provocateur-instigators that Oedipus and Ulysses should each rid the world of a menace. As the master painter and the architect were found guilty by their provocateurs, who represented society, Oedipus found the Sphinx guilty of destroying Greek culture through her obsession with killing. For us, she may be a symbol of man's impotency to control destructive impulses gone wild in a culture that is being consumed and obliterated by the misuse of power. The Sirens also aroused impulses that defied the intellect and knowledge inherent in the definition of human culture. Both Ulysses and Oedipus were able to use their courage and intellect to overthrow the impulse-ridden Sphinx and her sisters in crime, the Sirens.

To return to our theme, the attachment of the challenger to the Sphinx, as with the Sirens, is shown in her name. The word *sphinx* is derived from the Greek word *sphingo*, meaning to strangle, and from *sphingein*, to bind tight. Her riddle was the binding or strangling force that brought many young men before her, unable to resist the challenge of trying to outwit her. They could not, as the sailors could not resist the Sirens. With his hard-earned experience, Oedipus outwitted the Sphinx as Ulysses did the Sirens. If Oedipus and Ulysses had not used their mental powers to defeat their challengers, they too would have been murdered. But they saved their lives by knowingly resisting the attachment bonds held out by their challengers. In effect, they negated any attachment to them. Today, some potential suicide victims could also protect their lives by resisting the enticements of their instigators.

The suicides of the Sphinx and the Sirens were brought about by instigators who sabotaged their power game, defeating them through the power of thinking. Through the thoughtful analyses of the puzzles, the hero provocateurs not only escaped their own deaths but also defeated the false living and cleverness of their victims.

It seems that the Sirens should have been able to stop their singing or the Sphinx should have simply flown away rather than kill herself. But free choice was not open for them. Fate had determined otherwise.

These instigators seem heroic because they effected the deaths of those who scourged and destroyed cultures. This is a dilemma, and a current social puzzle as well. Their role in suicide raises an age-old question that remains a burning social issue today: does one ever have the right to kill?

All potential suicides face the challenge of avoiding self-inflicted death. As we shall see in the next chapter, some are able to escape their urge.

The Internal Instigator
Death in the Soul

Love taught my tears in sadder
notes to flow and turn'd my heart
to elegies of woe.

Alexander Pope (1688–1744)

The evidence is compelling that one individual may relate consciously or unconsciously to a significant other with projections of death. I have been amazed to realize that these projections are sufficiently strong so that a vulnerable person may introject them. The underlying process, often termed *introjective identification,* is easily observed in infants and young children as they experience the identification with their parents. As relatives may say, this child is "just like his daddy," "her aunt" or "her mother," and the child assimilates the projections. Those projections may become the basis of the child's selfhood. Some projections can fill a child with hope, goodwill and pride; identifications with positive traits may lead to the second, third or fourth generation of teachers, doctors and productive people. Other projections may become malicious when the message states, "You are a little thief, just like your uncle," or "You are as rotten as your aunt." The child may soak up, or introject, these labels or projections and feel impelled to act them out. Later on, we are not surprised to hear stories about the bad seed or the acorn that did not fall far from the tree.

The instigators that have been discussed so far have used the defenses of denial and repression followed by projection, as well as others, to contain their fears of death. The suicide victims have, in turn, accepted the projections and acted upon them. That is, they have taken into themselves the driving force toward death. The instigators that I will now discuss are internal rather than external, those that reside within the person as a part of the self.

I propose three types of internal instigators. The first arises during the victim's childhood or adolescence when a significant person dies. The internal instigator stems from the loss of an important person in their life, whether or not the person provided a secure or comforting attachment for the child. If that important person dies under disturbing circumstances, then the child may unconsciously identify not so much with the person's character as with the death itself. The introjection of the death turns fatal later on, when the victim is unable to still the grief and malaise caused by the death—except by following the same path to suicide.

Gregory Zilboorg recognized this phenomenon when he commented that the identifications with deceased persons during childhood are most likely to identify future candidates for suicide.[1] He relates the suicide of a twenty-two-year-old girl who jumped from the fourteenth floor of a building on the fourteenth anniversary of her mother's suicide. She was eight years old when her mother committed suicide. Although the girl was apparently happy and in a good mood the day before, she was driven to take her own life by unconscious forces that had begun with the death of her mother. This is the classic anniversary suicide of which we occasionally hear.

While Zilboorg does not comment on the point, it would be one assumption that the girl did not have a secure attachment with her mother. Further, if she was given neither an explanation that would have provided her with a cognitive framework to understand death nor emotional support to allay her grief, she could easily develop an identification with her mother's death. Her grief must have struggled on inside her, and she grew up lacking the personal strength to withstand her own developing compulsion to die. The stories of Sylvia Plath and Anne Sexton will illustrate this first kind of internal instigator.

The second type is an intriguing variation of the internal instigator, one illustrated by the story of a Vietnam veteran who carried his instigator around inside him for years until he committed suicide by successfully creating his own executioner.

In the third type, the suicide victim first kills someone else. Frequently this is someone the victim supposedly loves.

Many suicides begin with internalization, that is, "bringing some aspect of the external world into one's private mental life and having the representation of the external world exert an influence over one's thoughts and behavior."[2]

Death is not a person, and the term *attachment* usually applies to the quality of relationships between people. But attachments to things, to ideas or to nature are common. Freud termed these attachments a *cathexis*, which is explained in the *Dictionary of Psychoanalysis* as "the investment of mental or emotional energy in a person, object or idea."[3] I would like to propose the idea that one can have an attachment to death.

In the cases of anniversary reactions of suicide, the victim reenacts the suicide or death of a parent that occurred early in the person's life. The anniversary reaction usually symbolizes some part of the death, related to age or time of year of the death. It is often assumed that children "will outgrow it" or "don't understand anything," and their grief and loneliness are often ignored, even by the best of well-meaning adults. Several factors may linger within the person's psyche to make death, or suicide, seem an inescapable fate. First, if the child's confusion of thoughts or feelings about death—the child's sense of loss, the child's fear of further abandonment or the awe provoked by the intensity of the adults' emotions—is not clarified, death remains mystifying to the child. Next, if the child assumes some responsibility for the death of the parent because of incidents of displeasing a parent or having feelings of anger toward the parent, guilt keeps the death alive. The death may become even more frightening if a surviving parent or caretaker remains overwhelmed by grief and takes a prolonged time to recover from the loss without attending to the child's needs.

I also propose that the child's trauma is greater when the attachment has been insecure. Since one's primary attachments usually govern later attractions, it is the insecure attachment that will focus on death as the *real* event. The anxiousness is therefore exacerbated by the death, and in this regard, anniversary suicides seem to be brought on by anancastic ideas, that is, continued preoccupations with dying that have not freed the person to develop a good sense of the self.

In looking for examples of the internal instigator, I wanted to find people with sufficient biographical and autobiographical information to work with. After considering the suicides of several well-known figures, I chose Sylvia Plath and Anne Sexton, whose lives graphically depict the growth of powerful fantasized attachments and the emergence of the inner instigator.

In the stories that follow, an internalized instigator, apparently stemming from an attachment to the emotional abandonment by a parent during the victim's childhood, dooms the victim.

SYLVIA PLATH

> It is a love of death that
> sickens everything[4]

Sylvia Plath's suicide was a great loss to the literary world. Her writing was highly revealing and widely appreciated. Her suicide seemed to be a response to constant, driving inner forces. Her story opens up the world of an inner instigator.

Plath was overly concerned with death. Jacqueline Rose writes: "Plath herself has also become a figure for death. Death in the shape of a woman."[5] As Plath writes in the *Collected Poems*:

> Dying
> Is an art, like everything else.
> I do it exceptionally well.[6]

Then she goes on to say that while it may feel "like hell," she wants to make it real because it seems that death is a "call" for her.

Sylvia Plath was a child prodigy. She published her first poem at the age of eight. From then on, she made writing an outlet for her observations, her perceptions and her feelings. Those who knew her seemed unaware of the depth of her grief about living, for she most often seemed lively, dynamic and driven to write. After her second child, a son, was born, she would rise at 4:00 A.M. in order to have four hours to write, free of the responsibility of mothering.

The call of death pervades her writing. She confesses in her poetry that she has tried to kill herself every ten years, and maybe like a cat, she has nine lives to live. She also talks of dying when she was two; this may have been a reaction to the birth of her brother, Warren, who was two years younger than she. When she was ten years of age, she told a friend in confidence that she had tried to cut her neck. She showed him the scar. There is an allusion to this episode in one poem. Her suicide attempt at age twenty, while she was a college student, was serious. She made a third try ten years later when she drove her car off the road. She was not hurt. Finally the fourth attempt was fatal.

The reader cannot help but be overwhelmed by the strength of her words. Not all of her poetry focuses on death, for she was full of life and made each experience into words of beauty. But listen to the sadness in this poem:

> I do not stir.
> The frost makes a flower
> The dew makes a star,
> The dead bell . . . [7]

Anger also permeates her writing: "I am accused. I dream of massacres . . . hating myself, hating and fearing. . . . It is a love of death that sickens everything."[8] Many of her poems are about hate, a life where children hate their parents, a life where parents do not know how to parent or a life in which marriages fail.

Sylvia Plath was born October 27, 1932, to Otto and Aurelia Plath, who had married in January of that year. Her brother, Warren, was born thirty months later. Her father was a professor of German and biology. He was a loner, obsessive and quite unsocial, headstrong, intractable and with little empathy for others. Aurelia, on the other hand, was outgoing and social. She enjoyed books and read extensively to the children. She, too, was educated and taught English and German. Bound to her husband's wishes, her aim was to keep peace and quiet in the home, no matter the cost to herself.

Sylvia was an especially gifted child. Her mother reported that she tried to talk at six to eight weeks of age by imitating vowel sounds. She started elementary school at four years of age and by five was writing poems. At eight Sylvia had her first poem published in the school paper. She thrived in school, participating actively in school activities and receiving many honors during junior high and high school. In high school she was editor of the paper, *The Bradford*, wrote words for the class song and was received into the National Honor Society.

She entered Smith College as a freshman in 1950. She won prizes throughout college, including a guest editorship for *Mademoiselle*. The experiences in New York became the background for her novel, *The Bell Jar*. Rejection slips came her way, but she was unusually successful for a young person, having several poems and short stories published in journals such as *Seventeen* and *The New Yorker*. In spite of severe depression and the drastic treatment she received for it during her college years, she graduated summa cum laude, received the Clara French

Prize as an outstanding student in English and was elected to Phi Beta Kappa. She received a Fulbright scholarship that took her to Cambridge for a master's degree.

She also seemed to have a hysterical streak. While she was in New York, Sylvia was walking with a friend, Janet Wagner. The Rosenbergs were to be executed. This execution had concerned her deeply. Janet reported that at the exact time Sylvia thought they were to be executed, Sylvia "stopped and held out her arms to me and there were, raising up on her arms from her wrists to her elbows, little bumps. Soon, they sort of bled together like welts from burns."[9]

Returning home after an exciting month in New York with the *Mademoiselle* editors, Sylvia asked her mother to meet her at the station when the train, "her coffin," arrived. She was already exhausted, and then, finding out that she had been rejected for a writing class at Harvard, she became depressed. She wanted to die. During that summer, she wrote in her journal, "You [Sylvia] saw a vision of yourself in a straight-jacket, and a drain on the family, murdering your mother in actuality, killing the edifice of love and respect built up over the years in the hearts of other people."[10] During this same time period, her mother noted scars on her legs and asked Sylvia about them. She responded, "Oh, Mother, the world is so rotten! I want to die! Let's die together."[11]

Her mother took her to a psychiatrist who recommended electroshock therapy. This therapy proved to be disastrous. In addition to the excruciating pain, Sylvia suffered pangs of numbing loneliness lying alone in the hospital and was haunted by feelings of abandonment. She felt herself a failure. Coming home after the ill-administered therapy, she crawled into a hiding place in the basement, pulled a blanket around her, took about forty sleeping pills and fell unconscious. She was not found until two days later when her grandmother, going to the basement to do the laundry, heard a moan. She found Sylvia crouching, sick from the pills and vomiting, and saved her life.

This depression marked the onset of a life in which she had periods of depression and was preoccupied with thoughts of death and dying. As observed by her mother, Sylvia was very sensitive to any slight and could easily become irrationally angry. In one period of depression in her early days at Cambridge, Sylvia wrote in her journal, "Father, father, comfort me."[12] But it seems that she never discussed her father with any psychotherapist, nor had she ever received comfort from her father. The role that the loss of her father played was paramount in much of her life. After she lost one of her men friends, she wrote in her journal: "I rail and rage against the taking of my father whom I have never known. . . . I would have loved him; and he is gone."[13]

She met and married Ted Plath after a short three- to four-months' romance. Within thirty months, she had a daughter, a miscarriage and a son. She was becoming successful in having her poems published. Not long after the birth of their son, Sylvia discovered that her husband was unfaithful, and a divorce followed. Another suicidal incident occurred soon after, when she deliberately drove her car off the road. Neither she nor the car was damaged.

In 1963, amid a period of depression and with her psychiatrist unable to find a hospital bed for her, she took food into the children's bedroom, stuffed towels around their door and taped it. She then went to the kitchen and turned on the gas oven. Kneeling on the floor, she stayed there until she died.

What made this gifted, talented person choose to die? It is true that there was a history of suicide in her family heritage on the paternal side, but there is meager support for the hypothesis of genetic determinants as the basis for suicide.

What we do know is that her mother reported that Sylvia had never had a close father-daughter relationship. Indeed, her father had no intimate talks or activities with any of the children.[14] He was irascible with them, easily frustrated by childish noises and play and could not tolerate their mere presence. Knowing that, Sylvia's mother protected the children from their father. When he would come home, she would take Sylvia and her brother upstairs and keep them there, away from him. They would eat dinner up there, with their mother standing by. Then she would have her dinner downstairs with her husband. Sylvia and her brother would be brought down into the living room for half an hour while their father reclined on a sofa. They would recite some rhymes or Sylvia would play the piano; and then, with a perfunctory hug, they would be sent back upstairs to bed.

Her father's attachment to his children was at best a negative bond, for he denied them a secure love. Sylvia's mother had been startled when she learned that her husband cared for no one's feelings except his own. Still, Aurelia not only protected her husband from the children, she also demonstrated that he came first in her love and attention. Consequently, Sylvia's relationship with her mother was marred first by her brother's birth and then through the mother's obvious preference in giving attention to her father. As a result, any attachment to her father could only be fantasized and unreal.

When Sylvia was three or four, her father became sick and more ill tempered, and she saw even less of him. When she was eight, he suffered a prolonged illness that became a serious diabetic condition. He was treated too late and died.

Although Otto had never been a devoted father, there is no doubt that his death was traumatic for little Sylvia, as it robbed her of any chance whatever for a relationship with him. His death must have also stoked her fantasies and her preoccupation with death. When he died, she was angry, and is said to have responded that she would never speak to God again.[15] Sylvia suffered the ultimate rejection by her father, his death.

As her writing shows, she lived with death inside her at all times, even in seeking romances or loves. She had chosen Ted Plath as her husband, though their first sexual encounter had been so brutal that her face was battered and her neck red and injured.[16] Shortly after their marriage, Ted tried to strangle her. He released his hold only when she began to lose consciousness. Later, as the marriage fell apart, she was convinced that Ted wanted her to kill herself, and she told her mother about this conviction.

Sylvia's attachment was to death, rather than to a person. Death was an obsession even when life seemed to be going well. She sought and attained success and acknowledgment as a poet and writer, but her achievements did not alleviate the pull of death. In one poem, she writes: "daddy, I would have loved you." And in her poem "Daddy," she said:

> At twenty I tried to die
> And get back, back, back to you.[17]

This poem, written shortly before her suicide, expresses rage and anger toward her father for his authoritarianism; it also shows her yearning for a kindly father. In the poem, she captures the obsessive, torturing nature that was his, as well as giving expression to her intense preoccupation with death, as if it could provide the salve for the hurts of her soul.

In summary, Plath suffered an emotional abandonment by her parents. In her early childhood she could not have had the cognitive skills that would have enabled her to cope with the anxious attachment to her mother and disregard by her father. Neither did she seem to receive the comfort that might have alleviated the grief nor the explanations that could have provided an understanding of his death. Her inner isolation never abated. And so she lived a life of inner suffering and died because of it.

Unresolved grief becomes a power that may dominate anyone's life. Her marriage to Ted Plath and the abuse that she took from him seem an effort to quiet her own destructive impulses by letting someone else be responsible for her death. When such a creative person as Sylvia Plath describes grief, we inherit knowledge about the turmoil of an inner life and the steps that lead to suicide.

The following story of Anne Sexton reveals a similar life with much of the psychological pain that Sylvia Plath bore. Because both writers left a record of their thoughts and feelings, it is hoped that their stories will make it easier for us to recognize in others and perhaps ourselves the possible signs of self-destruction and enable us to develop a firmer hold on the meaning of life.

ANNE SEXTON

Anne Sexton and Sylvia Plath were both young women, both primarily poets, finding their way into publication at a time just opening to women writers. Both committed suicide. The sources for the information on Anne Sexton are in books by Diane Wood Middlebrook and Sexton.[18] Anne was born in Newton, Massachusetts, on November 9, 1928, to affluent parents, the third of three daughters. Among the three, she was the least able to conform to her parents' demands for propriety. Jane, the eldest, became Daddy's girl. She shared the passions of her father for automobiles and dogs. She, too, later committed suicide. Blanche, the second daughter, was the only one who went to college; she seemed the "smart one." Anne, the youngest, was active, noisy, fidgety and sloppy. Anne remembered being very lonely as a child. She had memories of being shut up in her room with a folding gate across the doorway so she could not get out. When she later wrote about this room, it was with terror. She claimed that the roses outside were like blood clots and the leaves rustling on the windowpanes were like tongues urging her to die. She wrote, "I was a nothing, crouching in the closet!"[19]

The family life was quite formal, including dressing for dinner. Living in the "flapper age," her parents were partygoers and party givers.

Even when there were no guests, the girls did not eat with their parents. A nurse who lived with the family until Anne's father died essentially reared them. As the girls grew a bit older, they were permitted to eat dinner with their parents; but Anne, who was noisy, rowdy and messy, did not eat with the family until she was eleven years old. About this time, great-aunt Anna Ladd Dingley, better known as Nana to the family, moved in with them. Anne became a special person to Nana, cuddling and sleeping with her. Nana called Anne and herself "twins." There was some hint, during Anne's therapy, of a sexualized relationship with Nana. At thirteen, Anne became more interested in friends and boys than in being cuddled by Nana. Later, Nana had a psychotic break and received electric shock therapy. In her confusion she was not able to recognize Anne. Nana disowned her, calling her "horrible," and once attacking her with a nail file. For the rest of her life, Anne felt somehow responsible for Nana's breakdown.

During her childhood, Anne's father started drinking far too much, became mean with his drinking and hated everyone. Her mother also drank excessively throughout her life, claiming it was only for the "social life." Her mother was cold, sarcastic and very rejecting of Anne, who claimed that she could never predict her mother's moods, which seemed to change suddenly. At least she knew what to expect when her father went on an alcoholic binge. Anne's mother was also writing and became very competitive with Anne. Suspecting that Anne had plagiarized some of her poems, her mother sent them to a college professor, asking his opinion. He replied that they seemed to be originals, leaving her mother still more envious. Her father also demeaned Anne's writing, stating that the letters that her mother wrote to him while he was traveling away from home on business were brilliant. "You are creative but she is brilliant."[20] It is interesting to me personally that as I write about Anne's mother, I sometimes call her "the mother," in clinical fashion, not "Anne's mother," and I have had to correct this several times. To me, the choice of language captures the distant relationship between Anne and her mother during her childhood years.

Anne was an active, noisy child and a problem to her quite formal parents. She was sent to a public school, rather than the private school that her sisters attended. When she entered junior high school she became the center of a group of girls, with the result that Anne's house became their social center. She was popular, even though she did not think so. She was on the swimming and basketball teams and was captain of the cheerleaders. She actually directed one play in school and was the star in others. As a senior, she began to write more formal poems, and some were published in the school literary magazine, *Splinters*.

Anne aimed to acquire a fiancé, which she did while attending a finishing school. She became engaged and was about to be married in a large, formal wedding, when she met another man, Kayo Sexton. They became lovers, and when she thought she had missed a menstrual period, they eloped, much to the dismay of Kayo's parents, who did not like Anne.

On the trip to North Carolina to be married, she discovered that she was not pregnant. They married anyhow. Kayo soon dropped out of college. In 1950 during the Korean War, he joined the Naval Reserve. Anne had strong sexual drives that seemed hard for her to contain. Early in the marriage Anne had been attracted to the husband of a friend. Upon learning this, her mother sent her to a therapist. While Kayo was overseas, Anne was quite free sexually, claiming that she just had to be with someone. These infidelities did not seem to disrupt the marriage. When Kayo was stationed in San Francisco, Anne joined him there, and she immediately became pregnant. They soon had two daughters. Later Anne did have a third pregnancy, but unsure that Kayo had fathered the child, she talked Kayo into letting her have an abortion. When Kayo was separated from the navy, he accepted a position with Anne's father and remained with his firm. They lived under the shadow of both their parents throughout their marriage.

Anne had great difficulty with motherhood, feeling overwhelmed and anxious about caring for two babies. Peter Fonagy makes a strong point about the generational transmission of attachment patterns.[21] Since Anne had not received secure mothering, it is small wonder that she had difficulty with her own children. She could not give the care she had not received. Kayo's mother, who was extremely fond of both the girls, came to the rescue and actually had the girls live with her for extended periods. Much of the time, she also stayed with Anne and Kayo.

Anne had a breakdown at about the age of twenty-eight. As Middlebrook wrote, Anne claimed that "she wasn't just tired and low; she was agitated, disoriented, and subject to fits of feeling 'unreal.' "[22] It seems that she became most anxious when Kayo was out of town and she would become fearful that she might kill her babies. Sometimes she would rage at Linda, her older daughter, choking and slapping her. It is easy to suppose that she acted out her rage at her mother's negligent care upon her own children.

Anne made several attempts at suicide, saying she wanted to get back to "the place where Nana was," and "I want to curl up and sigh, 'don't leave me.'" Her psychologist, Dr. Orne, encouraged her to relieve the pain by writing about her experiences in her poetry, hoping she would find a means of expression, and then of insight, for she had difficulty with free verbal expression. His constant support for her writing kept her alive. He stated:

> Anne had no resources that she could recognize. And that one goal of psychotherapy was to provide her the confirming kind of attention she had needed from her parents in order to develop a secure sense of herself. She felt parasitic, helpless, and profoundly angry.[23]

Anne saw him and other psychotherapists for several years. Her periods of dissociation, depression and severe anxieties often led her to the brink of suicide. Middlebrook reports from conversations with Dr. Orne,

> In particular, the dissociative states that were so prominent a feature in her case, her tendency to sexualize significant relationships, and the fluidity of the boundaries she experienced between herself and other people—fit the clinical picture of a woman who has undergone sexual trauma.[24]

Anne reported that her father would come into her bedroom at night when he was drunk and fondle her. Also in her therapy she claimed, "I'm my mother, only I did it and she didn't (write) . . . I think my father was kind of crazy, though not overtly."[25]

Anne was obsessed with death, with wanting to die. As she said to Dr. Orne, "suicide is addicting too."[26] This does not seem to be simply an adult obsession. In one poem, "The Death Baby," she writes, "My sister at six dreamt nightly of my death."[27] Also:

> I died seven times
> in seven ways
> letting death give me a sign,
> letting death place his mark on my forehead, *crossed*
> *over, crossed over*.[28]

And, "Death, You lie in my arms like a cherub."[29]

Although she reached a pinnacle of professional success as a poet and writer, her personal and private life retained much of its confusion and anger. She drank too much. She took medication to assure her sleep. About a year before her suicide, she divorced Kayo. Without him, she had no stability; although he, too, was given to angry outbursts, he had been there for her throughout all that time, through her infidelities, her emotional swings and fugue periods in which she might seem to behave rationally but which she could not recall later. Like Sylvia Plath, she was living with death as an introject, a part of herself that she both owned and disowned. It was an unwanted part of her being, yet one she was unable to reject.

On the day of her death, she saw her therapist, left her cigarettes and lighter tucked behind a bowl of daisies, had lunch with a friend, "a wonderful and silly lunch, and drove home."[30] She stripped her fingers of rings, took her mother's old fur coat from the closet, got a glass of vodka, went to the garage and closed the doors behind her. She turned on the ignition and the radio. In time, she died.

The relationship both Sexton and Plath had with their parents, and perhaps especially with their fathers, did not let them develop the ego strength to relate to men—or to themselves. That is, they suffered a disorganized attachment to their fathers: the fathers' illness or alcoholism, coldness and hostility and withdrawal could not provide them with a stable internal image of themselves. In addition, the insecure attachment to their mothers and the mothers' ambivalent attachment to them left both women with a mystified inner self. The introjection of the emotional abandonment by both parents left them with only one way out—an obsession with death, which ultimately led to suicide. Although the parents did not play an active role in their suicide, the victims' introjection of their parents' ambivalence seems to have become the internal instigators that made these two women murder themselves.

AN INNOCENT VETERAN

The spirit of storytelling has had varied basic themes and truths from millennium to millennium. The following modern story shares essential features and psychodynamics with the previous stories. It is a psychologically plausible suicide story that intrigues us because its unspoken ethics create an unavoidable but heartbreaking error.[31]

A tough Vietnam veteran has years ago withdrawn to the high mountains, living there by his wits, his main tool a bayonet he brought home from his combat tour "in country" during the war. One day, on a high narrow bluff with steep slopes plunging downward into deep gorges on all sides but one, he meets another lone hiker. The two men are alone up there, both seeking solitude, no other soul in sight. After a while their nearness to each other and their natural curiosity start them talking.

The other man is a slender philosophy professor who had been a conscientious objector to the Vietnam War. The veteran had been thrown into the roughest fighting in one of the most chaotic wars in our history. The veteran begins to chide the professor about his pacifism. The professor defends his war-protesting activities. The two discuss the respective merits of their causes: obeying your country's orders to fight in an unjustifiable war versus protesting and working against it. The discussion heats up rapidly, becoming a hostile debate and culminating in the veteran's outcry that he had loved the conscientious objectors for their cause, but that they had not loved him for his.

The debate gets mean, the veteran threatening the smaller man's life with his bayonet, provoking him with inflammatory speech, terrorizing him, insulting him, daring him to stand up for himself, goading him to attack with thrusts of his bayonet. The professor scrambles to get a pocketknife from his backpack. As the veteran rushes at him with his bayonet, the professor stabs the veteran deep in the belly.

While the veteran is lying bleeding on the bluff, he confesses that he had purposely brutalized the professor into acting as his executioner because this is the anniversary of a terrible misdeed, one that he has had on his conscience for seventeen years. Each year the memory has become more unbearable. "Call it atonement," the veteran says. Then he tells his story.

It is Vietnam. His troop has liberated a village from the Vietcong. The liberators line up the villagers along the road, a row of houses behind them. There is a ten-year-old girl among the villagers. The little girl suddenly steps out of the line and slowly walks toward the American soldiers, toward the veteran. He shouts, "Go back! Go back, back, back!" But she keeps coming. Why the hell doesn't she go back? As she draws near to him, she reaches into her blouse. Why doesn't she obey his order? What does she have in there? Have the Cong used children and old people in suicide attacks? Of course they have. She must have a hand grenade! The soldier can imagine the grenade flying at him, exploding, shrapnel flying, his buddies shredded, falling to the ground.

He runs his bayonet through her small body, carries her on it across the street, and nails her, as he puts it, to a house wall. There she dies, from that moment on to become his crucified, stigmatizing inner instigator, his grief haunting him for seventeen years of mental torture, turning him into a walking dead soul.

The veteran confesses that he provoked the professor to stab him and thus give him his death. For seventeen long years living as a condemned man, he had wanted to be stabbed by a weaker person as he had stabbed a weaker person, a child, so he could finally die, free of his instigator.

Having gained his heart's desire, one fatal stab wound for a stab wound, the veteran dissuades the professor from going for help and begs the professor to help him crawl to the edge of the cliff. Reluctantly, the professor helps him. The veteran rolls over the cliff and plummets down into the canyon, finally atoning for his misdeed, perhaps hoping to find a pardon for his unpardonable error. The professor leaves the bluff, innocent but marked for life.

What did the veteran find so unpardonable about his error? Had he not acted in good faith, in the line of duty? Yes. Probably. Perhaps. But he could never persuade himself of his innocence. The little girl whom he bayoneted to the wall had not been concealing a hand grenade in her blouse. She had been carrying her most precious possession to the veteran, to offer him as thanks for liberating her village. What she was hiding in her blouse was a can of Coca-Cola.

This searching for an executioner is not unlike the searches of Maggie and of Rita, both of whom taunted their husbands about keeping them alive (see Chapter 6). The professor had no choice. Quentin and Max did not accept the challenge; both had fled from the suicide.

I would like to take a minute to clarify the idea of an internal instigator. Within psychological thinking, the internalized person is comparable to a relationship with a person in external reality. These internalized persons are representatives of emotionally significant aspects of persons upon whom we have been dependent in early life. Attachments to our internal images are as important as to persons in real life and the incorporation of these persons in our early life are probably responsible for many of our personality characteristics. However, it is important to know that the incorporation does not resolve any problems arising from the interrelationship with that person. Rather, the incorporation simply transfers the problem from the outer to the inner reality so that the person will continue to be affected by the problems, but now within themselves rather than with a real person. As W.R.D. Fairbairn states, "Outer conditions ordinarily have very little influence in producing any fundamental change in inner situations except by way of confirming and intensifying them."[32]

Internal instigators arise from aggression against the self that has its origin in the introjection of hostility. The hostility hides within, one foundation of the self. The person lives with unresolvable anger brought on by grief. Trying to manage the grief warps the character and annihilates other reasons for existence. Losing this sense of one's self and being overwhelmed with grief, one's inner life becomes crazed in the battle for life. The internal instigator ultimately wins, forcing death as the choice against life.

Grief, in such instances, supplants a firm sense of the self. As we know, anger is a phase of mourning, and the anger against the parent who provides the insecure bonding compounds the grief with guilt.

Internalized instigators bring about the suicide in such instances: the felt rejection by both parents leads to the introjection of the parents' hostility toward the child. The child learns to hate himself or herself. The inner self becomes ever more dissatisfied and the call to death becomes more inviting. With this rejection and especially with the loss of a parent, the attachment that becomes the strongest is the attachment to death. Insecure attachments open the soul's door to death.

CHAPTER 12

The Internal Instigator II

Double and Triple Tragedies

The third type of internal instigator involves those who first kill someone else—frequently a lover, a spouse, one or more children, a parent, a rival, sometimes a whole family—and then commit suicide. Usually the killer has a fairly strong but ambivalent attachment to the victim, which makes the homicide-suicide difficult to comprehend. The newspapers relate many of these sad and frightening homicide-suicide events but rarely escort us down to the debris and swirling currents beneath the surface. In the ancient myths, however, there are stories that give some insight into the killer's motives, for example in the triangles of Eos, Procris and Cephalus and that of Evenos, Marpessa and Idas. But first, here is a case history of Tony and his wife, Lara.

TONY

At the time of the tragedies, Tony was a well-respected professor of Italian literature at a university. Tony had immigrated to the United States from Italy to study, and had successfully obtained his graduate degrees. He married Lara, and they soon had two sons. They seemed a happy, contented family. Lara's sister came for psychotherapy following the homicide of Tony's wife and man friend and the suicide of Tony. She was seen by a psychiatric resident whom I was supervising.

Lara, a professor of economics, was an exceptionally voluptuous woman, a vivid blond with seductive brown eyes. She was so beautiful that men stared at her as she passed. Some, in spite of themselves, found ingenious ways to meet her and invite her to bed. This amazed and amused her. She seemed naively unaware that her every movement was seductive and that her style of dress was inviting.

Probably she really did enjoy her alluring, emotional expressiveness that brought her much attention. Tony both enjoyed her appeal to other men and angrily resented her continued flair for seduction. As I write, I am reminded of the love-hate relationship that Maggie had with herself in the play *After the Fall*, and it seems certain that Lara entertained the same mixed feelings. And Tony felt the same pride-shame that Quentin had with Maggie.

When Tony and Lara's sons were about three years of age, Lara succumbed to another man's sexual advances. Tony discovered her unfaithfulness to him, confronted her about her disloyalty and ordered her from their home. Around midnight the next evening Tony took his gun, went to the man's house and shot both Lara and her lover. He then drove to his home, sat in his car, wrote a short note and shot himself.

The note read, "I can only kill myself. Lara was the only person who ever loved me and even she could not. Please take care of the boys."

Lara's sister did not know much about Tony's first eight years except that he had been a child during World War II in Italy. He witnessed bombings, destruction and killings. His mother was severely wounded and disabled, his father killed. He had grown up in the home of an extended family with his mother. He described his childhood as feeling like a "lost little boy," wandering about the town with no one to miss him.

Outwardly, Tony was a quiet, seemingly thoughtful person at peace with himself. Obviously that was not the case. His wife's betrayal was the shock that broke through his defenses and brought long-suppressed volcanic waves of rage to the surface. Overcome by fury and loss, he killed two people and then himself.

There are scores of stories of homicide-suicide. The turmoil a person experiences when lacking secure attachments leads to a lifelong search for a substitute, a lover, a partner or a friend. After fantasizing that one has found it, to be robbed of the attachment releases the hidden grief and the violence that rages against the self as well as against others. Rage hides behind grief. This is nothing new. But grief or depression cannot always defend against the rage.

The life of Heinrich von Kleist[1] provides another example. A German author whose writings have been more highly regarded after his death than before, he too endured losses, suffered inner confusion. His father died when he was ten; his mother also died when he was young. Early in life he sought friends who would enter into a suicide pact with him. His plays and stories deal with characters who often suffer from confused feelings and find themselves in desperate situations. As time went by and his writing could not allay his inner torment, he decided to kill himself. At her request, he first killed a friend, Henriette Vogel, a young married society woman who was incurably ill, and then shot himself.

The passions of lust and lost love seem to flip swiftly into aggression and revenge. The fury is hot, the anger cold as the actions are directed toward the grief of a lost love. The killer first kills love and then the killer.

RUDOLF AND THE PROSTITUTE

Roland Kuhn poignantly presents the origins of homicidal-suicidal impulses in the case history of a patient, Rudolf.[2] As a boy, Rudolf had been severely traumatized by deaths. His mother died when he was three years old. He had been so close to her that he had slept in her bedroom and spent his days playing on her bed. After her death, he repeatedly searched the house, looking for her. His father, too, was severely depressed following his wife's death, could not work and obsessively collected and hid objects. With nine children in the family, he needed care for the children, so he married the housekeeper. She was an alcoholic and grossly neglectful of the children. In his early school years, Rudolf was impressed by a picture of Jesus being tempted by the devil to jump, and in imitation, he jumped from his grandfather's hayloft, severely damaging a foot that was left permanently deformed. This probably was his first attempt at suicide. Rudolf's world was unsafe. He was a multitraumatized child—shocked by scars on his father's legs and his father's depression, forced to visit a deceased neighbor's coffin and to suffer the death of his grandmother and then, at twenty-one, the death of his father. His anxiety increased with each trauma: he tried to open the eyes of the corpses as if to undo their death (remember Paulette opening the eyes of the animals). He was fearful of the night and afraid of meeting the devil and had fantasies of murder and suicide that continued many years. Each incident had added to Rudolf's anxiety about death. He developed tremendous fears of falling; he could not cross bridges, afraid that he would fall into the canal; he was terrified of being eaten alive by rats—which had happened to a child in his neighborhood. As a teenager he was an usher in the church, collecting money. He stole some for cigarettes to buy some friendships, but was discovered. He was beaten by his father and by his schoolteacher and damned to hell by the priest. He remembered his anger at these punishments. During the forced confession, he vowed vengeance by murder. After these punishments he began to stutter, and his family and peers teased him for his halting speech.

After his father's funeral, he took the train to return to work, with a stop in Zurich. He was desperate. He wanted to kill and then kill himself. He found a prostitute, had intercourse with her and then pulled out a gun. She thought it was a cigarette lighter, but as she reached for it, the gun fired, wounding her in the neck. Rudolf called the police. During the trial he was declared irresponsible and placed under the guardianship of the state for extended therapy in a hospital.

His fantasies of suicide and murder continued for several years. He imagined crucifying himself in the woods, jumping into rivers, hanging himself, being a victim in a traffic accident, jumping in front of a train and other suicidal or fatal acts. He had to fight the compulsion to plunge from the gallery of the church, down into the midst of the congregation; he pictured himself lying smashed on the stone floors. During his five or six years in the hospital he continued to see himself as a murderer, toying with ideas of dissecting women or killing them by some other unspeakable means. Once, before he could carry out a suicidal plan to jump in front of a train, he had to wait an hour for the train to come. While waiting he went into a Catholic church, repeated the Lord's prayer and then continued praying with Gretchen's prayer from Faust. As he watched, the Virgin and Child took on a strange shimmer, as if they were alive. This experience, occurring on the twenty-third anniversary of his mother's death, seemed to have cured him of his compulsions toward suicide, for he never tried again.

After six or seven years, Rudolf was dismissed from the hospital. He finished a trade school and it is reported that, aside from occasional depressive periods, he was doing well and "discovering the beauties of the world." The significant details of Rudolf's life are available because of Kuhn's longtime involvement with this patient.

The story suggests, as Paulette's story does, that origins of suicidal and murderous impulses in a child arise from the multiple traumas around deaths they experience, the failure of any meaningful attachment and the unresolved grief. These experiences prove too much for the sensitivities of a child. The inner isolation that follows the experiences with death is compounded by the ensuing lack of emotional care. The confusion about death remains unexplained and inexplicable. In this condition they become compelled to reenact death over and over again, both in actions and in fantasies. They have assimilated death as the meaning of life. The moral of Rudolf's story is that compassionate, expert help may be able to save a life.

Homicides do not always lead to suicide. If that were so, we would have no need for the legal system to adjudicate and assign some killers to death or imprisonment. But when the homicide is followed by a suicidal action, it is obvious that the killing itself has traumatized the killer.

EOS, CEPHALUS AND PROCRIS

This is a love story.[3] Cephalus, son of Hermes and Deion, the king of Phocis, fell in love with Procris, a beautiful maiden. They married, both fervently in love. Unfortunately, Eos, the Goddess of Dawn, saw Cephalus while he was hunting, fell in love with him and carried him off to Syria. But Cephalus mourned for Procris, longing to return to her and her love. Clever and underhanded, Eos wanted to keep Cephalus. She filled him with doubts about the fidelity of Procris and challenged him to return, in disguise, to test her faithfulness. He finally agreed to the challenge, certain that no one else could seduce her. Eos provided Cephalus with jewels of such worth that they would be irresistible to any woman.

His identity concealed, Cephalus approached Procris with the magical jewels, asking for her love. She could not resist the temptation. Furious and saddened, Cephalus drove her away.

Procris was devastated by his trickery but more so by losing him. Wandering about as she was then forced to do, the beautiful Procris came under the protection of Artemis (or Minos), who gave her a dog that never lost a scent and a javelin that never missed its mark. He then sent her back to the angry and mournful Cephalus. This time it was Procris in disguise. When this new woman offered him the javelin, Cephalus took it, making the same mistake Procris had. Neither, it seems, could resist temptations so common to men and women. After Procris revealed herself to Cephalus, the couple joyfully reconciled their love as deeply as ever. But now, having lost their initial trust, they kept close watch on each other.

Cephalus often left her to go on overnight hunting expeditions, or so he said. Uneasy and suspicious, Procris and her dog followed him one day, hiding behind bushes and trees. She found him. He really was hunting, carrying the javelin that she had given him. He had been seeking his game for a long time without success. Naturally, when he heard a rustle in the bushes behind him, he quickly turned and threw the javelin that never missed its mark.

To his horror, it was Procris hiding in the bush. Cephalus was so overwhelmed with grief that he promptly took himself to the promontory of Leucas, the same cliff from which Sappho is said to have jumped to her death over the loss of Phaon, and threw himself into the sea.

As in modern life, faithfulness is highly regarded and easily lost. Jealousy and distrust had ruled the day for Procris and Cephalus. Jealousy by itself is traumatizing, destroying peace of mind through painful anxiety over a potential loss of love. The fear of abandonment impairs the attachment bonds, and for Procris and Cephalus, that fear of abandonment precipitated a homicide, however unintentional, and its companion, suicide. Unresolved grief brings violence, even against the self.

The next story is also about jealousy, a jealousy rooted in overinvolved parenting.

EVENOS AND MARPESSA

Evenos was the son of a mortal mother and Ares, the god of war.[4] Evenos was also a military man, a master of horses. His name means "reiner of horses." On a field of battle, mounted on his war chariot, he could chase down and lance anyone so unlucky as to be in his way. With his wife Alkippe (her name means "mighty mare") they had a daughter named Marpessa. Homer calls her "fair-ankled," and "Marpessa of the fair ankles."

Evenos had resolved that his daughter should remain a virgin forever. She grew up a beautiful maiden who loved to dance. In time, many suitors came to her. To keep Marpessa a virgin and close to him, Evenos challenged each of her suitors to compete with him in a chariot race. If the suitor won, he could marry Marpessa. If Evenos won, the vanquished suitor's head would be chopped off, a trophy for Evenos. With his magnificent horsemanship, Evenos won every race, and soon many skulls decorated the walls of his palace, not only as signs of his power but also as warnings to other suitors, much as the gargoyles on cathedrals are supposed to repel evil spirits.

Then along came a determined fellow named Idas, who fell in love with the fair-ankled Marpessa. Among her other charms, Marpessa's dancing enchanted him. Knowing the dangers, Idas' father, Poseidon, gave Idas a winged chariot that would outdistance any chariot, including Evenos' horse-drawn chariot. One day while Marpessa was dancing, Idas abducted her. She was delighted. Evenos was not. Evenos pursued the fugitive pair up to the river Lykormas, but was unable to catch those magical wheels with their winged supernatural horses. His best war-horses became exhausted and even under lashing could go no faster. As the couple flew away, Evenos' fury overcame him. He killed his horses for their failure to catch Idas. Then, because of his loss—and it seems to me a loss of power as much as the loss of his daughter—he drowned himself in the river, which became known as the River Evenos.

This tale of a father's rage over losing a daughter to a suitor, which is a normal loss of a child to adulthood, dramatizes the father's overwhelming lack of control over his impulses, especially over his sexuality and his daughter's. This lack of control leads to the pathological overprotective, overinvolved reaction of a parent jealous of his daughter's virginity.

When Marpessa escaped from him, Evenos lost his raison d'être, the meaningfulness of his life. Evenos' life had been dedicated to controlling his impulses and all other circumstances in his life, even when killing others (the suitors) was necessary to maintain that power. When Evenos lost control, the aggression that had driven him turned on himself, and suicide remained his only escape.

The strength of the compulsion to control is a measure of the explosiveness of the repressed aggression. Evenos' instigation to suicide lay within himself. Those other killings were justified as long as he was winning. Losing meant that he was abandoned to himself. Then, like Meles, he finally had to face himself as a murderer. In addition, because he lost the race and his sense of power with it, his was a self that he could not live with. His attachment was not to his daughter, but to his power. Had he been attached to his daughter, he would have welcomed her happiness with a fine suitor.

Evenos' attachment to his daughter was pathological, a nullifying attachment because he did not relate to her as the person she was or as a person in her own right, and it was a malevolent attachment in depriving her of suitors and of a normal life. It was not guilt over his actions of killing but rage arising from the loss of his daughter that led him to suicide. The trauma of killing maimed his conscience. He became his own instigator.

Ironically, the final chapter in the story of Evenos, Marpessa and Idas shows the generational impact of suicides. Marpessa and Idas had a daughter. When Idas was killed in battle, Marpessa committed suicide. In what might then be an anniversary suicide, the granddaughter later forfeited her life as well.

The tale of Marpessa with her fair ankles is not the only myth telling of a possessive father who murdered her suitors. Hippodameia was a name associated with owning many horses, and therefore being high-born.[5] This beautiful girl's incestuously jealous father, Oenomaus, gave his daughter's many suitors a head start in the races. However, upon overtaking them, he would fling a spear into their backs and kill them. Like Evenos, he had their heads cut off and nailed to the façade of his house.

Eventually, Hippodameia found a lover in Pelops. Instead of running away on a magic chariot, Hippodameia and Pelops murdered Hippodameia's father by removing the axle pin of his chariot, and he was killed in the race. But Hippodameia remained an angry, destructive and jealous woman, for not only did she connive to murder her father, she also helped to murder Pelops' illegitimate son, Chrysippus. She then committed suicide.

A MODERN WOMAN, HER FIANCÉ AND HER FATHER

In my practice, I had similar examples of pathological father-bonding, as well as mother-bonding. Nancy and Charles had come for premarital counseling. Nancy was a woman of thirty-nine who had been engaged to Charles, a man of forty-two, for over five years. Both were professionals. She was a marriage counselor, he a retail store manager. They sought couple counseling because they had not been able to marry, although both said they wanted to. During couple counseling, they reported lying all night in the same bed, cuddling and touching, but without actual intercourse. Both claimed to base their abstinence on religious beliefs.

Finally, after several sessions, Nancy stated that she could marry only when her father died. She felt indebted to her father because he had purchased an apartment for her—and not only an apartment, but also an automobile, furniture and other things. She would feel ungrateful to abandon him through her marriage.

Several sessions later, she acknowledged that she had a sexual debt to him as well. In her teens, he had provided her with her first sexual encounter, fondling her genitals but without intercourse, so that, he claimed, she would know what it was like to be with a man. Her anger over the incest was not available to her, although she would admit that it did not seem the right thing for a father to do. When it happened in spite of the severe religious and moral stance the family maintained, she rationalized that all fathers were supposed to do that for their daughters. Nancy was caught on the horns of an ambivalent attachment. Her adult sexuality was intertwined with her father. If he were to die, she thought that she could become sexually involved with another man.

As fortune would have it, her fiancé was enmeshed with his aged mother. This did not seem a sexual attachment, but Charles said he "could not stand to abandon her." His father had died when Charles was young, and he had been his mother's financial and emotional support since his adolescence. Further, his mother was now aged and chronically ill. She needed his care.

Both Nancy and Charles feared that if they married and thereby left their parents, it would kill the parents. This ambivalent attachment with their parents, as well as the anxiety-loaded attachment to each other, was not to be broken. Not surprisingly, both Nancy and Charles wished their parents dead and both had dreams of killing them. There was no freedom for themselves; they could not kill their parents by marrying. And they didn't. They decided to break off their relationship and counseling was ended.

Shortly after counseling ended, they had still another date. Charles took her for a ride in his new sports car along Highway 1, a road known for its steep curves and high cliffs. He missed a curve, sending them both to their deaths. The highway patrol claimed they must have been driving over eighty miles per hour.

This double suicide resulted from their inability to handle the violence and hatred toward their parents. Both Charles and Nancy had assimilated a damaged self that was dependent upon their merging with pathological parents. Their lives manifest a murder of the soul; they had so introjected the hostile, pathological symbiosis their parents demanded that the only release they let themselves find was death, which is what the parents had obviously and unconsciously desired. This seems the ultimate sacrifice—to kill themselves rather than their parents. They could gain their independence from their overattached parents only through this violent action. The parents had been unable to relinquish their need for their child. The attitude of these parents seems to be, "If I can't have you, then no one can!" Or, "Thou shalt have no one other than me!"

KENNETH

I am reminded of a young man named Kenneth whom I saw for several years in therapy. He was severely schizoid (or more probably suffering from Asperger's syndrome). He had no friends whatsoever throughout his school life and was often teased by other children because of his rather peculiar appearance and gestures. Although exceedingly intelligent, Kenneth had stymied his teachers, refusing to complete any assigned studies. He would not take any tests the teachers gave him, and yet on his own he would present them with essays that showed he knew more than was expected, especially in mathematics, science and history. He studied electronics, physics and music and read the encyclopedia. His conversation was replete with idiosyncratic words and phrases; for instance, little boys' feet were "charmful."

Psychotherapy had been suggested repeatedly throughout his childhood and adolescence, but his parents had never sought any help for him or for themselves. His high-school teachers threatened that Kenneth would not graduate unless his parents got help for him. This was no idle threat. When his parents reluctantly brought him for his first therapy session, it was obvious they had no hope for any behavioral or emotional improvement in him. With her plain dress and her hair pulled tightly back into a bun, his mother was a slight, mousy woman who seemed depressed but declared that she was all right and needed no help whatsoever. She was a withholding, quiet person without observable signs of anxiety. About sixty-five years of age, Kenneth's father seemed sickly and overworked, but he expressed some feelings, especially in wanting help for his son. Kenneth's parents reported that they had to give him anything that he wanted because otherwise he would break out into angry rages, striking at them if his wishes were not granted. They were both frightened by his narcissistic furies. His father feared for Kenneth's future and his wife's safety if he were to die because of Kenneth's vile temper.

At first Kenneth sat slouched in his seat and would not talk. He did, eventually, bring in some of his writing and poetry. It was full of unusual and elided words that helped to open a pathway to his soul. He was a loner—and with good reason.

His history, as told by his mother and father and later confirmed by his two older sisters, was the tale of an abandoned child, even within the family. He was born fifteen years after the birth of his next older sister, when his mother was forty-five and his father was fifty years old. Not only was Kenneth's conception a shock to them all, coming as late as it did, but his mother did not want him. She did not love him and denied him the warmth so necessary for an infant's development. She provided him the necessary physical care but no other stimulation. She maintained only a negative attachment to him.

Kenneth received very little social stimulation during the first three years of life. He was "fed and watered" and diapers were changed. There was no baby play, no cooing with him, no rocking, no response to his cries or laughs. His father and siblings were astonished at the mother's negligent emotional care of this baby, her only son. They felt helpless. As soon as he could, Kenneth began toddling around, checking out his surroundings. He did not talk at all until he was four, when he began to speak in complete sentences, to the surprise of the family. At five he was fixing electrical appliances in the home. There was, however, no joy in the air near him and consequently none in his heart.

Because of Kenneth's lack of trust in anyone, therapy with him was exceedingly difficult. It was also gratifying (a story in its own right). This much I can share at this time: the way to his soul was through his poetry. At first, I just listened to him read his poetry to me, eventually asked him to tell me what it meant to him, and then talked with him about it. The next step was to let him, know that some words that he used were not real words that could be found in the dictionary, and that if I were to understand him, perhaps he could try to use words that everyone could understand. Gradually, his speech and writing became more socialized; they were already filled with unexpressed emotion. Here is an example of his writing:

> This may be a situation where a child may have a real potpourri of internal caveats in an attempt to transcend to a sort ne plus ultra that all other dimensions of his character might be entwoed and enfolded and consolidated into compartment in his mind.

And another,

when one bubble swells into the other not when this one bubble is content to be realms burst and the universe becomes monstrous.

When he talked about this poem to me, Kenneth said that he had a dream that he was a bird alone in a tree and his mother scared him by turning out the light in his bedroom. He was then afraid of the monsters of the dark, as if the whole world was just fear.

After three years of treatment, Kenneth was still a loner, but he had become attached to therapy and, I think, to me. He would eagerly run from the car to lean against my door, his hands above his head, waiting to be admitted.

I tried to prepare Kenneth for my coming sabbatical—a longer absence than any I had taken previously. He was dismayed at my leaving, but he could not quite express the loss that he was feeling. To hold the gains he had made while I would be away, I referred Kenneth to another therapist who placed him in group therapy. This experience with others began Kenneth's seeking.

Kenneth became a seeker of social interaction. He would find his way to the college restaurant, sit there and watch others come and go. He got his driver's license, which was a significant accomplishment for him, but it frightened me because his impulsiveness and rage still erupted all too quickly against anyone crossing his path.

His behavior now brought to mind the story of Aisakos and Hesperie. Aisakos, a Trojan prince, had been reared in isolation in the forest and remained there, without relationships with other people.[6] He hungered for companionship, but he had no skills for approaching anyone. He fell in love with Hesperie, a nymph, and began to chase her endlessly. Frightened, she always ran from him. One day while running from Aisakos' pursuit, Hesperie stepped on a snake, was bitten and died. Aisakos was smitten with grief over her loss and hurled himself from a high cliff down into the sea, intending to kill himself. Because of his innocence in love, Tethys, the "lovely queen of the sea," denied him the privilege of death. Rather, Tethys caught him gently in her arms and covered him with feathers so he floated on the waves. By and by, Tethys transformed Aisakos for all eternity into a *Mergus*, a bird that dives incessantly.

From a need like that of Aisakos, Kenneth started cruising, seeking, stalking people, male or female. If someone took his fancy, he would follow that person, never speaking to him or her. One day a college student without transportation asked Kenneth to take him to a party.

When the man promised that Kenneth would be the guest of honor, Kenneth agreed. It turned out to be a pot-smoking party. Kenneth tried a joint. The young man asked to borrow his car. In his eagerness for friendship, Kenneth agreed. This friend drove his car from California to Oregon, had an accident that totally destroyed the car and then abandoned it along the highway. Kenneth never heard from him again, but the state made Kenneth pay for towing the car away.

This did not stop Kenneth's seeking. He continued observing and stalking. Occasionally he would rage against the persons who ran from him, who were obviously frightened by his intense interest. He followed little boys in the park, sexually aroused by their "charmful" feet. He chased after women walking by his house and old men who would sometimes talk with him. Once he was arrested. He had stalked a woman for a couple of days. Jumping out from behind a bush as she walked by, he grabbed her breasts. Fortunately for her, she ran and called the police. Kenneth told me that he wanted to take her home and lock her in the garage. Then he could have someone all to himself. What would he do with her? He was not sure; maybe he would have to kill her.

Interested in people? Yes. Socialized? No. Sadly enough, his father died about this time and his mother, against all recommendations, abruptly discontinued therapy. I had carefully and thoroughly warned the mother of his rage and especially the possibility of his acting out his rage against her, but she chose to keep him at home. Two years later Kenneth wounded his mother and then shot himself with a gun his father had left behind. He died, still a tormented soul.

Kenneth had always felt persecuted, and he really had been persecuted when his mother had deprived him of affectionate care as a baby. He was neglected again when his parents were reluctant to get him any professional help. For that and many other reasons, his attachment was not to his mother. In his poetry she was a feeding machine. His attachment was to his own empty core, an isolated center of his self that had no imago, only the uncomforted rage of his infant isolation. This rage, I believe, was not the usual infantile rage per se; it was a primordial rage about and for existence. It is a rage that precedes the infantile rage, which is the only possible reaction to emptiness. I well imagine that in more physically barren situations, it would eventually result in a defeated withdrawal from life itself, as in anaclitic depressions.

Ironically, neither Aisakos' nor Kenneth's self-core could become inhabited; their attachment was to their emptiness. If anyone tried to fill that emptiness, a killing rage would be turned against that person. Theirs was a rage for existence, which in the long run had let them live, even though they had suffered the death of their soul.

Attachment is, at the least, a psychological phenomenon in human relations, and most probably a psychophysiological phenomenon. Ronald Fairbairn avers that the real aim of the instincts in life is "the establishment of satisfactory relationships with objects [persons]."[7] Fairbairn then states, "I regard aggression as essentially a tendency called into operation in the setting of libidinal situations involving frustration or rejection, viz. 'bad object' situations."[8] I maintain that the frustration over the absence or loss of an "accepting" attachment provokes grief. This grief contains the elements of aggression that is turned toward the rejecting person as well as toward the self. Homicide and suicide may follow. In many instances of suicide, repressed grief holds an insidious need for power over persons and their relationships. Such repressed grief contains an undergirding dynamic that continues throughout life and destroys a stable sense of the self. To understand these triple tragedies is not to excuse them. The homicide-suicide deaths, as we have seen, arise from pathological attachments, whether to a child, spouse or friend. Rejection becomes impassioned into jealousy. The inner turmoil is fed by a weakened ego that cannot gratify the hostile impulses. The result is a loss of self-control. My thesis is that the inner instigator is an alien part of the self that surges into a death-seeking action with the loss of attachment. It is a rejecting self that denigrates love and living, success and achievement.

CHAPTER 13

Cult Instigators
The False Path

The path from error to enlightenment, from false ideas to truth and reality, often proceeds over a dark chasm of the unknown. We ponder choices that lead to disappointment and death or to fulfillment and life. Often a whole group or nation must make a choice, must bridge the gap that would lead to life or death. When a group or nation is misguided, when it ignores the truth it has already experienced, when it ignores the fact that every life is dear, that nation is destined to chaos and to wander aimlessly. When leaders ignore the message of truth and reality, the nation becomes like the lemmings that race over the cold steppes and do not even stop at the precipice of the cliff. They throw themselves en masse into the ocean below to be killed. They cannot stop. Humankind needs not only the power to choose but also the power to desist and resist, to step back from the cliff's edge, from a dangerous leader and a dark path. When infamous leaders work under the guise of agents of Providence, desperate followers see only the light of the promise. They follow blindly. These leaders have a charisma that lures and entices followers, sadly enough often to death. The leaders are paragons of self-destruction and the destruction of others. They spur their followers to join them in death, a mutual suicide to occur when the leaders reach their narcissistic combustion point. This point comes when the leaders face within themselves the malevolent ingratitude that colors their lives. This ingratitude is manifestly perverse. Life, in truth, like a stroke of luck, is really a gift. The death leaders reject the gift, instead being ungrateful, vindictive humans.

Cicero calls gratitude the mother of all other virtues. Psychologically that seems true, as gratitude appears to be one of the earliest of all virtues. It is gratitude that excites the smile of an infant, and the beauty of that smile of gratitude starkly contrasts with the leaders' faces of discontent. The ability to "praise the bridge that bore you" distinguishes those with gratitude from those with ingratitude. But the death leaders condemn that bridge and wander from it in angry steps. Often they have a painful feeling that some ill fate has denied them a life they deserve. They blame their parents and most often their fathers for their miserable fate. They nurture revenge against life itself. At the same time, they search for power over others to force their followers to bow to them in gratitude. Later they will lead these grateful followers over the cliff.

Death leaders bite the hand that feeds them. They secretly or openly hate those who submit to their wishes even though they crave the adoration they missed in their early lives. Their hunger for power is insatiable. They tie their followers to their apron strings with promises of free milk, free love, free sex and life ever after. The leader and the led are perversely attached; theirs is a mutual attachment to death, often a conscious commitment to a joint doom. Then they become the exterminator and annihilator of each other. Today, fear of such cultish groups and the destruction they cause grips the whole world by the throat.

Numerous cases of mass suicide and of mass homicides have occurred in recent decades. These cases dramatically illustrate the macabre power of attraction and provocation of the charismatic doomsday leader. Young people who are wounded and starved of self-esteem easily fall victim to the opiate of power-through-love, which such leaders offer. The leaders, for their part, seek love-through-power. Unconsciously they realize that there is no unconditional love, for they have never received it. One promise that the leader can deliver is "power through death." This is the perversion of any love pact. Freedom is narrowed for the followers. Their only "freedom" is to follow, to reflect the being of the leader—in thoughts, feelings and actions. They must share their leader's greatest delusion, that death brings freedom and exquisite happiness.

Others who can value the bridge that carried them over the water are better protected against self-destruction. They are grateful for life. They are protected against suicide because, as the Chinese proverb says, "He who never forgets the source while drinking from the stream is connected to living."[1] The death leaders and followers, however, have burned all their bridges, and their connection to their heritage is at best ungrateful and morose. Not surprisingly, followers are jealous of any favor or love given to any other fellow converts.

Suicide victims in cults fall prey to the untenable promise of fatherly protection and motherly tender loving care. The leaders themselves are often the neediest of all, the most lovelorn persons. They look to the followers for security and love, but mistake or accept submission for adoration.

When there is a threat to the leader from either within or outside the group, the death pact is carried out. Then, security must bring mutual death. The tragedy of Jonestown was set off by a threat from outside. Other charismatic leaders give the signal for carrying out the pact when forced to encounter their own fallibility and lack of gratitude for life. We hear about torches, shots, fires, poison, drowning. The public is at a loss to understand. A perverse narcissism has suddenly devastated an entire community, it is, a self-mutilating preoccupation. The elan of life is distorted into a longing for self-extermination, for the annihilation of a detested life.

The always smoldering, perverse narcissism flares up whenever the self-anointed leaders perceive that their seductive power over disciples is waning. Then the leaders are pushed to the most extreme test of their power. Their defense against this anxiety, usually of their own demise, is to assume a superhuman origin for themselves. Spurred on by their own devils, their anxieties, the doomsday leaders portray themselves to their disciples as gods.

The following stories provide examples of death-leaders, from both myth and reality. Our investigation begins with the Pied Piper.

THE PIED PIPER OF HAMELIN

The Pied Piper of Hamelin—a story that apparently has some factual basis—personifies the charisma that can lead not one, but many people to their deaths.[2] It is 1284 A.D. The town of Hamelin suffers from a plague of rats, and the Mayor offers a reward of a thousand florins to anyone who can rid the town of them. A man dressed in bright red and yellow colors appears and promises that he can rid the town of the rats. At night he begins to play a soft, strange tune on his flute. The rats are lured from their hiding places and follow the Piper to the river. He walks into the river; the rats follow him and drown.

When the Pied Piper tries to collect his reward, the Mayor refuses, saying that no melody on a flute deserves a prize. Miffed, the Piper leaves town only to return on a Sunday morning, now dressed as a hunter with a strange red hat. It is St. John's and St. Paul's day. The adults are all in church. The Piper now plays a different strange melody on his flute and a great number of boys and girls (the story counts 130) follow him, including the Mayor's grown daughter. They follow him out of town to a cave in a mountain where he and the children disappear, never to be seen again. The essence of this story may be factual, for old writings on the walls of several houses in Hamelin say that on July 26, 1284, a piper led 130 children out of town, to be lost on Köppen Hill.

The Pied Piper represents the special, almost magical, charisma that some other leaders possess. Their followers are deaf to the music of any voice other than that of their leaders. The music of these leaders has a hypnotic appeal, which deafens the sounds of reason or greater reality. Followers worship at their feet and follow them even unto death. These are death leaders. They are instigators of suicide.

The myth of the Pied Piper includes the story of two children who escaped. One was deaf and could not hear the music; the other was blind and could not see to follow. And so the myth tells us that death leaders can be resisted. If the music is not sweet to the ears and the path is not clear to the eyes, people can escape the powerful urge to follow the doomsday leaders. These leaders have been legion throughout the ages of mankind, and many have followed them.

The pull of death is a theme in ancient stories as well as modern ones. Consider the role of Hegesius, who was leader of the Cyrenian School, located in Alexandria during the time of Ptolemy Sotir.[3] The Cyrenes endorsed a pessimistic philosophy of life, a variant of hedonism. They claimed that life is without pleasure and full of pain. Hegesius carried the surname *Peisithanatos*, meaning a proponent of death. The Cyrenian's most ambitious goal for life was to gain protection against grief and *empfindungslosigkeit*, that is, a state of non-feeling, after death. Hegesius, with his charm and logic, convinced many that life was not worth living, that suicide was preferable. So many of the followers of his philosophy committed suicide that the number of deaths came to the attention of the authorities. They recognized his "black power" and expelled him from Alexandria. He was an instigator of suicide, a death leader. With these suicides on his conscience, or perhaps because he had lost the followers who gave him love through power, he later killed himself.

We can recognize a duality in the natures of these charismatic leaders that springs from the fact that they offer the promise of love and life but ultimately the cry for death. For example, in certain Hindu myths, the god Vishnu has several incarnations: one of them is the benevolent Krishna and another is the dark-sided Jagan-nath.[4]

Krishna is the most charming and human of Vishnu's incarnations. It is said that all the herdsmen's wives and daughters were in love with the enchanting Krishna. When he played his flute, the women left their work, their homes and even their husbands to join Krishna in the forest along the Yamuna River. There they danced with him, each woman thinking she had Krishna as her exclusive partner. Because so many of these women were in love with Krishna, he multiplied himself into many forms. Thus, each woman had the illusion that she was Krishna's sole love.

But like the death leaders in modern times, Vishnu had a dark side, the Jagan-nath. This Sanskrit word means "Lord of the Universe." A shrine to Jagan-nath was completed in the 1100s at Puri, in the state of Oressa in India. The shrine contained a crudely carved, brightly colored wooden idol, forty-five feet high. Each summer this image of Jagan-nath was placed on a large cart that had sixteen wheels. The idol was then pulled through the streets to its summer temple. During this sojourn, pilgrims would rush to the idol and cast themselves under the cart, there to be killed. They believed this death was an act of piety, invoking the god's blessings and sending them straight to heaven. While this is not a stated practice of the religion, it has given us the word *juggernaut*. The *Oxford English Dictionary* defines juggernaut as "customs, institutions, and so forth, beneath which people are ruthlessly and unnecessarily crushed." This call to death is the dark part represented in the Jagan-nath.

Like Vishnu, the doomsday leaders turn out again and again to be charismatic and death leading. The two-natured persona of the leaders often denies rational explanations. On the one hand, the death leader is full of charm and a convincing wisdom. He smiles, he plays his haunting, strange melody. People are intrigued and follow. His words and message seem golden. Promises are many and usually based on Providence—promises of love, wisdom, riches, a fulfilling and eternal life. These leaders are the idealized parental figure come to life. But their other persona is punitive and dark. From this side, the leader demands a commitment to death at the signal of the leader. Their death-leading impulses are suppressed only as long as unremitting devotion is accorded the leaders, and the followers nurture the leaders' needs for self-aggrandizement.

The power of the pathological narcissism of the leader ultimately brings death to the followers. Each member is chosen to provide a reflective mirror for the leaders; the members are to reflect the leaders' thoughts, feelings and desires. In turn, the reflections justify the living of the leaders. In the beginning the leader seeks only the death of the spirit of each follower. As they become "his" or "hers," the followers lose their reasoning abilities because the emotional adoration of the leader clouds and obscures their rationality. The followers submit to any wishes of the leaders in order to secure unconditional love. Husbands give their wives and fathers give their daughters to the leader, spiritually and physically. Homelands may be abandoned, relatives and friends forgotten. All is abandoned for the love of the narcissistic death leader and the promise of an Eden.

Most often, love and Providence are the chief messages the death leaders give—the promise of pure love as the return for total adoration of the leader and the promise of eternal life. Submission to their charm and then to the dogma gradually chokes the thinking and results in the murder of the souls of the followers. Finally, the requisite commitment—to follow the leader to death—becomes easier to accept. The leaders' unconscious intent is to spur the followers to share their death, for they have long been frightened of death.

Death occurs at the time when the leaders' unconscious anxieties about death or punishment flood their existence. A dissociative state or psychotropic drugs often facilitate their well-planned escape to death. Providence justifies death.

The following are a few examples of the instigators to suicide and their charisma.

THE INSTIGATORS OF DEATH: THE CULT LEADERS

There are four cult leaders who can help us define and then understand the personalities that lie behind the need to provoke others to die.

The Peoples' Temple: Reverend James Jones

The Reverend James Jones is a prime candidate for consideration because the Jonestown tragedy marked the beginning of a sense of horror in our times.[5] The deaths of these thousand people linger in our consciences; also, the suicide bombing of the 9/11 tragic attack against our greater society heightens our horror. Both show the peril that occurs when death leaders act out their death-driving wishes.

James Warren Jones led about one thousand to death. The members of his church had practiced self-killing until it became ritualized. It was just another action that was part of their form of worship. The self-killings began with the murder of some visitors to Jonestown, including California congressman Leo Ryan and others. They had been urged by a defector, Tim Stoen, to visit to investigate the group. As the visitors were preparing to board the plane to return home, all were killed.

Jones then called his group together and announced that the outside world had coerced them into their planned leaving from the earth, via self-killing. A vat of Fla-Vor-Aid, mixed with potassium cyanide, sedatives and tranquilizers (including Valium, Penegram and chloral hydrate) was brought into the assembly building. He organized the members into lines, had the parents give the infants and children the drink first and then directed the adults to drink the poison. All died except a few who ran away from the mass suicide and survived.

Jones was born in Crete, Indiana, on May 13, 1931, the only child of James Thurman Jones and Lynett Putnam. His father was a disabled veteran and unable to work; his mother was a waitress and later a factory worker. The family lived in a shack without plumbing. His father was abusive, both physically and emotionally. The increasing dissension between his parents led to a divorce when James was fourteen. His mother moved to a nearby town with James, who then worked and boarded in a hospital in order to finish high school. Eventually James received a Bachelor of Education degree from Butler University.

The forces that shaped his development into an instigator included the hostility between his parents and their attitudes toward him and toward life. His father, an ardent racist, supported the doctrine of the Ku Klux Klan; by contrast, his mother was very liberal and progressive in her political views. She was skeptical about organized religion or any god in the sky, but she was firmly convinced of spirits, evil and good. It is not clear to what extent his mother was emotionally stable. Neither parent attended church.

His insecure attachment to an anxious mother, his hatred of his father and his hostility-ridden home all gave rise to an insatiable thirst for love. He developed charm early in life, learning how to work his way around people and to allay their anger. He early discovered that others who needed love would follow him. As an adult, he was a suave, if slightly sinister figure. He dressed in a sweeping red robe and wore dark glasses to maintain an aura of mystique when preaching. He had an ability to impress people of all walks of life with his presence, if not his beliefs. His extraordinary charisma resulted in his selection as a preacher in a Pentecostal Church in Indianapolis when he was only twenty-three years old. Charm is a central attribute of death-leaders.

As he assumed leadership of people, he claimed to be able to discern the spirits and to know the thoughts of others. He professed supernatural healing powers and avowed he could heal illnesses by the touch of his hand. With each claim of supernatural powers, his anxieties over self-deception increased and threatened to break into consciousness; in effect, he was suffering from his own "disinformation." To protect himself, he escalated his delusions and found temporary escape in the fact that his delusions were convincing to many love-starved people who clung to his every word. He considered himself the reincarnation of both Jesus and Lenin. He developed a belief called Translation, avowing that his followers would all die together and be moved to another planet for a life of bliss. The self-killing pact was an integral requirement in the contract for becoming a member of his cult.

Death leaders share experiential similarities to other instigators of suicide. An early chaotic life experience with death or loss, through deprivation, neglect or trauma, creates an inner chaos that seeks a structure in external life. The formation and organization of cult groups under the death leaders' control satisfies this need to impose order on their social environment. The following descriptions of two other cult leaders show how homicidal impulses are carried out by the planned suicides, or murders, of their followers. As with Jones, the attachment to their followers is not only malevolent, it is also a usurping attachment, for in order to perpetuate dependency upon them as leaders and upon the group as the family, the leaders usually require that members sever all ties with their families.

The White Brotherhood: Mari Devi Khristos

The White Brotherhood cult was formed under the supreme leader named Mari Devi Khristos and a cohort, Yury Krivonogov, who had taught Mari paranormal practices at the Kiev Institute of Human

Soul.[6] Yury called himself St. Baptist Johann Swami. With Mari as the leader, they developed their dogma and programs, using paranormal activities to convince others of their metaphysical powers. Basic to their beliefs was the conviction that contemporary civilization would soon be destroyed, bringing a "Golden Era" in which only 140,000 true believers were destined to live. However, that Golden Age would not come until at least 12,000 of Mari's followers had sacrificed themselves and committed suicide for their beliefs.

By 1993 Mari and Yury had developed a strong organization mostly consisting of discontented, disaffected and naïve youths. The youths were told they must leave their families to become true members of the White Brotherhood and that the Living God Mari and the Teacher Swami were their real parents. Much brainwashing took place, subjecting the new members to brutal methods of mind control, with the use of psychological and psychotropic means. The members quickly turned into submissive puppets who were willing to believe the dogma and to carry out any request of the leaders. This usurped attachment seemed to serve as a devilish defense against Mari's own sense of loss and abandonment.

One day a group of these youths was instructed to gather in front of St. Sofia Cathedral in Kiev in preparation for a mass suicide. Fortunately, the city police intervened quickly enough so that their ill-devised suicide pact was not carried out. Mari, with others, was convicted and imprisoned for four years for "seizure of a state institution, organizing mass disorders and preaching a religion harmful to health."

The mixture of aggression, as in the sacrificial suicidal-killing of their followers; delusions of self-aggrandizement as in assuming the role of god; and the search for power and money via the brainwashing techniques—all are familiar actions of death-leaders. Mari had been reared by her grandparents; little is known of what had happened to her parents. She had already been a leader in adolescence, in charge of the local communist group for youth. She had one son during a short marriage but abandoned his care in order to fortify her power in the cult. In the cult's beliefs, members were to be pure and unsullied by human longings. To maintain her role as god, Mari considered herself unsullied by human desires, especially sexual feelings. To maintain this myth, her followers attempted to kill her son in a bus explosion. In light of her delusions about her god-ness, the attempted murder of her son and the desired suicide of her followers, Mari can be considered a seriously disturbed person, whether psychopathic or psychotically deluded.

The Order of the Solar Temple: Luc Jouret and Joseph Di Mambro

Formed under the leadership of Luc Jouret and Joseph Di Mambro, the Order of the Solar Temple was another murder-suicide cult.[7] Luc Jouret was a discontented, medically trained man who for ten years had been a peripatetic explorer of alternative health approaches, including Eastern mysticism and homeopathy. Joseph Di Mambro was a confidence trickster who had been in legal trouble with French authorities from early adolescence.

In their dogma, death was considered the ultimate stage of personal growth. It was a ritualized, fiery burning of the body that would provide a return to and entrance into the "Great White Sirius." The members were told that they had been reincarnated from this planet with a specific mission on earth. The members were supposed to take back to the "Source" all the consciousness that they had gained while experiencing life in this world.

Their setup included advanced electronic and mechanical gadgets that were props for the mystical trances induced by the leaders. Members bought their way into higher stages in the cult, paying for the hooded magical cloaks, engraved swords and other medallions that were required. A sum of $500,000 would provide the promise of salvation during the ritualized death and $1 million would give the member a magical charm to ensure a place at the head of the line as they entered into eternity. As the "spiritual" trances were found out to be faked and as it became obvious that the leaders were using the money for their own purposes, their power was threatened. It was time to die. Three who had fled to Quebec were murdered by stabbing on October 4, 1994; twenty-two others were found dead in a burning house in a small Swiss village, dressed in colored ceremonial robes and laid out in a sun-shaped circle with feet pointing inward. Then another twenty-five members were found dead by an injection of drugs. Finally, in December 1995, sixteen more were found dead, lying in the same star-shaped pattern and doused with inflammable liquid to ensure death by fire. This stark obsession with death ruled these people who gave up their worldly goods to die in the "right" way. It was death wrapped in many layers of delusional thinking.

Luc Jouret, born in the Belgian Congo in 1945, had received a medical degree from the Free University of Brussels. It could be said that he drifted in and out of the solar systems of ancient sects to find one for himself. Rilke suggested that wandering is a form of mourning, and Jouret seemed to be ever in search of something. He did marry and have a son, but the son died four days after birth and his wife left him, compounding his losses. He distrusted everyone, and eventually distrusted Di Mambro as well. In 1994 he fled to Quebec to avoid possible arrest by authorities. He seems to have become increasingly paranoid and self-oriented, requiring sex with a selected woman before every presentation or ritual to assure his powers.

Joseph Di Mambro had been on the run from French authorities for embezzlement, fraud, swindling and tax evasion since his teenage years. He orchestrated the electronic frauds of the spirit world on his followers. When Jouret and Di Mambro sensed that they might be exposed, the insult to their sense of power and to their narcissistic image brought their anxieties to the fore. These death leaders then resorted to the final proof of their power over the members, the transit to the other world, to Sirius. This, of course, meant group death. The leaders used both murder and the prescribed ritualistic suicides for their members and for themselves.

Heaven's Gate: Marshall Applewhite

"Death is not the enemy of life but life itself," preached Marshall Applewhite, the leader of the Heaven's Gate cult.[8] It was a time to die for God. Applewhite averred that a space ship would follow the Hale-Bopp comet and transport the group to their true home. To get on board, thirty-nine individuals killed themselves on a ranch in San Diego, California, on March 26, 1997. They were all dressed in black pants, flowing black shirts, new Nike shoes and a purple shroud to cover their faces. Their faces were glowing with joy and glee. Each had apparently ingested phenobarbital mixed with applesauce or pudding, downed a shot of vodka, and then placed a plastic bag over his or her head. They were lying on their backs on bunk beds. Their house was immaculate. They even left behind video and Internet information documenting their preparedness for leaving this world and being transformed into their real bodies. These were willing suicide victims, killing themselves at the signal of the leader. This was mass suicide.

The group was intensely symbiotic, made to be overly dependent upon each other. Personalities were lost in the fusion of ideas and actions. Members gave up their identities, assuming new names and renouncing their former lives and material possessions. They became sexless and genderless; no human attractions or sexual relations were allowed or wanted. Fitting the pattern of cults, the group became strictly regimented. For inductees, every moment was ritualized with brainwashing procedures for every waking activity.

The leader, Marshall Applewhite, seemed an intelligent person, with a master's degree from Austin College and eventually some experience teaching in a university. He was an overachiever academically and socially. Called a "born leader," he was the president of school organizations. Even as a boy, he seemed to enjoy an interpersonal power that could get people to believe anything. Born on May 17, 1931, Applewhite was the son of a peripatetic Presbyterian minister who seemed unable to hold a congregation. His father wandered from town to town starting new churches so that family seldom remained in one town for more than three years. Little else is reported of his childhood. It is known that the family was not economically stable. They lived in a "shack" like everyone else in the little town of Spur, Texas. Applewhite grew up with a strong hatred of his father, which permeated his adult life. For a psychologist, it is difficult not to conjecture about the reasons for that hatred. It is clear, however, that Applewhite's hatred led to a profound hatred of himself, of the world and of broader world events. Applewhite believed the ethnic cleansing in Europe and Africa was simply pruning out the spiritually dead. He said the same about the gang killings in the world's cities—the killings were ridding the world of unwanted, undesirable, unspiritual humans. He became quite paranoid, believing in an international conspiracy in which the politicians, the wealthy and the church leaders were programming people to their own ends.

He did get married, but his marriage ended in a divorce. He was beset by homosexual urges. It seems that his homosexual activities played a major role in terminating both his marriage and his position at a university. After failed attempts at treatment, he had himself castrated to put an end to these urges. Some others in his cult followed suit. He believed that sexual attractions and feelings were evils that would tie him to this earth. His delusions grew as the influence over his followers increased. These delusions led to their suicides.

The leaders of mass suicides share many characteristics with one another and with other instigators. First, as we have seen, they are all damaged persons, devoid of the secure love and attachment that are requisite for grateful living. The early experience with deprivation, neglect or trauma creates an inner chaos that seeks a pattern for living. The formation of cult groups satisfies the leaders' need to have a social environment that they can control.

Another most important trait is the charismatic pull they exercise over others. They are charming. Charm seems a primary personality trait of the death-leaders. Charm has a number of meanings—to powerfully attract the senses and the mind; to soothe, to fascinate; to subdue and to conjure. Interestingly enough, charm originates from the Latin, *carmen*, to sing, and the French, *canere*, to sing. And sing they do, much as the Pied Piper played his pipes. They have a song that attracts others.

Their words are songs of unconditional love and a life of peace, of life after death, of the imminent destruction of the world and of salvation for the chosen few. A hypnotic quality is induced by the sheer duration of the song or the meditations, and then the words become hypnotic simply by repetition, like the *om* in some meditations or by the rise and fall of the emotional tenor.

Charm wins an anxious mother's attention and affection, but at a cost to the other feelings of the child. For these death leaders, the infantile need to calm the mother's anxiousness brings a disastrous emptiness. It is a lone-ness that provided no accepting "other" for them because they primarily learn to appease a negative, non-giving other. They learned well how to subdue the destructive feelings of others and basked in the power this brought them.

To charm also means to subdue. Charm subdues the destructive, aggressive and fearful impulses of others. For such children, parents serve as negative objects for their inner world and, in order to calm the dread of rejection, delusional beliefs are developed that permit some inner control. The delusions are then used to control the fears of others.

Charm can be a defense against aloneness. The ability to entice others is rewarding, and death leaders utilize enticement as their power. "Fuse with me and you will find happiness. Love only me and you have my unconditional love." This is a destructive aggression against others; it is an act of violence against the being and integrity of their followers. "Fuse with me" is a powerful message to those seeking an inner relief from their aggressive drives, but it is unsatisfying to others who have experienced the rewards of some reciprocal bonding. These latter are those who leave the cult.

When the attrition rate among followers becomes too great, the leaders' power is threatened. This brings out sadistic impulses, for their hatred is too cold and too old to be hot anger. Finally, the leaders reveal their hidden motive—the loss of life for all, leaders and members alike.

Charm is the instigators' tool in usurped attachments. Their infantile sense of omnipotence is reinforced with each successful recruitment. Clever words—compounded by skillful manipulations through meditation, hypnosis, mind-altering drugs, even financial contributions—enforce their followers' attachment and reinforce the instigators' own delusional sense of power. Their primitive superego defines evil or unworthiness as any affront to their narcissistic pleasure. The instigators' degree of pathology (and consequently that of their followers) is a direct function of the distance of their removal from societal participation in thought and action.

Exploitative relationships such as in terrorist organizations require more in-depth treatment than this book permits. However, I propose that exploitative leaders are given or assume power because they promulgate a conviction or belief held to be an undeniable truth, a holy cause—the only reason for living and dying.

The followers' attachment force is to the abstract, righteous cause. Because of their damaged earlier attachments, the leaders deny personal attachments to their followers—except as the followers are loyal to and champion the cause. The followers, spurred on by a righteous cause, develop an adolescentlike, hero-ideal crush on the leaders. The cause may be social, political, economic, religious or even idiosyncratic. Assuming an omnipotent position, the exploitative instigators seldom place themselves in harm's way. Instead, they demand their followers' unquestioning fidelity, to the point of their death in battle or their suicide. The cause demands martyrdom.

As the Pied Piper legend suggests, escaping the charm of the death-leaders is possible. The next chapter describes how some fortunate people who have escaped become even more grateful for life.

CHAPTER 14

Instigation Foiled
Getting Out Alive

Then the devil conducted him
to the holy city and had him
stand on the loftiest point
of the temple, saying to him,
"If you are the Son of God,
throw Yourself down."

Matthew 4:5–6, *Modern Language New Testament*

Instigators to suicide do not always succeed. While the instigator's attachment to a person may contribute to a social field in which to play out death anxieties, the person need not respond as the instigator might wish. Victims can, and do, break the attachment, sever the relationship and save themselves.

It is critically important for all of us who are vulnerable to these potential death threats to learn how we can help thwart such malevolent drives among ourselves and how therapists can best serve patients on the brink of suicide or of instigation.

The next stories show us how instigation can fail: the temptation of Jesus, the myth of Eros and Psyche, the story of Inge Morath and a tale about a soldier.

THE TEMPTATION OF JESUS

If there ever was a First Instigator, the role model for all instigators to follow, it had to be Satan. Satan fits well the criteria for instigators. Initially one of the angels, he had sinned grievously. The lore states that he was an envious, power-driven angel that God cast out of heaven to fall into an existence far worse than death. Injured in his fall, he limps and has a cleft foot, like a goat's hoof. His stigma is reminiscent of the misshapen foot of Oedipus and the lameness of Ulysses. This stigma and the trauma of banishment from Heaven produced the First Instigator, with revenge and jealousy boiling in his heart. Jesus was a perfect candidate.

Early in his ministry, Jesus went into isolation to fast and to meditate. After forty days, he was hungry. Instigator Satan saw his chance and appeared before Jesus. Satan challenged Jesus to prove his divinity by turning stones into bread so that he could eat. Jesus refused, saying, "Man does not live by bread alone, but by every word that proceedeth out of the mouth of God."[1]

Next, Satan dared Jesus to jump off a high tower to see whether God's angels would catch him. Jesus again refused.

In the third and final challenge, Satan promised that if Jesus would fall down and worship him, he would give Jesus the whole world. Jesus' response was, "Get thee hence, Satan," at last telling the instigator Satan to leave him alone. Satan's tests of Jesus' strength failed; Jesus did not succumb to false promises.

Many a suicide victim tests another's love with the hope of rescue. Of course, the test is not fair. These tests may take many forms. Procris and Cephalus tested each other's love, with the result that one accidentally died at the other's hands. Both Maggie and Rita tested the love of their mates by threatening suicide. The tests did not work.

Children test the love of their parents in many ways. I am now reminded of the many stories that children tell while taking the Thematic Apperception Test during a diagnostic assessment. They frequently tell a story of a child running away from home because the child feels angry and unloved. Once gone, the parents will find out how much they really love and miss this wonderful child; the parents will search high and low until they find their child and then give their child everything the child wants, which to the child means love. In other stories children tell, the child is lost, never to be found, with the parents happy that the child is gone. The child fears, perhaps knows, he or she is unloved. Arthur Miller poignantly described the self-defeating impulses of running away when he wrote, "Running away from home is a form of suicide designed to punish everybody."[2] Many adolescents who have run away from home in recent years may have chosen to disappear and to punish their parents, rather than act out their violence against them. Running away, while a form of violence against the parents, results in a suicide of the soul. For these adolescents, it seems they or their parents fail the test of love.

We have seen how the tests of love may backfire against the suicide victim. Max tells his wife and the therapist that Rita should know he loves her but that he refuses to tell her so. Hearing this, Rita stages a suicide. Maggie, too, in *After the Fall* is similarly hypersensitive. Never trusting that love could be hers, she plays her suicidal game of taking pills.

Tests of love may be initiated by the instigator or by the suicide victim. As Satan demonstrates, the test for the victim is total submission in order to gain the instigator's love. For the suicide victim, the test is often a desperate, potentially fatal, act to compel the instigator to prove his attachment to the victim.

The stories that follow show ways that the impulse to suicide can be forstalled.

PSYCHE AND EROS

Once upon a time there was a king who had three beautiful daughters. Like Cinderella, the youngest one was beautiful beyond compare. People worshipped her instead of Aphrodite, which made Aphrodite so angry and jealous that she ordered Eros, her son, to punish Psyche by making her undesirable to all men except the ugliest monster he could find on earth.[3] But when Eros saw Psyche, he was so stunned by her beauty that he dropped his golden arrow and pricked her heart. Then again by accident, he pricked himself with his magic arrow and immediately fell in love with her. In disobedience to his mother, he ordered Psyche's father to dress Psyche in a bridal gown and to leave her on a lofty mountain crag.

Whoever would fall from such a height would perish without fail. But the West Wind, Eros' servant, gathered her up, wedding dress and all, and carried Psyche down to a green valley. From there Psyche found her way into an enchanted castle where Eros was waiting. They made love often, but each time only in the dark. She never got to see him. Although her every wish was fulfilled, she soon felt lonely and asked her lover for permission to invite her two sisters to the castle for a visit. With considerable foreboding, the god granted her request.

The sisters visited three times, and three times Eros' servant, the obedient West Wind, carried the sisters on the round trip from the cliff to the castle and back. During their third visit, "consumed with the gall of swelling Envy,"[4] the sisters persuaded the now pregnant Psyche that her invisible husband was a monster. They laughed, taunting her about her marital arrangement and telling her that she was married to a monster, a dragon who is fattening her up so he could devour her. They urge her to cut off his head in his sleep.

Psyche could not keep the mocking voices of her sisters out of her head. She grew curious about her husband, knowing that it was prophesied that she could only marry a monster. One night, carrying a lamp and a razor, she slipped toward the sleeping monster, and saw the gorgeous god lying before her. The razor flew out of her hand. Seized by desire of him, with her hands quivering, she spilled a drop of the lamp's boiling oil "from the point of its flame."[5] It burned deeply into the god's winged right shoulder, wounding him gravely. He flew away.

Psyche woke up back on the mountain crag, wracked with grief over her shameful actions toward her husband. Although she was carrying their child, she resolved to die for her misdeed and leaped from a steep bank into a river below. The river, however, caught her softly and carried her to a meadow, where the god Pan advised her against further deadly plunges.

Psyche stigmatized the god of love in the most literal sense of the word, branding him, traumatizing him and making him an instigator.[6] Both in love with Eros and oppressed by her mourning, Psyche searched for him, determined to find him or die. Along the way, however, helpful and redeeming forces recognized her true worth, innocence and love for Eros. They repeatedly shielded her from death.

After long wanderings, Psyche finally arrived at the palace of jealous Aphrodite, who received her most ungraciously and set her four impossible tasks. The first was to sort an astronomical number of mixed grains in one day; ants helped her with this task. The second task was so daunting that Psyche again wanted to jump into a river, but a reed dissuaded her and helped her. The third task also drove Psyche to the brink of suicide, but she allowed herself to be helped by an eagle.

The fourth and final task was to fetch a day's ration of Proserpina's beauty ointment from the underworld. It seemed impossible to come back from any descent into the underworld. Psyche despaired so utterly of this task that she headed straightaway to the top of a tower, determined to plunge to her death. But the tower began to speak, counseling Psyche against the deadly plunge. The tower taught her the path to the underworld. Once there, Psyche obtained the beauty unguent for the cruel and jealous Aphrodite.

Eros pleaded for help from Zeus himself. After all this travail and with Aphrodite's blessings, Psyche reunited with Eros, became immortal and gave birth to their daughter, Pleasure.[7]

To return to the sisters: With Psyche gone, first one sister and then the other vied to be the bride of Eros and to enjoy his love and his wealth. They were so avaricious and self-centered that they convinced themselves they could succeed, even though they wanted him only for their own pride and glorification.

Eros instigated their suicides. He challenged each sister in turn to prove her love by jumping off the cliff. In blind obedience to their own pathological fantasies, each sister jumped off the cliff, convinced that Eros would prefer her to Psyche and fully expecting the West Wind to once again carry her to Eros' castle. No West Wind carried them; no wings of Eros broke their fall. They tumbled into the void, unrescued and unloved. The sisters, for whom their own husbands were never good enough, were dashed to pieces on the rocks, tragic victims of greed and insatiability. In a seemingly fitting end, in the myth, vultures devoured their innards.

The existential purpose of Psyche's sisters could be characterized by the catchword "death-wishing"; that is, they wished their sister dead. Death-wishing is that malicious, subversive, undermining cupidity which proceeds from selfishness but which in the last analysis causes the ill-wishing person's own destruction.

Psyche's sisters could not stay away from their instigator Eros just as the Sirens could not let go of their instigator Ulysses, Sappho could not give up the showman Phaon, the Sphinx could not flee Oedipus and Evenos could not escape his beheaded rivals. The victims all clung to their instigators like addicts to their needles.

How does Psyche, or anyone, avoid suicide? The answer is to know love and gratitude. Psyche truly loved Eros but in her naïveté she fell prey to her older sisters' rapacious jealousy. Eros loved Psyche. Each time Psyche despaired over the task given her and wished to kill herself, it was Eros, the voice of love, that saved her. She could hear it. And

Eros could speak love to her when she needed it. Psyche had the capacity to be grateful for Eros' love.

It seems rather simple to state, and perhaps it is overdone in current literature, but one cure for suicidal impulses is to develop a *gratitude for life*. To grasp onto life as the ultimate gift.

Another characteristic of Psyche that enabled her to overcome her self-destructive thoughts was the openness to accept help and counsel from others. Psyche readily listened to the benign voices in nature and from within her own depths. She heard the voices of life awakening the well-meaning intentions within her, perhaps stemming from her childhood when she had listened good-naturedly to family wisdom. Thanks to her openness to the universal unconscious strivings for life, she could hear the voices of the river god and Pan, the reed, the eagle and especially the tower, who taught her the way to the underworld, that is, to the unconscious.

The story of Psyche and Eros has a happy ending. The symbolic message of the story appears to be that innocence may be favored, that Eros and Psyche, love and soul, belong together, and together give birth to Pleasure.

THE STORY OF INGE MORATH

Arthur Miller's third wife, Inge Morath, was an internationally known photojournalist. She figured recognizably as Holga in *After the Fall*, and Miller wrote of her again in his autobiography, *Timebends: A Life*.[8] The present portrayal draws on both works. Inge Morath emerges as a compelling personality whose admirable conduct in life is in high contrast to the somber thesis of this book.

The fictional Holga hailed from Salzburg. So did Inge Morath. In *After the Fall*, Holga embodied what every other character, including Quentin and Maggie, had lost: *hope*. Arthur Miller first met the real-life Inge Morath in Reno, Nevada, where she had come to photograph the shooting of a movie, *The Misfits*, with Marilyn Monroe in the cast. Marilyn liked Inge Morath at once, especially for her considerate kindness and lack of journalistic aggression. In turn, Inge Morath seems to have photographed Marilyn with real affection.

Arthur Miller wrote that he perceived Inge Morath as a noble-looking woman, both shy and strong. He says she was a handsome, beautiful woman, a socially distinguished lady with "austere pride."

He sensed a "conflicted sensitivity" in her. She was a survivor in the disconcertingly double-edged sense of that word, with fear as her indomitable protective friend in troubled times and grief tormenting her to repudiate her good fortune once she was delivered from those troubles. Consequently she met the future with a questioning faith and unquestionable fortitude and faced her past with painful probing. Here is some of her story.

Inge Morath was born in Graz near Salzburg, Austria, in 1923. Her parents were both scientists, her father a professor. She refused to join the Nazi student organization and was forced by the Nazis to work in a factory assembling plane parts in Berlin at a time when it was bombed daily. Working alongside Ukrainian women who were also forced laborers, she was with many whom no one was likely to miss were they to be killed by the bombs. One day at the factory, a gate was bombed open, and along with others she simply walked out. Although she had little reason to believe that any of her family had survived or were still living in Salzburg, she headed south toward her home in Austria. It was a long trek. She was part of the many streams of people during the end of the Reich who sought rides on trucks, trains, bicycles or horse-drawn wagons; who needed food and some human decencies from others as they all plodded to what used to be their homes. After many days of tired walking, she came to a bridge. Completely despondent, she climbed the rail to drop to her death in the water, as many had done, when suddenly an older man appeared, a soldier on crutches, crippled by the war. In psychological terms, he certainly fit the picture of a traumatized man. His wounds and infirmity could have embittered him. Yet seeing this woman ready for death, he gathered the strength to overcome any ill will and rancor that could have resulted from his infirmities. Like Camus' lawyer, he could have become a passive instigator. Instead, he became Inge Morath's ministering guardian angel, ordering her never to give up hope. Apparently aware that she might repeat her suicide attempt, he took her in tow and had her follow him. After many days and nights on the road, the two reached Salzburg. Her memory had failed and she could no longer recall the house where she had lived. The crippled soldier led her down one block after another, coming at length to an area that felt familiar to her. He scoffed at the idea that she belonged in this affluent neighborhood, for she was this "scabby girl in rags." They started to go on when she recognized a brass knocker, knew it was her house and ran to the door. Amazingly, her mother answered the knock. Inge turned around to invite the soldier into their home, but he had already disappeared as if ascended into the sky.

What a contrast between young Inge Morath's socially timid yet paternally protective, stout-hearted soldier and Camus' brilliant, socially lionized but heartless "judge-penitent." What a contrast between the old soldier and Quentin, whom the dying Maggie calls "Judgey" in Miller's play and who was driven to instigative fury by his stigma. And were not Inge's traumas sufficient to put her at risk of becoming an instigator, a bitter death-wisher of others? Inge was fortunate. She was rescued by a man who knew about suffering and whose help she was able to accept. Somehow this encounter detoxified her misery; it implanted hope in her heart.

While this story alone is clear evidence that not all stigmatized individuals become instigators, there is more to be learned. Her gratitude for life led her onward. The rest of the story is this: an unknown German soldier had saved her from drowning; in gratitude to life and hope, she in turn saved a famous American soldier from death.

Inge was working for *Paris-Match* and *Life*, photographing the making of *The Unforgiven*, a film John Huston was shooting in the Mexican backcountry. The picture starred Audie Murphy, America's most decorated World War II hero.

One morning Huston and a few friends were hunting ducks on the shore of the large mountain lake where part of the film is set. Huston wanted her to take pictures of his kills as they dropped out of the air. Inge, however, grew bored with the noise of the shotguns and the pellets falling down on her and her new telephoto lens. She went wandering off.

She noticed two specks far out on the water and what looked like erratic thrashing. Through her camera's powerful lens, she made out what looked like someone struggling around a rocking boat. She called to Huston and the hunters. They refused to respond. After all, this was Audie Murphy out there! He surely knew how to take care of himself. With him was the film company's plane pilot, two strong men who could survive any danger. Inge just saw two helpless men. Seeing one man struggling in the water, she tore off her clothes except for her panties and bra, jumped into the cold water, and swam about half a mile before she reached Audie Murphy, who was exhausted by his fight to stay afloat. He could not swim.

Nor could the pilot swim. The pilot was not able to keep the boat stable and help Audie Murphy into the boat, lest the boat turn over as well. Inge reached the sinking Murphy, had him hold on to her bra strap, and pulled him to land. And then she swore furiously at the indifferent hunters.

She had towed Audie Murphy to safety just as she had been towed away from her leap to death. She repaid her debt of gratitude. Just as the German soldier had bested his war stigma to become a ministering angel rather than an instigator, so had Inge Morath healed her trauma with the elixir of hope. In gratitude, Audie Murphy gave her his dearest possession, a watch that had been with him throughout the entire war. She wore it constantly.

Here, then is a potent example of the failure of instigation. The German soldier, certainly stigmatized and traumatized by his experiences, held on to hope. Hope was his gift to the forlorn young Inge Morath. From hope comes gratitude for life and for the life of others as well.

And now for a lighter story.

LIEUTENANT GUSTL

The following story has the surprise ending of an Edgar Allan Poe tale.[9] The author, Arthur Schnitzler, was possibly Austria's finest twentieth-century playwright, novelist and storywriter. He corresponded with Sigmund Freud and had a deep interest in psychology. In this story, free association of ideas replaces chronological narration; it is perhaps the first important stream-of-consciousness story in European literature. The form is similar to Camus' *The Fall*, for both use monologues. It shows some of the potentially ludicrous aspects of the instigator-victim relationships. It leaves me with a smile of relief. I will tell this story in the present as the lieutenant experiences it.

Lieutenant Gustl is attending a concert. He is quite restless and self-absorbed, mostly bored because he really does not know what is going on. He believes the concert could be a mass. It isn't. It is an oratorio. He would not be there except that a friend whose sister sings in the chorus gave him a ticket. "Patience, patience!" he tells himself. "It will be over sometime. The singing is beautiful but maybe I am not in the mood." He does not know how to behave in the audience. He is afraid to move, to look at his watch lest he appear bored. He is paralyzed by his ignorance of what good manners might be in the opera house. He cannot even take a note from his pocket to read lest he call attention to himself. His gaze now is on the beautiful girl sitting in a box opposite him. He thinks she is beautiful, but then his thoughts turn to Steffi, his lady friend. Why did she have to be with her husband tonight instead of coming with him?

He is annoyed by the applause given the singers. "Bravo! Bravo!" everybody is yelling; but he joins in. At last it is over. Everybody is standing up to leave! Good! His eyes are still fixed on the beautiful, obviously wealthy girl that he wants to know. He has to know her! But first he must stop to pick up his coat at the checkout counter. He is impatient and yells at the clerk, "You there, No. 224! It's hanging right *there*! Are you blind? It's hanging there!"

An obese man blocks his way; Gustl cannot get his coat fast enough to permit him to follow the lady. "Patience," the man says. "Don't push. You're not going to miss anything." But Gustl becomes even more impatient and turns around. The fat man is Habetswallern, the master baker. Gustl knows him very well. How on earth can a simple baker come here to a concert?

Unable to calm him down, the baker says, "Lieutenant, if you make the slightest disturbance, I'll pull your saber out of its scabbard, smash it and send the pieces to your regimental headquarters. Do you understand, you fool?" The German expression that the baker uses is *Dummer Bub*, which translates as "stupid fool" and a standard phrase for a challenge to a duel. By now the baker has the hilt of the lieutenant's saber in his hand.

The lieutenant's downfall is launched. From here on, he is overwhelmed by doubts about himself, his honor and his life. "Did the baker really challenge me to a duel? Of course he did. What am I to do? My life is now ruined." Gustl leaves the opera house in a daze, puzzling over whether he has really been challenged to a duel but knowing all the while that by the military code of honor, indeed he has been.

What should he do? Throughout that night, Gustl is distraught. Should he report it to his commanding officer? No, of course not; he would then have to fight. Could he go to his favorite café and ask his fellow officers? No; what a fool he would seem. Does anyone else know, besides himself, about the affront? He could not tell. How could he go ahead with the duel? It would be certain death. He is not fit to fight a duel; after all, he is only a clerk. But tomorrow comes so soon.

It is eleven o'clock. "I should have some supper," he thinks. "I have to just kill myself and then I would not have to fight a duel. This is what the baker wants! I should just kill myself, commit suicide. It is the only honorable way out. The paper would read, 'Suicide of a Young Officer. The motives are veiled in obscurity.'" Gustl becomes convinced that he must kill himself, that there is no other way out of the duel. Further, he cannot take the chance that in the morning when his superiors find out about the duel, they will take back his commission. They would never be his seconds! And so his musings go on and on. He cannot even go to have his supper.

Gustl falls asleep on a park bench, only to awaken several times with alarm. Pedestrians pass by. Are they looking for him? He is frightened, suspicious of all. How can he get out of this predicament? He thinks about several possibilities. He could visit his family, especially his favorite sister, but decides that is impossible. It would be too difficult. He could escape to America and then return later when everyone has forgotten it. But that will not work either. Then he muses over all the possible women he might have had . . . to no avail. Many will think he killed himself because he had too many debts; but that is not so.

He awakens to a mild, warm morning and to the necessity of killing himself. His thoughts return. Will Steffi bring flowers to his grave? He needs to talk to someone before he dies, maybe a priest. That will not work either. Now a policeman salutes him and he has to return the salute. He even says "Hi" to him. He considers that it was too bad that he never really got to fight in a war. Perhaps he could have become a hero, even if he became a dead hero.

On and on go his tortured ramblings. He finally convinces himself that he could have a café au lait before he shoots himself. He sits by the window, the first customer, but pulls the curtains so no one can see him.

And then the waiter says, "Have you heard, Lieutenant?"

"What?" For the love of God, does he know something already about the duel and him?

"Mr. Habetswallern . . ."

Gustl's thoughts are confused. He fears what the waiter will now say. Perhaps even the waiter knows that he is to be in a duel.

". . . had a stroke last night at twelve."

He can't believe this. "Is he dead?"

"Of course. He was dead on the spot!"

Gustl is overwhelmed. He has never been so relieved or so happy. He repeats, "He's dead—he's dead! No one knows a thing, and nothing has happened. What shall I do? I am so happy, so happy!" Lucky Lieutenant Gustl is saved fortuitously from his instigator!

This is a delightful story in some ways and an unusual one, because its stream-of-consciousness style gives insight into the thoughts of a suicide victim. It depicts the agony of the potential victim who is thinking of death. These musings are typical for a person being prompted by another to commit suicide: anger against the instigator, memories of past events, thoughts of what will be missed in life, sorrow for the loss, pity for oneself. Although the story is told in a light, comical tone, Gustl's anxiety contemplating his fateful decision accurately reflects the agonies of people contemplating suicide.

Instigators sometimes fail in their intent. Perhaps the baker also had a sleepless night, for this time the instigator seemed to bring about his own undoing. As we have seen, often the instigator, suffering from his own anguish, takes his own life after successfully instigating the suicide.

Instigation often fails. Four important factors appear to be involved when the temptation to suicide is foiled. First is the nature of the attachments in which the victim is involved; second, the victim's ability to maintain hope despite the vicissitudes of life; third, the capacity of the victim to be open to and seek counsel; and fourth, the ability of the victim to discover the meaning of life for himself or herself.

The force of an instigator can be foiled by the potential victim when that person finds the strength to resist the attraction, that is, to recognize that the relationship is enchaining rather than freeing for life. The ability to resist requires a conscious awareness of and acceptance of the unhealthiness of an attachment. It involves resisting the false songs of the Piper or the Sirens, even though they seem so inviting.

When despair begins to replace hope, the victim's only real chance is to center on himself and find a basis for hope. Often enough, disappointments in one's love life can be regarded in a positive light, for the disappointments can lead to an understanding of the reasons for the failure. The gained insights lead to hope and to being able to create a better attachment next time. Hope is a prime requisite for living. Psyche had many trials before she could trust herself and know her own strength, even to go through hell itself. Hope provides the energy for struggling on, for seeking the path of life.

Often, as we have seen, the ability to accept or seek counsel is critical. Sometimes the help comes through a stranger, as it did for Inge Morath. Family members or trusted friends often reach out a supporting hand. Help may arrive through a psychotherapist who can provide the emergency guidance and then lead the person onto a path for living. Communities now have inaugurated crisis resources that are available to those considering the pull of death. These are "hot lines" for potential suicide victims who need temporary support in resisting the Siren's song. Community crisis centers are usually open for telephone calls twenty-four hours a day.

One must hold on to a meaning of life for one's self. While this may involve contact and support from other people, the essence of the focus center must be on the self. "What do I want from life for myself? What can I give to life?"

Persons who would avoid the call of the instigator must develop sufficient knowledge of the self and sufficient ego strength to recognize the projections or expectations that others place upon them, and to see that the source is from outside themselves. This is often the work of psychotherapy, which can help the person in crisis explore the issue, facilitate the person's growth and move ahead to the stage when the individual can proceed to learn, safely, on his own.

Ultimately, to be healthy, the individual must learn that gratitude for life is the essence of living.

CHAPTER 15

Loving Attachment to Life

Think of yourself as dead.
You have lived your life.
Now take what's left and live it properly.

Marcus Aurelius, *Meditations*

Instigators and suicide victims are complementary partners who sustain each other as long as their reciprocal needs are met. Of course, things can go wrong in any relationship. It is a rare individual who has not, at some time, wished another person would disappear or drop dead. To wish someone dead, however, rarely causes a suicide. It takes more than a casual surge of anger to affect another's person's life so strongly.

In this book I have tried to describe the origin of instigations to suicidal actions and the nature of attachments that instigators are destined to develop. I have tried also to highlight factors that lead to unsuccessful instigations. Some suicidal actions are provoked by others who project their pathological attachments onto another person. These are most visible instigators. Sometimes, however, the instigative forces are incorporated within the victims themselves; these forces may be more elusive, but no less deadly. My strongest hope for this book is that we will begin to recognize the role that instigators have in suicides. Perhaps then it will be possible to work through, and ultimately beyond, the continually repeated patterns that might otherwise lead to additional tragedies.

The very idea that one person can instigate the death of another individual is awesome, and many people will shy away from it. No one, including myself, really wants to believe there is someone who can induce a suicidal action.

But, as the myths show us, instigation is an old, old idea, found in the earliest accounts of civilization; modern stories and case histories show beyond a doubt that the phenomenon is all too real. The murderous impulses that are contained within the instigators are poisonous both to themselves and to those whom they victimize.

Four types of instigators have been identified: active, passive, provocateur and internal instigators. *Active* instigators hold conscious murderous impulses against the suicide victim. They are thick-skinned narcissistic people with corollary superego deficits that develop through defensive identifications with their own traumatizing agent. The resulting self-idealization lets them justify their aggression.

Passive instigators are thin-skinned narcissistic personalities whose deficiencies of conscience develop during an abusive, traumatic infancy. They are left with an internalized, pervasive sense of being bad and deserving the punishing trauma. Over-sensitive to any slight, their misinterpretations of a loss of love provoke excessive guilt as well as hostility. The subsequent repression of grief and anger conceals their hostile, murderous impulses from themselves but not from the vulnerable victim who introjects and acts upon the hostility with suicide. The instigator's guilt about the victim's suicide is excessive, releasing the primitive internal chaos of the original trauma and destroying some ego functioning.

Provocateur instigators propel a suicidal action by their determined efforts to unmask the evils in another. They have a reactive hostility toward supposedly protective others whom they feel have humiliated or failed them. They are driven by sadistic impulses to undermine another in order to prove that their hostile scorn for (parental) ego ideals is justified. Their self-righteous mask serves to defend against knowing the evil within themselves.

Finally, *internal* instigators have an obsession with dying. Death becomes a self-fulfilling fantasy. The guilt over another's death, compounded by grief, drives them to seek punishing relationships with others. Their ego defenses are so sufficiently tenuous that they can function at a borderline level of reality. Naught can satisfy their death obsession, only death.

In identifying the attachments of instigators, I found several pathological types of attachment which, I believe, are more general and do not apply only to instigators of suicide. These attachments include the malevolent, nullifying, fantasized, negative, ambivalent, usurped and exploitative attachment. In the *malevolent* attachment, the instigators have obvious evil intent toward others. Terrorist leaders seem to have this attachment toward their suicide-bombers. Instigators who ignore others, even though the other persons are part of their lives, act out the *nullifying* attachment. It is exhibited by those who say, either in action or words, that they don't want to have you around, or who act as if you are not present. A subcategory of the nullifying attachment is the *fantasized* attachment in which the partner is expected to act out the instigator's idealized blueprints for the victim. In spite of the most obvious evidence to the contrary, the instigator feels fully justified in anticipating that their sons and daughters will become the perfect princes and princesses, or their partners will be the kings or queens of their dreams. The reality of the person in front of them is sweetly denied or angrily banished from their sight. They react only to their projections, whether the projections idealize or demonize the other person.

The *negative* attachment is easy to recognize, because it is an open dislike of someone else. It usually manifests itself clearly in words such as "I don't like you" or "I don't love you anymore." The instigator may deny these feelings, but their actions are rejecting and punitive toward the other person. *Ambivalent* attachments fluctuate between warm feelings of fusion with the other and hateful reactions when the other person's needs come to the fore.

Individuals who demand a submission at the cost of annihilating any other attachments use both *usurped* and *exploitative* attachments. Cult leaders, including high-powered religious leaders, often cloak themselves in the trappings of supernatural authority. Narcissistic to the core, the basis of their leadership is a hatred of all. Anyone who follows them falls into the trap of a one-way attachment, giving up relationships with all others to follow—and ultimately be exploited—by their leaders. Exploitative attachments include any relationships in which the leaders unethically use other people to accomplish their own aims. Their disciples are often pushed to their death, while the leaders live on, aloof from any dangers to themselves. Cults, terrorist organizations and even some churches often misuse their members' lives.

I have tried to show that instigation is an adaptation to traumas in the lives of some people. The trauma endured by the instigators is sometimes physical, sometimes psychological and often both. The trauma infects the instigators with a fear of death, of a basic distrust of others' motives, and of anxieties of eventual abandonment. The need for instigators to take control of their own lives gradually develops into a sense of power as they learn to manipulate others to fulfill their needs. The power is sometimes outwardly expressed and sometimes more subtly, as in an angry withdrawal. At any time, however, the power is malevolent and seeks revenge.

Basic to the psychological make-up of instigators is the primitive grief that has resulted from trauma. It is a grief about dying and death, evoked by those early experiences that challenged their attachment to others and their actual existence. The grief colors their lives and is resurrected with each relationship for they become attracted to those who evoke feelings similar to those feelings already within themselves. And so we have an interrelationship: a grief-driven person attracts the grief-driven individual. Both are set up for further problems.

Instigators are self-oriented, lacking those initial experiences that permit openness to others or to the world. In this respect, they can only act *out*, not act *with* another person or within the world. Relationships provide the proving ground for their fearful expectations when the stage is set outside the self with others. At other times, the stage is within the self as an introjected image becomes the battle place for life.

If anything can be learned from this investigation, it is that the impact of a bad experience has long term effects. The incorporation of a tragic experience instills an anticipation of its repeat and impairs personality development or relationships with others. Neither children nor adults "grow out of" or forget the shocks of their lives. We can, however, with due care forestall permanent psychic damage.

I have tried to present a realistic picture of instigators, but I do not feel sympathetic toward any of them. I can only abhor the cult instigators of mass suicides or the terrorist leaders who find it easy to send others to their death in support of the leaders' philosophies.

Gustave Flaubert (1882) had an insight into suicide and instigation in a letter he wrote to Louise Colet: "We want to die because we cannot cause others to die, and every suicide is perhaps a repressed assassination." It may be that each person carries some seeds of instigation. Arthur Miller was also aware of these depths of the psyche when he said that only with the awareness and knowledge of our own evil can we be free from being dominated by it.

Often psychotherapists avoid dealing with the evil of their patients, especially patients who seem to be cooperative with the work of therapy. It is then easier for therapists to avoid an encounter with the patients' evil, their hatred, their homicidal or suicidal impulses. For instance, I have watched therapists work with incestuous families, never approaching the problem of the incest itself, let alone the feelings of the offended child. With our good intentions, therapists want to have positive regard for the patient and, unconsciously, side with the patient's defenses against their "evil." I feel that too often we wait for patients to initiate discussion of their destructive feelings, which may never happen if their defenses are successful even with therapists.

One goal of therapy must be to help people face themselves, to know their own violence as well as their grief. The therapists must first be able to accept the violence inherent in all mankind and in themselves. The destructive, hostile, angry, mean, malicious, hurting, killing characteristics of all of us need to be recognized as part of the human condition. Only by knowing this aspect of ourselves, and then of our patients, will we, or anyone, be able to live with warmth, love and freedom.

This book has been difficult for me to write because of the innuendos and chords of dissonance that it might bring to any who have experienced the shock of a suicidal person. I have wanted to bring understanding and hope to us all. For the social scientists among us, it has been my desire to open a field of investigation that is too easy to overlook. For the psychotherapists, my hope has been to help all our patients have a firmer, more gratifying view of life.

I will end as I began—with the hope that this book will help to alleviate the terrible suffering of suicide victims, their survivors and their instigators.

Notes

Chapter 1. Fatal Attachments

1. There have been a multitude of studies on the attachment of infants to parents and the behaviors of the infant toward the absence and then return of a parent. The reader is referred to the following book for a summary:

Jude Cassidy and Phillip R. Shaver, *Handbook of Attachment: Theory, Research, and Clinical Applications* (New York and London: The Guilford Press, 1999).

2. In the surgeon general's report of May 2, 2001, on suicide in the United States, the surgeon general presented overwhelming evidence that suicide is more devastating and destructive to the lives of individuals than are illnesses such as AIDS or even homicide. These statistics were taken from the Internet at www.mentalhealth.org/suicide.

3. John Donne, *Biathanatos. A Declaration of that Paracoxe, or Thesis, That Self-homicide is not so naturally Sinne, that it may never be otherwise* . . . , eds. Michael Rudick and M. Pabst Battin (New York: Garland Texts, 1644/1982), xcvii, 4.

4. For a more complete look at the history of suicide and the social attitudes about suicide, the reader is referred to the 1995 book by Georges Minois, *History of Suicide: Voluntary Death in Western Culture*, trans. Lydia G. Cochrane (Baltimore and London: Johns Hopkins University Press, 1999).

5. Epicurus was a Greek philosopher (342–270 B.C.) who taught that suicide was an honorable end to life, especially when a person is overcome by fears of the gods and of death. Because good and evil lie in sensations and because death ends sensation, suicide is good.

6. I will not attempt to cover the rich history of the philosophy, attitudes and resulting actions concerning suicide. There are excellent books that provide thoughtful overviews and analyses of the cultural responses to suicide, among them *The Savage God: A Study of Suicide* by A. Alvarez (New York and London: W. W. Norton and Company, 1990) and *History of Suicide: Voluntary Death in Western Culture* by G. Minois (Baltimore and London: John Hopkins University Press, 1995).

7. Simon Fanshawe, "Children on a Field Trip Understood the Suicidal Lure of Beachy Head," *San Francisco Chronicle*, January 24, 1999.

8. Pierre Boelle and Antoine Flahault, "Suicide Trends in France and UK," *The Lancet*, Vol. 353, April 17, 1964, p. 1364.

9. P. S. Yip and R. C. Tan, "Suicides in Hong-Kong and Singapore: A Tale of Two Cities," *International Journal of Social Psychiatry* 44(4) (Winter 1998): 267–279. They report, "Jumping from a height was the commonest method of suicide."

10. A. Alem, D. Kebede, L. Jacobsson and G. Kullgren, "Suicide Attempts among Adults in Butajira, Ethiopa," *Acta Psychiatrica Scandinavica Supplementum* 397 (1999): 70–76.

11. Alec Roy, "Family History of Suicide," in *Essential Papers on Suicide*, eds. J. Maltsberger and M. Goldblatt (New York and London: New York University Press, 1996), 549–561.

12. M. Asberg, L. Traskman and P. Thoren, "5-HIAA in the Cerebrospinal Fluid: A Biochemical Suicide Predictor?" in *Essential Papers on Suicide*, eds. J. Maltsberger and M. Goldblatt (New York and London: New York University Press, 1996), 342–355.

13. Sigmund Freud, "Mourning and Melancholia," in *Sigmund Freud Collected Papers*, Vol. 4, trans. Joan Riviere (New York: Basic Books, 1917/1959), 162.

14. Karl Menninger, *Man Against Himself* (New York: Basic Books, 1938).

15. M. Straker, "Clinical Observations of Suicide," *Canadian Medical Association Journal*, Vol. 79, 473–479.

Chapter 2. Instigators

1. This story was printed from *Reuters News*, July 2001, as reported in the *Santa Barbara News-Press*.

2. *Los Angeles Times*, January 15, 2003, B3.

3. Carlos Parada, *Genealogical Guide to Greek Mythology*, http://hsa.brown.edu/~maicar/Eros.html 2002.

4. Since the early work of David Levy on the failure to thrive among infants, mental health professionals have recognized the importance of not only the presence of another but also the attachment and bonding to another, especially in infancy and early childhood. For more information on attachment the reader is referred to the three volumes by John Bowlby, *Attachment and Loss. Vol. 1, Attachment* (New York: Hogarth Press/Basic Books, 1969/1982); *Vol. 2, Separation: Anxiety and Anger* (New York: Basic Books, 1983); and *Vol. 3, Loss: Sadness and Depression* (New York: Basic Books, 1980).

5. Please see the following for the story of Timagoras and Meles:

John Donne, "Hero and Leander," in *John Donne Poems*, The Franklin Library (New York: Oxford University Press, 1932).

Anthony S. Mercatante, *The Facts on File Encyclopedia of World Mythology and Legend* (New York and Oxford: Facts on File, 1988), 317.

Ovid, *Heroides and Amores*, trans. G. Showerman Loeb, Classical Library (Cambridge, Mass., and London: Harvard University Press, 1963), Book XIX.

Carlos Parada, "Eros," in *Genealogical Guide to Greek Mythology*, http://hsa.brown.edu/~maicar/Eros.html, 2002.

6. Edwin S. Shneidman, *Comprehending Suicide* (Washington, D.C.: American Psychological Association, 2001), 155.

7. The sources for this story are:

Christopher Marlowe, *Hero and Leander* (London: Adam Islip, 1998).

Anthony S. Mercatante, *The Facts on File Encyclopedia of World Mythology and Legend* (New York and Oxford: Facts on File, 1988), 317.

Carlos Parada, "Eros," in *Genealogical Guide to Greek Mythology*, http://hsa.brown.edu/~maicar/Eros.html, 2002.

8. Carlos Parada, "Hero and Leander" in *Genealogical Guide to Greek Mythology*, http://hsa.brown.edu/~maicar/hero.html.

9. Marlowe, *Hero and Leander*, 116–120.

10. Ibid., 15–16.

11. Ibid., 83–88.

12. Ibid., 377–378.

13. Ibid., 174.

Chapter 3. Terrorized Children

1. Francois Boyer, *Les Jeux Inconnus* (The Secret Game), trans. by Michael Legat (New York: Harcourt, Brace and Company, 1950).

2. This seems reparation for the grief over her dead parents, for the dead demand to be duly buried. They exact compliance by threatening the wrath of the gods for disobedience. To illustrate: When Odysseus and his men left Circe's island, they abandoned their youngest sailor there. This dull fellow had gotten drunk and broken his neck in a headlong fall from the palace roof. He was not given a proper burial. Later, Odysseus met this "unwept and unburied" sailor's ghost in the Underworld. The ghost implored Odysseus to correct his sin of omission by burying the ghost's neglected corpse. Odysseus dutifully sailed all the way back to Circe's island. There he and his crew burned the fallen sailor's corpse, heaped a mound over his ashes and planted his oar on the sepulchral mound and pillar.

3. Adam Robinson, *Bin Laden: Behind the Mask of the Terrorist* (New York: Arcade Publishing, 2001).

Chapter 4. Passive Instigators

1. Sigmund Freud, *Standard Edition of the Complete Psychological Works* (London: Hogarth Press, 1953–1965), Vol. 18, 191–192.

2. Albert Camus, *The Fall* (New York: Random House, 1956).

3. Ibid., 70.

4. Ibid., 48.

5. Ibid., 45.

6. Ibid., 67.

7. Ibid., 91.

8. For a thorough review of the work on attachment, the reader is referred to the book *Handbook of Attachment: Theory, Research, and Clinical Applications* edited by Jude Cassidy and Phillip R. Shaver (New York and London: The Guilford Press,

1999). Cassidy provides a succinct summary of the concept of attachment in Chapter 1, "The Nature of the Child's Ties," 3–20.

9. Anthony Bateman, "Narcissism and its relation to Violence and Suicide," in *Psychoanalytic Understanding of Violence and Suicide*, ed. Rosine J. Perelberg (London and New York: New Library of Psychoanalysis, 1999), 109–124.

Chapter 5. Passive Instigators II

1. R. E. Gould, "Suicide Problems in Children and Adolescents," *American Journal of Psychotherapy* 19 (1956): 228–246.

2. Joseph C. Sabbath, "The Suicidal Adolescent—The Expendable Child," in *Essential Papers on Suicide*, eds. John T. Maltsberger and Mark J. Goldblatt (New York and London: New York University Press, 1996), 185–199.

3. Willa Cather, "Paul's Case." in *The Troll Garden: Short Stories* (Lincoln, Neb., and London: University of Nebraska Press, 1983), 102–121.

4. Ibid., 105.

5. Ibid., 114.

6. Jack Novick, "Attempted Suicide in Adolescence: The Suicide Sequence," in *Suicide in the Young*, eds. Howard Sudak, Amasa B. Ford and Norman B. Rushforth (Boston: John Wright/PSG, 1984), 125.

Chapter 6. Ambivalence and Instigators

1. M.D.S. Ainsworth, M. Blehar, E. Waters and S. Wall, *Patterns of Attachment: A Psychological Study of the Strange Situation* (Hillsdale, N.J.: Erlbaum, 1978).

2. Judith Feeney, "Attachment and Couple Relationships," in *Handbook of Attachment: Theory, Research and Clinical Applications*, eds. Jude Cassidy and Phillip R. Shaver (New York and London: The Guilford Press, 1999), 364.

3. Ibid., 357–359, passim.

4. Jeffrey Simpson, "Attachment Theory in Modern Evolutionary Perspective," in *Handbook of Attachment: Theory, Research and Clinical Applications*, eds. Jude Cassidy and Phillip R. Shaver (New York and London: The Guilford Press, 1999), 133.

5. Arthur Miller, *Timebends: A Life* (New York: Harper & Row Publishers, 1987), 527–528.

6. Arthur Miller, *After the Fall: A Play in Two Acts* (New York: Penguin Books, 1964/1978).

7. Ibid., 111.

8. Ibid., 41–42.

9. Ibid., 28.

10. Ibid., 76.

11. Ibid., 74.

12. Ibid., 41.

13. R. Plutchik, provides more information about emotional development in *A Psychoevolutionary Synthesis* (New York and London: Harper & Row, 1980).

Chapter 7. Self-Attached Instigators

1. The sources used for the investigation of Sappho include: A.F.S.A. Chalmers, "Addison, Account of Sappho: Her Hymn to Venus," in *Prefaces: Historical and Biographical*, Vol. 7 (Boston: Little, Brown and Company, 1855).

Mary Robinson, "Sappho and Phaon," in *Legitimate Sonnets, with Thoughts on Poetical Subjects and Anecdotes of the Grecian Poetess* (London: S. Gosnell, Copyright by the Rector and Visitors of the University of Virginia, 1796/1994).

John Addington Symonds, *The Greek Poets* (New York: Harper & Brothers, Publishers, 1901).

Henry Thornton Wharton, *Sappho: Memoir, Text, Selected Renderings and a Literal Translation*, 3rd edition (London: John Lane, 1895).

2. See Ovid, Heroides 15 in Ovid, *Heroides and Amores*, trans. G. Showerman, The Loeb Classical Library (Cambridge, Mass., and London: Harvard University Press, 1963), 181.

3. Harold Isbell, trans., *The Poems of Ovid* (New York: Penguin Books, 1990).

4. Please refer to Anthony Bateman's discussion of Rosenfeld's concept of thick- and thin-skinned narcissism in "Narcissism and Its Relation to Violence and Suicide," in *Psychoanalytic Understanding of Violence and Suicide*, ed. E. Rosine Perelberg (London and New York: Routledge Press, 1999), 109–124.

5. John Addington Symonds, *The Greek Poets* (New York: Harper & Brothers, Publishers, 1901).

6. Bateman, "Narcissism," 112.

7. Ibid., 112–114, passim.

Chapter 8. Passive Instigators III

1. Henry James, *Roderick Hudson* (London: Penguin Books, 1875/1986).

2. *Merriam-Webster's Collegiate Dictionary*, 10th Edition (Springfield, Mass.: Merriam-Webster, 1997), s.v. "gift."

3. Please refer to the *Oxford English Dictionary* and the *Oxford Dictionary of English Etymology* for these definitions.

4. James, *Roderick Hudson*, 53.

5. Ibid., 196.

6. Ibid., 251.

7. Ibid., 378.

Chapter 9. Provocateur Instigators

1. The reader is referred to the considerations of violence and suicide in the borderline character in Anthony Bateman, "Narcissism and Its Relation to Violence and Suicide," in *Psychoanalytic Understanding of Violence and Suicide*, ed. Rosine Perelberg (London and New York: New Library of Psychoanalysis, 1998/1999), 109–124.

2. Joseph Ponten, *Der Meister* (The Master) (Stuttgart and Berlin: Deutsche Verlags-Unfalt, 1920).

3. E.T.A. Hoffman, "The Jesuits in G," in *Nachstücke*, trans. von W. Cremer (Berlin: Verlag der Schillerbuchhandlung, 1816).

4. Ponten, *Der Meister*, 121.

5. Ibid., 122.

6. Ibid., 122.

7. Ibid., 123.

8. Peter Baker, "One Death Altered the Path of Presidency," Whitewater Special Report 1999, http://www.washingtonpost.com/wp-srv/politics/special/clinton/stories/forster072098.htm.

9. Mega Garvey, "Accused Priest Who Killed Self Is Remembered at Mass," *Santa Barbara News*, April 4, 2002.

Chapter 10. Heroic Provocateurs

1. The story of the Sirens and Ulysses are taken from the following sources.

Apollodorus, *The Library*, Vol. II, trans. J. G. Frazer, The Loeb Classical Library (Cambridge, Mass., and London: Harvard University Press, 1989, 1990), 1, 3, 4.

Apollonius Rhodius, *Argonautica*, trans. R. D. Seaton, The Loeb Classical Library (Cambridge, Mass., and London: Harvard University Press, 1988), 4, 891–921.

Ovid, *Metamorphoses*, Vol. II, trans. F. J. Miller, The Loeb Classical Library (Cambridge, Mass., and London: Harvard University Press, 1984), 5, 552–563.

Pausanias: Description of Greece, trans. W.H.S. Jones (Cambridge, Mass., and London: Harvard University Press, 1977–1980), 9, 34–35.

2. See Sirens at: http://www.thanasis.com/sires.htm;+Ulysses.

3. The story of Oedipus and the Sphinx is found in many sources. Among those used are:

Apolladorus, *The Library*, Vol. II, 3, 5, 8.

Hesiod, *The Homeric Hymns and Homerica*, trans. H. G. Evelyn-White, The Loeb Classical Library (Cambridge, Mass., and London: Harvard University Press, 1982), 326–329.

Anthony S. Mercatante, *The Facts on File Encyclopedia of World Mythology and Legend* (New York and Oxford: Facts on File, 1988), 493.

Ovid, *Metamorphoses*, 7, 759.

Roy Willis, Ed., *World Mythology* (New York: Henry Holt and Company, 1992), 163.

Chapter 11. The Internal Instigator

1. Gregory Zilboorg, "Considerations on Suicide with Particular Reference to That of the Young," in *Essential Papers on Suicide*, eds. John T. Maltsberger and Mark J. Goldblatt (New York and London: New York University Press, 1996), 71.

2. Raymond Corsini, ed., *Concise Encyclopedia of Psychology* (New York: John Wiley & Sons, 1987).

3. Nandor Fodor and Frank Gaynor, *The Dictionary of Psychoanalysis* (Greenwich, Conn.: Fawcett Publications, 1958).

4. Sylvia Plath, *The Collected Poems*, ed. Ted Hughes (New York: HarperPerennial, 1981), 181.

5. Jacqueline Rose, *The Haunting of Sylvia Plath* (Cambridge, Mass.: Harvard University Press, 1991), 3.

6. Plath, *Collected Poems*, 245.

7. Ibid., 255.

8. Ibid., 181.

9. Paul Alexander, *Rough Magic: A Biography of Sylvia Plath* (New York: DaCapo Press, 1991), 113.

10. Ibid., 113.

11. Ibid., 118.

12. Ibid., 176.

13. Ibid., 183.

14. Ibid., xiv.

15. Ibid., 32

16. Ibid., 184.

17. Plath, *Collected Poems*, 223.

18. The reader is referred to the following book for the information used in this section on Anne Sexton:

Diane Wood Middlebrook, *Anne Sexton: A Biography* (New York: Vintage Books, 1991).

19. Ibid., 8.

20. Ibid., 20.

21. Peter Fonagy, "Transgenerational Consistencies of Attachment: A New Theory," paper to the 1999 IPA Pre-Congress on Psychoanalytic Research, Santiago, Chile, July 23–24, 1999.

22. Middlebrook, *Anne Sexton: A Biography*, 31.

23. Ibid., 43.

24. Ibid., 57.

25. Ibid., 49.

26. Ibid., 217.

27. Sexton, *The Complete Poems*, 354.

28. Ibid., 356.

29. Ibid., 357.

30. Middlebrook, *Anne Sexton: A Biography*, 396.

31. Dinky Dau. This is a one-half-hour dramatic program broadcast by Channel 10 KYEH on the evening of November 8, 1992 and received in the San Francisco Bay area via cable TV.

32. The interested reader is referred to the works of W.R.D. Fairbairn for further investigation of the effects of early attachment on the development of psychic structures. See W.R.D. Fairbairn, *From Instinct to Self: Selected Papers of W.R.D. Fairbairn, Vol. I Clinical and Theoretical Papers*. David E. Scharff and Ellinor Fairbairn Birtles, eds. (Northvale, N.J., and London: Jason Aronson, 1994).

Chapter 12. The Internal Instigator II

1. Evan Goodwin, "little blue light—Heinrich von Kleist," Littlebluelight (May 16, 2003 Edition), Evan Goodwin (ed.), http://www.littlebluelight.com/lblphp/intro.php?ikey=14.

2. Roland Kuhn, "The Attempted Murder of a Prostitute," in *Existence, a New Dimension in Psychiatry and Psychology*, eds. Rollo May, Ernest Angel and Henry Ellenberger (New York: Simon and Schuster, 1967), 365.

3. The sources for the story of Cephalus and Procris include Edward Tripp, *The Meridian Handbook of Classical Mythology* (New York: Meridian Press, 1970).

4. The sources for the story of Evenos and Marpessa are: Apollodorus, *The Library*, trans. J. G. Frazer, Vol. I, The Loeb Classical Library (Cambridge, Mass., and London: Harvard University Press, 1989, 1990), 59 passim.

Pausanias, *Description of Greece*, trans. W.H.S. Jones, 5 volumes, The Loeb Classical Library (Cambridge, Mass., and London: Harvard University Press, 1977–1980), Vol. 4, 2, 7.

J. E. Zimmerman, *Dictionary of Classical Mythology* (New York: Bantam Books, 1964, 1964, 1985), s.v. "Marpessa."

5. Robert Graves, *Larousse Encyclopedia of Mythology* (London: Paul Hamlyn, 1959), s.v. "Hippodemia." Her name, Hippodemia, means "a horse tamer." See also Zimmerman, *Dictionary of Classical Mythology*, s.v. "Hippodemia," p. 128.

6. Ovid. *Metamorphoses*, edited by F. J. Miller. The Loeb Classical Library (Cambridge, Mass., and London: Harvard University Press, 1985) Vol. II, pp. 778–795.

7. W.R.D. Fairbairn, *From Instinct to Self: Selected Papers of W.R.D. Fairbairn*. David E. Scharff and Ellinor Fairbairn Birtles, eds. (Northvale, N.J., and London: Jason Aronson, Inc., 1994) Vol. I, p. 113.

8. Ibid.

Chapter 13. Cult Instigators

1. Arthur Miller, *Timebends: A Life* (New York: Harper & Row, 1987), 4.

2. Sources for this story include:

Jacob Grimm and Wilhelm Grimm, *Der Rattenfänger von Hameln* in *Deutsche Sagen* (Berlin, 1816/1865).

Jonas Kuhn, "Johan Kuhn's Pied Piper Homepage," www.ims.uni-stuttgart.do/~jonas/pi (August 9, 2001).

3. Sources for this story are:

Georges Minois, *History of Suicide: Voluntary Death in Western Culture,* trans. Lydia G. Cochrane (Baltimore and London: Johns Hopkins University Press, 1999), 44.

The Oxford Classical Dictionary, eds. N.G.L. Hammond and H. H. Scullard, 2nd Edition (Oxford, U.K.: Clarendon Press, 1970), 492.

4. Please refer to the following sources for the tales of Jagan-neth:

Michael Jordan, *Encyclopedia of Gods: Over 2500 Deities of the World* (New York and Oxford: Fact on File, Inc., 1993).

Samuel Kramer, ed., *Mythologies of the Ancient World* (New York and London: Anchor Books, Doubleday Dell Publications, 1961).

J. Larousse, *Encyclopedia of Mythology*, trans. Richard Aldington and Delano Ames and revised by a panel of editorial advisors (London: Paul Hamlyn Ltd., 1996), 380–381.

William Whiston, trans., *The Works of Josephus, Book 7* (New York: Hendrickson Publishers, 1987), on www.pbs.org/wgbh/pages/frontline and www.mfa.gov.il/mfa/go.asp.

5. The information for the Jonestown story comes from:

The Dictionary of American Biography, Supplement 10 (New York: Charles Scribner's Sons, 1976–1980), 391.

John R. Hall, "Apocalypse at Jonestown," *Society* 16(6) (1979): 52–61.

Steve Rubenstein, "Jonestown Tragedy Recalled in Oakland," *San Francisco Chronicle*, November 1993.

http://www.religiousmovements.lib.virginia.edu/nrt. December 28, 2002, "Peoples Temple (Jonestown) Special Report!!"

6. The following sources have been consulted for the information on the White Brotherhood:

Eliot Bornstein, "Articles of Faith: The Media Response to Mari Devi Khristos," *Religion* 5.3 (July 1995): 249–266.

The Fortean Times, "The New Barbarians," July 2001. See www.rickross.com/reference/rs/rs30.html.

Alexandra Sorokino, "Beware. Sects. Goddess at Liberty," *Moskovskii komsomolets*, August 28, 1997.

7. The sources for the material about the Solar Temple include:

John Hall and Phillip Schuyler, "The Mystical Apocalypse of the Solar Temple," in *Millennium, Messiahs and Mayhem*, eds. Thomas Robbins and Susan J. Palmer (New York: Routledge, 1997), 285–311.

J. Stephen Hedges, "How an Obscure Cult Mixed Computers, UFOs and New Age Theology So Its 39 Members Could Take the Ultimate Journey," *U.S. News & World Report*, April 7, 1997, 26–59.

Jean Francois Mayer, "Our Terrestrial Journey Is Coming to an End: The Last Voyage of the Solar Temple," *Nova Religio*, 1999, April 2/2.

8. The sources for the story of Heaven's Gate include:

Howard Chua-Edan, "Imprisoned by His Own Passions," *Time*, April 7, 1997, 40–41.

Elizabeth Gleick, "The Marker We've Been . . . Waiting For," *Time*, April 7, 1997, 31–35.

John Hallinan, "Applewhite Sought Cure for His Homosexual Urges from Young Overachiever to Cult Leader," *Time*, March 28, 1997.

Chapter 14. Instigation Foiled

1. Matthew 4:4.

2. Arthur Miller, *Timebends: A Life* (New York: Harper & Row, Publishers, 1987), 47.

3. The sources for the story of Psyche and Eros include the following:

Apuleius, *Metamorphoses*, Vol. I, 5, 9, edited and translated by J. A. Hanson, The Loeb Classical Library (Cambridge, Mass., and London: Harvard University Press, 1989), 327.

The Oxford Classical Dictionary edited by N.G.L. Hammond and H.H. Scullard (Oxford, U.K.: Clarendon Press, 1970).

Edward Tripp, *The Meridian Handbook of Classical Mythology* (New York: Plume, 1974).

4. Apuleius, *Metamorphoses*, "*gliscentis invidiae falle flagrantes . . . ,*" 239.

5. Ibid., "*evomuit de summa luminis sui stillam ferventisolei super umerum dei dexterum,*" 5, 23.

Notes

6. The Greek word *stigma* is a mark made by a needle, a tattoo mark, a brand-mark. The Latin *stilla* is a diminutive of *stiria*, meaning icicle, here used by Apuleius. It is a viscous, fatty, pointed drop. Cf. English *distill*.

7. The Latin name for Psyche's daughter was Voluptas.

8. The sources for the material in this section include:

Arthur Miller, *After the Fall: A Play in Two Acts* (New York: Penguin Books, 1964).

Arthur Miller, *Timebends: A Life* (New York: Harper & Row, 1987).

9. Arthur Schnitzler, "Lieutenant Gustl," in *Five Great German Short Stories: A Dual Language Book*, ed. and trans. by Stanley Apelbaum (New York: Dover Publications, 1900), 104–164.

Selected Bibliography

Ainsworth, M.D.S., M. Blehar, E. Waters and S. Wall. *Patterns of Attachment: A Psychological Study of the Strange Situation*. Hillsdale, N.J.: Erlbaum, 1978.

Alem, A., D. Kebede, L. Jacobsson and G. Kullgren. "Suicide Attempts among Adults in Butajira, Ethiopa." *Acta Psychiatrica Scandinavica Supplementum*, 397 (1999): 70–76.

Alvarez, A. *The Savage God: A Study of Suicide*. New York: W. W. Norton and Company, 1990.

Apollodorus. *The Library*. Vol. I. Translated by J. G. Frazer. The Loeb Classical Library. Cambridge, Mass., and London: Harvard University Press, 1989, 1990.

Apollodorus. *The Library*. Vol. II. Translated by J. G. Frazer. The Loeb Classical Library. Cambridge, Mass., and London: Harvard University Press, 1989.

Apollodorus. *The Library*. Vol. III. Translated by J. G. Frazer. The Loeb Classical Library. Cambridge, Mass., and London: Harvard University Press, 1990.

Apollonius Rhodius. *Argonautica*. Translated by R. D. Seaton. The Loeb Classical Library. Cambridge, Mass., and London: Harvard University Press, 1988, 4, 891–921.

Apuleius. *Metamorphoses*. Translated by J. A. Hanson. 2 Vols. The Loeb Classical Library. Cambridge, Mass., and London: Harvard University Press, 1989.

Asberg, M., L. Traskman and P. Thoren. "5-HIAA in the Cerebrospinal Fluid: A Biochemical Suicide Predictor?" In *Essential Papers on Suicide*, edited by J. Maltsberger and M. Goldblatt. New York: New York University Press, 1996, 342–355.

Avery, C. B. *The New Century Classical Handbook*. New York: Appleton-Century-Crofts, 1962.

Baker, Peter. "One Death Altered the Path of Presidency." Whitewater Special Report, 1999. http://www.washingtonpost.com/wp-srv/politics/special/clinton/stories/forster072098.htm.

Bateman, Anthony. "Narcissism and Its Relation to Violence and Suicide." In

Psychoanalytic Understanding of Violence and Suicide, edited by Rosine Perelberg. London and New York: New Library of Psychoanalysis, 1999, 109–124.

Boelle, P., and A. Flahault. "Suicide Trends in France and UK." *The Lancet*, Vol. 353, April 17, 1964.

Bowlby, J. *Attachment and Loss. Vol. 1, Attachment.* New York: Hogarth Press/Basic Books, 1969/1982.

Bowlby, J. *Attachment and Loss. Vol. 2, Separation: Anxiety and Anger.* New York: Basic Books, 1983.

Bowlby, J. *Attachment and Loss. Vol. 3, Loss: Sadness and Depression.* New York: Basic Books, 1980.

Boyer, F. *The Secret Game (Les Jeux Inconnus).* From the French, translated by Michael Legat. New York: Harcourt, Brace and Company, 1950.

Brown, P. H., and Patte B. Barham. *Marilyn.* New York: Signet Penguin Books, 1993.

Camus, Albert. *The Fall.* New York: Random House, 1956.

Cassidy, Jude, and Phillip R. Shaver. *Handbook of Attachment: Theory, Research and Clinical Applications.* New York and London: The Guilford Press, 1999.

Cather, Willa. "Paul's Case." In *The Troll Garden: Short Stories.* Lincoln, Neb., and London: University of Nebraska Press, 1983.

Chalmers, A.F.S.A. "Addison, Account of Sappho: Her Hymn to Venus." In *Prefaces: Historical and Biographical,* Vol. 7. Boston: Little, Brown and Company, 1855.

Cicero. *De Finibus Bonorum et Malorum.* Vol. SVII. Translated by H. Rackham. The Loeb Classical Library. Cambridge, Mass., and London: Harvard University Press, 1983.

Corsini, Raymond, ed. *Concise Encyclopedia of Psychoanalysis.* New York: John Wiley & Sons, 1987.

Der Kleine Pauly, Lexikon der Antique auf der Grundlage on Paulys RE. Translated by K. Ziegler and W. Sontheimer. 5 volumes. Munich: Deutscher Taschenbuch Overflag, 1979.

Die Kinder—und Hausmärchen der Brüder Grimm (o.J.). Translated by V. F. Panzer. Wiesbaden: Emil Vollmer Verlag.

Donne, John (1644). *Biathanatos. A Declaration of that Paradoxe, or Thesis, That Self-homicide is not so naturally Sinne, that it may never be otherwise . . .,* edited by Michael Rudick and M. Pabst Battin. New York: Garland Texts, 1644/1982.

Donne, John. "Hero and Leander." In *John Donne Poems.* The Franklin Library. New York: Oxford University Press, 1932.

Evans, B. *Dictionary of Mythology. Mainly Classical.* New York: Bantam, Doubleday, Dell, 1991.

Fanshawe, Simon. "Children on a Field Trip Understood the Suicidal Lure of Beachy Head." *San Francisco Chronicle,* January 24, 1999.

Feeney, Judith. "Attachment and Couple Relationships." In *Handbook of Attachment: Theory, Research and Clinical Applications,* edited by Jude Cassidy and Phillip R. Shaver. New York and London: The Guilford Press, 1999.

Fodor, Nandor, and Frank Gaynor. *The Dictionary of Psychoanalysis.* Greenwich, Conn.: Fawcett Publications, 1958.

Freud, A. *Das Ich und die Abwehrmechanismen.* Munich: Kindler Verlag, 1964.

Freud, Sigmund. *Collected Papers* Vol. 4. Translated by Joan Riviere. New York: Basic Books, 1917/1959.

Freud, Sigmund. "Mourning and Melancholia." *Standard Edition of the Complete Psychological Works*. London: Hogarth Press, 1920/1961. Vol. 18, 157–172.

Freud, Sigmund. *Standard Edition of the Complete Psychological Works*. London: Hogarth Press, 1953–1965. Vol. 18, 191–192.

Garvey, Mega. "Accused Priest Who Killed Self Is Remembered at Mass." *Santa Barbara News*, April 4, 2002.

Goodwin, Evan. "little blue light—Heinrich von Kleist." Littlebluelight (May 16, 2003 Edition), Evan Goodwin (ed.), http://www.littlebluelight.com/lblphp/intro.php?ikey=14.

Gould, R. E. "Suicide Problems in Children and Adolescents." *American Journal of Psychotherapy* 19 (1956): 228–246.

Graves, Robert. *The Greek Myths*. 2 vols. London: Penguin, 1960.

Graves, Robert. *Larousse Encyclopedia of Mythology.* London: Paul Hamlyn, 1959.

Grimal, P. *A Concise Dictionary of Classical Mythology*. Translated from S. Kershaw after A. R. Maxwell-Hyslop. Oxford, U.K.: Basil Blackwell, 1990.

Hall, John, and Phillip Schuyler. "The Mystical Apocalypse of the Solar Temple," In *Millennium, Messiahs, and Mayhem*, edited by Thomas Robbins and Susan J. Palmer. New York: Routledge, 1997.

Harrison, J. E. *Prolegomena to the Study of Greek Religion*. Princeton, N.J.: Princeton University Press, 1991.

Hesiod. *The Homeric Hymns and Homerica*. Translated by H. G. Evelyn-White. The Loeb Classical Library. Cambridge, Mass., and London: Harvard University Press, 1982, 326–329.

Hoffman, E.T.A. "The Jesuits in G." in *Nachstücke*. Translated by W. Cremer. Berlin: Verlag der Schillerbuchhandlung, 1816.

Homer. *The Iliad*. Translated by A. T. Murray. Vol. I. The Loeb Classical Library. Cambridge, Mass., and London: Harvard University Press, 1988.

Homer. *The Odyssey*. Translated by A. T. Murray. Vol. II. The Loeb Classical Library. Cambridge, Mass., and London: Harvard University Press, 1984.

Isbell, Harold, translator. *The Poems of Ovid*. New York: Penguin Books, 1990.

James, Henry. *Roderick Hudson*. London: Penguin Books, 1875/1986.

Jamison, K. R. *Night Falls Fast: Understanding Suicide*. New York: Alfred Knopf, 1999.

Jens, H. *Mythologisches Lexikon. Gestalten der griechischen, römischen und nordischen Mythologie*. Munich: Wilhelm Goldmann Verlag, 1960.

Jordan, Michael. *Encyclopedia of Gods: Over 2500 Deities of the World*. New York and Oxford: Facts on File, Inc., 1993.

Kaplan, H. I., and B. J. Sadock, eds. *Synopsis of Psychiatry*. 8th ed. Philadelphia: Lippincott, Williams, and Wilkins 1998.

Kerenyi, C. *The Gods of the Greeks*. New York: Thames and Hudson, 1988.

Kramer, Samuel, ed. *Mythologies of the Ancient World*. New York and London: Anchor Books, Doubleday Dell Publications, 1961.

Kuhn, Roland. "The Attempted Murder of a Prostitute." In *Existence, a New Dimension in Psychiatry and Psychology*, edited by Rollo May, Ernest Angel and Henry Ellenberger. New York: Simon and Schuster, 1967.

Lamer, H. *Wïörterbuch der Aantike mit Berücksichtigung ihres Fortwirkens*. Foreword by P. Kroh. Stuttgart: Alfred Kroner Verlag, 1989.

Larousse, J. *Encyclopedia of Mythology*. Translated by Richard Aldington and Delano Ames. Revised by editorial advisors. London: Paul Hamlyn, Ltd., 1996.

Lewis, C. T., and Short, C. *A Latin Dictionary*. Oxford, U.K.: Clarendon Press, 1966.

Liddell, H. G., and Scott, R. *A Greek-English Lexicon*. Revised by H. S. Jones. Oxford, U.K.: Clarendon Press, 1990.

Lucian of Samosata. *The Works of Lucian of Samosata*. Translated by H. W. Fowler and F. G. Fowler. 4 volumes. Oxford, U.K.: Clarendon Press, 1905.

Maltsberger, John T., and Mark J. Goldblatt. *Essential Papers on Suicide*. New York and London: New York University Press, 1996.

Marlowe, Christopher. *Hero and Leander*. Printed by Adam Islip for Edward Blunt, 1598/1998.

Mecke, G. *Franz Kafkas offenbares Geheimnis: Eine Psychopathographie*. Munich: Wilhelm Fink Verlag, 1982.

Menninger, Karl. *Man Against Himself*. New York: Basic Books, 1938.

Mercatante, Anthony S. *The Facts on File Encyclopedia of World Mythology and Legend*. New York and Oxford: Facts on File, 1988.

Merriam-Webster's Collegiate Dictionary. 10th ed. Springfield, Mass.: Merriam-Webster, 1997.

Middlebrook, Diane Wood. *Anne Sexton: A Biography*. New York: Vintage Books, 1991.

Miller, A. *After the Fall: A Play in Two Acts*. New York: Penguin Books, 1964/1978.

Miller, A. *Timebends: A Life*. New York: Harper & Row, 1987.

Minois, Georges. *History of Suicide: Voluntary Death in Western Culture*. Translated by L. G. Cochrane. Baltimore and London: John Hopkins University Press, 1995.

Mitscherlich, A. *50 Jahre spater: Einige Empfehlungen an den Leser*. Foreword to Freud's *Psychology of Everyday Life*. Frankfurt: Fischer, 1964, 11.

Mitscherlich, Alexander, and Mitscherlich, Margaret. *The Inability to Mourn with Which Is Associated a German Way of Loving*. New York: Grove Press, 1975, 3–68.

The New Testament. Hg., ubers v. erlautert v. P. Dr. K. Rosch, O. M. Cap. Paderborn: Verlag von Ferdinand Schoningh.

Novick, Jack. "Attempted Suicide in Adolescence: The Suicide Sequence." In *Suicide in the Young*, edited by Howard Sudak, Amasa B. Ford and Norman B. Rushforth. Boston: John Wright/PSG, 1984, 125.

Ovid. *Fasti*. From J. G. Frazer. Revised by G. P. Goold. The Loeb Classical Library. Cambridge, Mass., and London: Harvard University Press, 1989.

Ovid. *Heroides and Amores*. Translated by G. Showerman. The Loeb Classical Library. Cambridge, Mass., and London: Harvard University Press, 1963.

Ovid. *Metamorphoses*. Translated by F. J. Miller. 2 volumes. The Loeb Classical Library. Cambridge, Mass., and London: Harvard University Press, 1984.

The Oxford Classical Dictionary. Edited by N.G.L. Hammond and H.H. Scullard. Oxford, U.K.: Clarendon Press, 1970.

Parada, Carlos. "Eros." In *Genealogical Guide to Greek Mythology*. http://hsa.brown.edu/~maicar/Eros.html. 2002.

Paul, Alexander. *Rough Magic: A Biography of Sylvia Plath*. New York: DaCapo Press, 1991.

Pausanias. *Description of Greece*. Translated by W.H.S. Jones. Cambridge, Mass., and London: Harvard University Press, 1977–1980.

Pindar. *The Odes of Pindar including the Principal Fragments*. Translated by J. Sandys. The Loeb Classical Library. Cambridge, Mass. and London: Harvard University Press, 1989.

Plath, Sylvia. *The Collected Poems*. Edited by Ted Hughes. New York: Harper Perennial, 1981.

Plato. *The Collected Dialogues including the Letters*. Translated by E. Hamilton and H. Cairns. Princeton, N.J.: Princeton University Press, 1987.

Plutchik, R. *A Psychoevolutionary Synthesis*. New York and London: Harper & Row, 1980.

Ponten, J. *Der Meister.* Stuttgart and Berlin: Deutsche Verlags-Unfalt, 1920.

Quintillian. *Institutio Oratoria*. Translated by H. E. Butler. 4 volumes. The Loeb Classical Library. Cambridge, Mass., and London: Harvard University Press, 1969–1986.

Ranke-Graves, R. *Grieschische Mythologie, Quellen und Deutung*. 2 volumes. Reinbek bei Hamburg: Rowohlt, 1960–1961.

Robinson, Adam. *Bin Laden: Behind the Mask of the Terrorist*. New York: Arcade Publishing, 2001.

Robinson, Mary. "Sappho and Phaon." In *Legitimate Sonnets, with Thoughts on Poetical Subjects and Anecdotes of the Grecian Poetess*. London: S. Gosnell, Copyright by the Rector and Visitors of the University of Virginia, 1796/1994.

Room, A. *NTC's Classical Dictionary: The Origins of the Names of Characters in Classical Mythology*. Lincolnwood, Ill.: National Textbook Company, 1990.

Rose, H. J. *A Handbook of Greek Mythology.* New York: E. P. Dutton, 1959.

Rose, Jacqueline. *The Haunting of Sylvia Plath*. Cambridge, Mass.: Harvard University Press, 1991.

Roy, Alec. "Family History of Suicide." In *Essential Papers on Suicide,* edited by J. Maltsberger and M. Goldblatt. New York and London: New York University Press, 1996, 549–561.

Sabbath, Joseph C. "The Suicidal Adolescent—The Expendable Child." In *Essential Papers on Suicide,* edited by J. Maltsberger and M. Goldblatt. New York: New York University Press, 1996, 185–199.

Schafer, R. *Retelling a Life: Narration and Dialogue in Psychoanalysis*. New York: Basic Books, 1992.

Schank, R. C. *Tell Me a Story.* New York: Charles Scribner's Sons, Macmillan Publishing Co., 1990.

Schnitzler, Arthur. "Lieutenant Gustl." In *Five Great German Short Stories: A Dual Language Book* edited and translated by Stanley Appelbaum. New York: Dover Publications, 1900.

Seyffert, O. (1894). *Dictionary of Classical Antiquities*. Revised by H. Nettleship and J. E. Sandys. Cleveland and New York: Meridian Books, 1967.

Shneidman, Edwin S. *Comprehending Suicide*. Washington, D.C.: American Psychological Association, 2001, 155.

Simpson, Jeffrey. "Attachment Theory in Modern Evolutionary Perspective." In *Handbook of Attachment: Theory, Research and Clinical Applications,* edited by

Jude Cassidy and Phillip R. Shaver. New York and London: The Guilford Press, 1999, 134.

Sirens and Ulysses. http://www.thanasis.com/sires.htm+Ulysses.

Smith, William. *Smaller Classical Dictionary*. New York: E. P. Dutton, 1958.

Straker, M. "Clinical Observations of Suicide." *Canadian Medical Association Journal*, 79 (1958): 473–479.

Symonds, John Addington. *The Greek Poets*. New York: Harper and Brothers, Publishers, 1901.

Tripp, E. *The Meridian Handbook of Classical Mythology*. New York: Penguin, 1974.

Vergil. *The Eclogues and Georgics of Virgil*. Translated by C. D. Lewis. Garden City, N.Y.: Doubleday and Company, 1964.

Wharton, Henry Thornton. *Sappho: Memoir, Text, Selected Renderings, and a Literal Translation*, 3rd edition. London: John Lane, 1895, and at www.classic persuasion.org.

Whiston, William, trans. *The Works of Josephus, Book 7*. New York: Hendrickson Publishers, 1987.

Willis, Roy, ed. *World Mythology*. New York: Henry Holt and Company, 1992.

Yip, P. S. and R. C. Tan. "Suicides in Hong-Kong and Singapore: A Tale of Two Cities." *International Journal of Social Psychiatry* (Winter 1998): 267–279.

Zimmerman, J. E. *Dictionary of Classical Mythology*. Toronto, New York, London, Sydney and Auckland: Bantam Books, 1985.

Index

Adolescence, 52–54, 60, 67–68
After the Fall, 76–80
Aisakos, 151–153
Alvarez, A., 8, n.8
Anteros, 15
Aphrodite, 18, 88–90
Applewhite, Marshall, 164–165
Aristotle, 7
Attachment, 22; ambivalent, 18, 49–50, 55, 69–74, 80–84, 106, 136, 148–150, 183; exploitative, 51, 154–183, 183; fantasized 48–49; 66, 183; malevolent, 5, 46, 106–107, 146, 152, 183; negative, 5, 45–47, 57, 59, 62, 93, 130, 183; nullified, 47–48, 65–66, 78, 80, 146, 183; self-attached, 50, 85–95; usurped, 51, 183

Berta, 110–113
bin Laden, Osama, 31–33
Bob and Jane, 38–41, 45
Boyer, Francois, 26–29

Camus, Albert, 41
Cather, Willa, 60–61
Charles and Nancy, 147–149
Clamence, 41–44

Cult, 23, 154–167

Eos, Cephalus and Procris, 144–145
Eros, 15, 170–173
Evenos and Marpessa, 145–147

Fall, The, 41–45
Freud, Sigmund, 9, 38

Gottfried, 110–113
Gottschalk, 109–113
Gratitude, 155, 173, 176
Grief, 34, 59, 97, 101, 132, 145, 153
Gustl, Lieutenant, 176–179

Handyman, 113–117
Heaven's Gate, 164–165
Hero and Leander, 18–22
Hoffman, E.T.A., 109

Instigation, 3, 17, 22–24, 29, 179–182
Instigators, 3, 4 17–18, 25; active, 22, 37, 108, 182; external 22, 182; internal, 23, 124–127, 138–39, 140, 182; passive, 23, 37–38, 41–46, 69–70, 80–82, 90, 108–109, 182; provocateur, 23, 108–119, 121–123, 182

Jagan-nath, 158
James, Henry, 96, 97
Jane and Bob, 38–41, 45
Jennifer, 63–66
"Jesuits in G, The" 113–117
Jesus, 169–170
Jones, James, 159–161
Jouret, Luc, 163–164

Katy, 15–18
Kenneth, 149–153
Khristos, Mari Devi, 161–163
Kuhn, Roland, 142

Leander, 18–22
Leslie and Suzanne, 91–94

Marpessa, 145–147
Mary, 30–31
Max and Rita, 72–76
Meaningfulness, 90–91
Meister, Der, 109–113
Meles and Timagoras, 14–15, 17, 21
Miller, Arthur, 76, 170, 173–174, 184
Morath, Inge, 173–176

Nancy and Charles, 147–149
Narcissism, 89–91, 93–95, 154–159
Norris, 96, 101–106

Oedipus, 121–123
Order of the Solar Temple, 163–164

Paul, 60–63
Paulette, 26–29, 35

Peoples' Temple, 159–161
Phaon, 87–90
Pied Piper, 156–158
Plath, Sylvia, 127–132
Plato, 7
Psyche, 170–173
Ponten, Josef, 109

Quentin, 76–80

Roderick Hudson, 11, 97–101
Rowland, 98–101
Rudolf, 142–144

Sappho, 85–91
Sexton, Anne, 132–136
Shneidman, Edwin, 15
Sonny, 52–60
Sphinx, 121–123
Suicide, 5–12
Suzanne and Leslie, 91–94

Timagoras and Meles, 14–15
Timebends, 173
Tommy, 1–3
Tony and Lara, 140–142

Ulysses, 119–121

Vietnam Veteran, 136–138
Vishnu, 158

White Brotherhood, 161–163

Zilboorg, Gregory, 125

About the Author

VIOLA MECKE is a clinical psychologist with more than 40 years' experience in research, private practice and teaching. She is a Clinical Professor Emerita in the Department of Psychiatry and Behavioral Sciences at Stanford University Medical School and Emerita Professor of Educational Psychology at California State University, Hayward, California where she was the coordinator of the Child Clinical and School Psychology program. She is a Diplomate of the American Board of Professional Psychology and a Fellow of the Academy of Clinical Psychology.